Who Is Worthy of Protection?

Oxford Studies in Gender and International Relations

Series editors: J. Ann Tickner, University of Southern California, and Laura Sjoberg, University of Florida

Enlisting Masculinity:
The Construction of Gender in U.S. Military Recruiting Advertising during the All-Volunteer Force
Melissa T. Brown

Cosmopolitan Sex Workers:
Women and Migration in a Global City
Christine B. N. Chin

Intelligent Compassion:
Feminist Critical Methodology in the Women's International League for Peace and Freedom
Catia Cecilia Confortini

Gender and Private Security in Global Politics
Maya Eichler

Gender, Sex, and the Postnational Defense:
Militarism and Peacekeeping
Annica Kronsell

The Beauty Trade:
Youth, Gender, and Fashion Globalization
Angela B. V. McCracken

From Global to Grassroots:
The European Union, Transnational Advocacy, and Combating Violence against Women
Celeste Montoya

A Feminist Voyage through International Relations
J. Ann Tickner

The Political Economy of Violence against Women
Jacqui True

Bodies of Violence:
Theorizing Embodied Subjects in International Relations
Lauren B. Wilcox

Who Is Worthy of Protection?

Gender-Based Asylum and US Immigration Politics

Meghana Nayak

OXFORD
UNIVERSITY PRESS

OXFORD
UNIVERSITY PRESS

Oxford University Press is a department of the University of Oxford. It furthers the University's objective of excellence in research, scholarship, and education by publishing worldwide.

Oxford New York
Auckland Cape Town Dar es Salaam Hong Kong Karachi
Kuala Lumpur Madrid Melbourne Mexico City Nairobi
New Delhi Shanghai Taipei Toronto

With offices in
Argentina Austria Brazil Chile Czech Republic France Greece
Guatemala Hungary Italy Japan Poland Portugal Singapore
South Korea Switzerland Thailand Turkey Ukraine Vietnam

Published in the United States of America by
Oxford University Press
198 Madison Avenue, New York, NY 10016

Library of Congress Cataloging-in-Publication Data
Nayak, Meghana.
Who is worthy of protection? : gender-based asylum and US immigration politics / Meghana Nayak.
pages cm. — (Oxford studies in gender and international relations)
Includes bibliographical references and index.
ISBN 978-0-19-939762-4 (hardcover : alk. paper)
1. Refugees—Government policy—United States. 2. Asylum, Right of—United States. 3. Women's rights—Government policy—United States. 4. United States—Emigration and immigration—Government policy I. Title.
JV6601.N38 2015
325.73—dc23
2015007496

9 8 7 6 5 4 3 2 1
Printed in the United States of America
on acid-free paper

CONTENTS

ACKNOWLEDGMENTS

We never know how readers will react to or critique our work. But what will stay with me is the amount of support and encouragement I received during the entire process. I am grateful for the opportunity to name the people without whom this book would have been impossible.

Angela Chnapko, my editor at Oxford University Press, is a kind and thoughtful person in the difficult, unforgiving industry of academic publishing. I will always appreciate the humane way she guided the process. Laura Sjoberg and Ann Tickner, the series editors of Gender and International Relations, are formidable in terms of their scholarship and how they act as genuine, supportive peers. I am also indebted to the two peer reviewers who gave me feedback that catalyzed a necessary and liberating overhaul of the first draft.

I am thankful to Pace University for a sabbatical in the spring of 2013, which allowed me to collect and analyze asylum cases. Sarah Adams at the Center for Gender and Refugee Studies at the University of California–Hastings generously provided access to data, thanks to the labor of the staff at this center, and answered technical questions. Pace University's Scholarly Research Committee awarded me a grant to fund the costs of this data collection. Under the auspices of the Pace University Provost Faculty-Undergraduate Research Grant, I was able to ask my student Jessica J. Meredith to help with data collection and analysis for chapter 2. I enjoyed working with Jessie, and serving as advisor for her independent research project on undocumented immigration was inspirational for my own writing process.

My student Klaudia Remiszewska kindly agreed to design the book cover. Klaudia interned with an immigration rights organization and witnessed firsthand the difficulties asylum seekers face. I am so proud that I can showcase her art.

I mention Chitra Aiyar throughout the book. Her work as a lawyer on gender-based asylum cases inspired much of this project. I am grateful

that she put aside time to answer questions, to hold me accountable, and to discuss the persuasiveness of my claims. I also thank the many lawyers and advocates who did not wish to be named or acknowledged but gave me crucial and challenging feedback. I extend my deepest gratitude to the people whose stories of migration and activism fuel my commitment to collaborative feminist praxis.

Several people read parts of or the entire book, making very useful suggestions. Of course, only I am responsible for the contents. But my treasured readers are Saskia Aykil, Roohi Choudhry, Emily Hardt, Susan Hansen, Jennifer Haydel, John W. Price, Carrie Booth Walling, and Lauren Woolley.

It is a joy that some of my former students at Pace University read my manuscript, applying the critical eye they honed in my classes to what they read. They gave me necessary feedback and reminded me of the delight of maintaining relationships with students after they graduate. I extend my gratitude to Katelyn (Katie) James, Alejandra Lopez, Whitney Macdonald, and Annamaria Santamaria.

Of course, friends and family showed me support, encouragement, and interest just when I needed it. I thank Helene Meyers, Eric Selbin, Susan Kang, Jess Geevarghese, Lizzie Elston, Tom Cannell, Catherine Beebe, and my relatives in Houston, Los Angeles, Toronto, Bombay, Canberra, and Sydney. Finally, I thank my husband, Andrew, for his unwavering belief in me.

Who Is Worthy of Protection?

CHAPTER 1
Introduction

It is the summer of 2014, and I stumble across news headlines every day about the increasing numbers of unaccompanied children and undocumented adults crossing into the United States. Some articles make provocative claims about the alleged threat these non-citizens carry: "Illegal immigrant kids expose federal agents to lice, scabies, tuberculosis and chicken pox."[1] Others argue that these particular migrants are escaping gang violence in Central American countries and are thus bona fide refugees.[2]

As a scholar of international relations (IR), I see the debate about migration as one about how the US government should negotiate competing pressures. On the one hand, the United States professes the need to secure borders. It might exercise its right to control its borders by deporting migrants with the goal of deterring future undocumented immigration.[3] On the other hand, the United States commits itself to upholding a basic human rights obligation, encapsulated in refugee law, to ensure the right to protection for those who would otherwise be returned to countries where their lives might be threatened. If it sees these migrants as legitimately fleeing persecution in their home countries, it might attempt to provide "safe haven" by facilitating increased access to grants of asylum, or legal protection from deportation.[4] In other words, the United States faces the tension between the *restriction* and the *protection* of non-citizens.

Who is worthy of protection? For many, the answer depends on whether one sees non-citizens as "good" migrants, vulnerable asylum seekers worthy of protection, or as "bad" migrants, criminal illegal aliens, deserving nothing more than fear and contempt. This distinction is a precarious, illusory one, often pivoting on how someone relays his or her reasons for

migrating. But who will be given the opportunity to tell his or her story to the governmental officials and immigration judges tasked with handling deportation proceedings or adjudicating asylum claims? Whose story will be convincing?

In international and US refugee law, people may apply for asylum if they can demonstrate a well-founded fear of persecution in their countries due to race, religion, nationality, political opinion, and membership in a particular social group. Notice that gender is not on this list. Indeed, gender is generally missing from the debates about the tension between immigration restriction and obligations to protect those fleeing persecution. Gender-related persecution comprises any type of violence that targets someone because of *gendered expectations* (such as forcing boys to join gangs or punishing women for their choices), *in gendered ways* (such as violence that includes sexual assault), or *due to non-conforming gender identities and sexual orientation* (such as police targeting lesbian, gay, bisexual, and transgender [LGBT] communities). Countries, immigration rights organizations, and feminist advocates around the world are increasingly acknowledging that gender violence is a form of persecution that should warrant grants of asylum protection. However, as asylum seekers try to prove their credibility and the legitimacy of their gender-based claims, they face the harrowing and difficult task of convincing immigration officials or judges that gender violence is not a personal or unfortunate problem but constitutes persecution.

This book confronts the question "Who is worthy of protection?" by examining gender-based asylum cases. Gender-based asylum offers an incredible opportunity for the United States to acknowledge and address gender-related persecution and to demonstrate protection of those fleeing persecution. However, due to the politics of immigration restriction *and* the "missing" category of gender, asylum/immigration officials and judges put an added burden on asylum seekers with gender-related claims to prove that they are deserving of legal protection. My critical investigation of these cases provides crucial lessons about the *construction* of "worthiness."

I argue that different types of violence generate correlating typologies of "worthy victims," or expectations about how asylum seekers should demonstrate their credibility and the legitimacy of their claims. In the chapters that follow, I conduct a comprehensive, comparative study of the most common types of gender-based asylum cases in the United States. I identify three main frames of "worthy victims": *autonomy, innocence, non-deviance.*

In my case studies I unexpectedly found that types of violence considered to be very different share similar "worthy victim" frames. As I show

in the rest of the book, we thus learn about new dimensions about how gender violence operates. I first demonstrate that *domestic violence* and *female genital cutting* cases both entail expectations that asylum seekers prove they are *autonomous*. These asylum seekers should express independence by showing how they reject not only their countries but also their family members. They are expected to vilify their loved ones.

Second, *trafficking* and *coercive sterilization/abortion* cases both expect a demonstration of *innocence*. Innocence means helplessness and making good, moral decisions. Asylum seekers fleeing trafficking undermine their cases if they participate in criminal activity, such as voluntary sex work or smuggling. Those escaping coercive sterilization/abortion need to prove they are married women dutifully protecting their "unborn children." The potential loss of unborn children is valued more than the harm done to women by coercive reproductive policies.

I also discovered that the third worthy victim frame, *non-deviance*, emerges in cases of *persecution due to sexual orientation and gender identity*. Sexual orientation and gender identity are different issues, but they tend to be grouped together as the persecution targets non-gender-conforming people. Ironically, these asylum seekers flee countries due to persecution because their identity is perceived as immoral or deviant; but once they stand in front of an asylum officer or immigration judge, they discover that in the United States, too, they are expected to prove that they are "normal" or fit certain perceptions. A judge might ask, "Are you really gay? You don't look it." These asylum seekers also confront a maze of homophobic and transphobic laws and practices that deter them from using the system.

The importance of interrogating these worthy victim frames is in understanding their long-lasting impact. *The first effect of these frames is the significant delimiting of which stories of asylum seekers are deemed credible.* In order to increase their chances of receiving asylum, asylum seekers might need to participate in narratives that are traumatizing to them. Asylum seekers are also incentivized to lie and exaggerate to tell the "right" story, which contributes to perceptions that asylum seekers are fraudulent and seeking to exploit the asylum system. These "worthy victim" distinctions also perpetuate the idea that undocumented immigrants, those without authorization to live, work, or be in the United States, are *always unworthy* and thus never eligible for access to social services or protection from deportation. The undocumented immigrant without an asylum claim has the same unsettled legal status as an asylum seeker who is still in the middle of the legal process, but if the asylum seeker receives asylum, she or he is perceived to be more worthy of inclusion in the United States than "illegal aliens."

Second, the frames are useful for how the United States exercises power. The US government uses these frames to justify the exclusion of non-citizens who do not meet these expectations, to demonstrate its capacity to protect those who are worthy, and to justify its right to shape other countries' policies on gender violence. While the United States finds it important to secure its borders, it is simultaneously politically expedient to show that it can protect *some* "worthy" non-citizens, particularly from gender-based persecution. It does so in order to demonstrate that it is "better" than other countries for women and sexual minorities. In turn, the United States links its alleged superiority in protection to its capacity and right to influence other countries, and in some cases, global organizations.

In the pages that follow, I explain the theoretical underpinnings of this book, my methodology, and a description of the book's chapters. My argument about the use and effects of worthy victim frames ultimately points out *three types of distinctions* at work in the asylum process: (1) between types of gender violence/persecution; (2) between "good" and "bad" non-citizens; and (3) between "better" and "worse" countries in global politics. I situate my investigation in a *feminist IR framework*, which offers the conceptual and theoretical tools for understanding these three distinctions. Feminist IR helps us explore the politics of naming and classifying gender violence and its victims; how and why distinctions (particularly along lines of gender, sexuality, and race) are made among non-citizens; and why the United States finds it important to show that it protects persecuted women and sexual minorities, while simultaneously trying to restrict the entry of non-citizens. I contend a *critical*[5] feminist IR investigation of asylum and undocumented immigration is long overdue.

I also invite asylum lawyers and advocates into the conversation. When I first started this book, Chitra Aiyar, a friend and asylum lawyer who has successfully argued gender-based asylum cases, asked me: "How will critical feminist theory help me win my case?" In other words, she kindly asked me the point of my book for practitioners. My answer is that lawyers and advocates directly deal with the necessity to present asylum seekers as the right kind of victim, and the feminist analysis I provide traces the emergence and impact of worthy victim frames. Ideas of "worthiness" draw upon *and* strengthen notions that we can find in popular discourses, laws, policies, and human rights/feminist activism. I thus provide clarity on the asylum process and suggest ways for academics and legal practitioners to collaborate to intervene in this *discursive climate* with new legal and political understandings. Specifically, I discuss pragmatic possibilities

for challenging the worthy victim frames and for feminist knowledge to play a role in the legal process.

THE IMPORTANCE OF A FEMINIST IR INQUIRY OF ASYLUM AND UNDOCUMENTED IMMIGRATION

A feminist IR framework gives us a unique lens for exploring the tragedies experienced by non-citizens as they deal with the categories foisted upon them. This interdisciplinary body of scholarship focuses on how gender matters in global politics, what is done to bodies in the context of power struggles, how the state is gendered, and how feminists address and deal with gender, race, sexuality, class, and other differences as they play out in international and transnational relations and geopolitics.[6] My feminist investigation of the asylum process thus builds on but goes beyond what other scholars have already explored: gender as an important category of persecution, the gendered experiences of female asylum seekers, and the gender-differential effects of asylum policy.[7]

Feminist IR scholars look for women and gender in global politics, only to consistently find that it is hard to make sense of the world *without* a feminist lens, particularly because gender works in often "unseen" and hidden ways.[8] Certainly in the course of researching this book, looking for gender in asylum cases revealed all kinds of twists and turns in what I thought I knew about how the United States operates. I find a feminist IR perspective particularly useful because, as Enloe remarks, feminist IR "isn't a static thing. It is something you try to *do* . . . to engage in the hard and invigorating work of doing feminist IR means to think and re-think, to listen and re-listen, to explore and re-explore."[9] Exploring the effects of gender on global politics, and vice versa, allows feminist IR scholars to contribute to how we think about and can remake the world.

Gender-based asylum is a unique and rich opportunity for feminist IR exploration. First, gender claims invite and require feminist analysis of how sovereign power works. Since asylum cases require proof that gender persecution occurred and that the asylum seekers' countries participated in or condoned this violence, gender-based asylum claims force one to grapple with *what* gender violence is, and to figure out how to assess another country's position on gender violence. Gender-based asylum also requires us to think about how and why a country like the United States that is so committed to immigration restriction finds it useful and important to increasingly legitimize gender-based asylum. Further, asylum is an

act of international relations as it requires one country to grant sovereign protection to a foreign national.

Second, gender-based asylum is a part of larger global feminist efforts for "gender justice," or opportunities of legal redress for and recognition of survivors of gender-related violence. Feminist activism helped bring about the very possibility of gender-based asylum in the United States, Canada, Australia, and several other countries. Feminist and human rights advocates often reach out to the media and galvanize the support of citizens and civil society organizations to pressure their governments to intervene in pending or denied gender-based asylum claims or to adopt gender-friendly legislation and guidelines. These advocates also push for better interpretations and application of the law. For example, they encourage asylum officers and immigration judges in their countries to consider international human rights documents, feminist legal analysis of how gender violence is persecutory, and key cases of gender violence in the International Criminal Tribunal for the Former Yugoslavia, the International Criminal Tribunal for Rwanda, and the International Criminal Court.

Gender-based asylum also illustrates the linkages between domestic and international law. The codification of gender crimes, in the Rome Statute of 1998, which created the International Criminal Court (ICC) in 2002, has created space for activists to shape asylum policies benefitting those fleeing the kind of persecution detailed in this treaty.[10] Others argue that it was actually international refugee law's recognition of gender-related persecution that influenced the delegates drawing up the Rome Statute to include gender when conceptualizing crimes.[11] Accordingly, the ICC could learn from the triumphs and problems within refugee and asylum law to better understand and interpret gender crimes.[12] In effect, anyone interested in the inclusion and recognition of gender crimes in multiple law regimes should examine gender-based asylum.

I use feminist IR to conceptualize and assess the effects of using "worthy victim" frames. In the pages that follow, I first draw upon feminist IR research in the naming, addressing, and preventing of gender violence, to posit that we should figure out how distinctions made between types of violence are connected to the construction and "framing" of "worthy victims" of gender-based violence. Second, I show how feminist IR, particularly when it draws upon insights in postcolonial feminist studies, helps us see how gender violence is "racialized." In other words, gender violence is sutured to ideas of "us," "them," and what allegedly happens "here" (freedom and dignity) and "there" (conflict and oppressive traditions). Understanding the racial undertones of how we discuss and understand

gender violence gives us more precise and critical tools for exploring the classification of non-citizens and survivors of violence. Third, feminist IR, by focusing on how countries respond to gender violence for politically expedient reasons, helps us understand how and why the worthy victim frames are entry points for countries to exert influence over other countries. Finally, feminist IR's focus on feminist agency and on how knowledge is contestable and contested provides space to explore how to mitigate the effects of worthy victim frames by challenging the construction of these frames in the first place.

Distinctions between Types of Gender Violence

Feminist IR scholarship is at the forefront of examining how domestic, regional, and transnational feminist advocates try to get powerful players to take gender violence seriously.[13] Keck and Sikkink's *Activists beyond Borders*, a key piece of scholarship in the feminist IR canon, explains how feminist advocacy networks introduced "violence against women" into the lexicon of the United Nations and international law as a way to bring together several different kinds of campaigns about "many practices that in the early 1970s were not understood to be connected."[14] Keck and Sikkink quote an activist's comments: "The violence theme is very evocative. No woman can help but feel it as her own. I don't think any one of us can say that she has never felt violence against her. It crosses all our lives."[15]

They find that transnational advocacy networks organize most effectively around "issues involving bodily harm to vulnerable individuals, especially when there is a short and clear causal chain (or story) responsibility."[16] They argue that while there might be contestation over what counts as this kind of harm, this issue resonates across the world. Violence against women can strike a chord and generate feelings of empathy, familiarity, and solidarity.

But what are the politics of naming and responding to gender violence? Weldon and Htun illustrate the enduring power of autonomous feminist mobilization, through particular commitments to end gender violence, in institutionalizing women's human rights.[17] Feminist advocates shape and amplify norms about gender violence. Thus it is crucial to explore the persuasive power of feminists. For example, the use of not only "violence against women" but also "gender-based violence" or "gender violence" occurred as international women's rights activists wanted to signal that some types of crimes keep *gender power relations intact*: male domination

and female subordination.[18] We could perhaps, thanks to the work of feminist activists, easily name rape, domestic violence, and forced marriage as typical examples of violence that demonstrate male domination and female subordination.

However, Nayak and Suchland argue that gender violence is not a "ready" category; we do not necessarily know what is meant by the term unless given the context.[19] For example, the terms "wartime rape" and "honor killings" are often used in self-explanatory ways, without exploring whether those who experience or fear these types of violence would all explain it in the same way.[20] Gender-based violence is a shifting category that depends more on the politics of those who describe this violence than on some positivist acquiring of knowledge about what violence constitutes.

The very term gender-based violence indicates that *gender* is doing some work here. So what is happening when advocates deploy gender as the *cause* of violence? What is it about gender that provokes violence? Why would someone be punished and targeted for being a woman, for being in a same-sex relationship, for making a choice about his or her own body? When people experience gender violence, we learn through their experiences what "gender" is, meaning which powerful forces and discourses delimit what "men" and "women" are supposed to be and how they are supposed to behave, love, and live.[21]

But different types of violence do not necessarily get attention because of the egregiousness of the violence but rather because the violence (or the understanding of it) has a political currency that prompts people to respond. Perhaps the labeling of and responding to a form of gender violence promotes a commitment to end patriarchy. Perhaps it justifies militarized intervention into a country with which one disagrees. Perhaps it reflects myopic understandings about how we think people are treated around the world. Perhaps it makes "us" look like human rights leaders.

So when various advocates, organizations, and countries acknowledge and address gender violence, we also learn about *their* ideas about what gender is. Their responses tell us their dominant ideas about who counts as a victim, who does not, and what types of harmful experiences are understood as "gendered." So it matters not just *that* but *how* we respond to gender violence.

Scholars who study gender violence propose that there are frames, narratives, and stories as to how gender violence is understood and categorized. Sally Engle Merry explores how the transnational discourses in global United Nations conferences or in international nongovernmental organizations about what counts as gender violence get "translated"

and remade in local contexts.[22] In another essay, Merry writes that naming violence means "to develop a framework that explains it and offers solutions," involving "subtle cultural technologies" that shape the kind of responses that occur.[23] True argues that the causes of gender violence should be understood in the context of multiple political economies, such as free trade zones, international financial institutions, labor markets, households, and socioeconomic conflict over resources and subsequent peace-building efforts.[24] If we do not look to political economy, we are then limited in addressing how to end gender crimes.

In this book, I discuss "framing" as the process of "making sense of a complex reality in order to provide guideposts for knowing, analyzing and acting."[25] *A frame is a way of consistently narrating ideas about what comprises gender violence, drawing upon preexisting discourses about the causes and effects of gender violence.* Various players involved in addressing gender violence can contribute to the strengthening of some frames or the articulation of competing, alternative frames. Frames are not always explicitly stated but can be identified by analyzing how political actors talk about and respond to issues.

I find most helpful Montoya's work on the use of frames in European Union policy documents about combating and addressing gender violence.[26] Montoya first identifies several ways of understanding violence against women that constitute particular "frames." She then analyzes the policy documents for the presence of the frames. The frames include (1) "human rights," which looks at violence against women as a human rights issue; (2) "gender equality," wherein violence is understood as a "manifestation of gender inequality"; (3) "universal," when the violence is discussed as widespread and global; (4) "inclusive," such that different marginalized groups are included in antiviolence measures, like the availability of information in different languages; and (5) "exclusive," where some forms of violence are labeled as "different," cultural," or "barbaric." She also identifies "nonfeminist" frames such as "criminal," "economic," and "health," regarding different approaches to understanding violence against women.[27] She draws upon critical frame analysis methodology, which identifies the biases and presumptions that shape the discourses that then become part of policy. Critical frame analysis requires the tracing of key "conceptual prejudices" held by those who shape policy, including differing ideas about how gender intersects with other constructs such as race, age, or sexuality, and whose voices, perspectives, and experiences are included in policy discussions.[28]

As an example, Montoya explores whether policymakers frame trafficking as a "criminal," law-and-order issue, or as a gender equality issue.

Both frames draw upon distinctions made about what constitutes gender violence; they posit different understandings of the causes of trafficking and lead to different ideas about how to address the problem. This methodology allows exploration of multiple, intersectional ways to understand gender, as well as an examination of the political decisions that activists and political players make when they put gender issues on the agenda.

Using Montoya's scholarship as a point of departure, I include a focus on the *victims* of violence. Feminist IR scholars show that when we look at how advocates, countries, and organizations address gender violence, they are also articulating and strengthening discourses about "victims" that include some people and leave out others. For example, to some, only women are truly victims of gender violence, which is why Carpenter asks whether and how men can count as "civilians" in discussions about civilian harm and casualties during war.[29] Still, Enloe notes the persistence in examining gender violence as what happens to "womenandchildren."[30] She uses this term to indicate the conflation of women with their children, which presumes not only that all and only women are caretakers but also that women and children are interchangeable as helpless and innocent victims, despite evidence that women also participate in violence. Such presumptions explain why some asylum officers or immigration judges may assume that straight men would never apply for gender-based asylum.

Koomen studies the use of testimonies given by victims, noting that institutions such as the International Criminal Tribunal for Rwanda mediate, translate, and ultimately appropriate victims' stories to legitimize their own prosecutorial work.[31] Hierarchical interactions get perpetuated between tribunal personnel seeking stories of violence, and witnesses who have experienced or seen violence. This means that we must view narratives about violence in the context of how they were elicited. In other words, victims' stories may not quite match their own experiences, or may get used in ways that leave the victims' needs and interests behind.

After reading these compelling studies, I realized that it was imperative to reveal the construction of "worthy victims." Who is seen as "deserving" of asylum protection? The process of gender-based asylum, which is allegedly *about* acknowledging gender violence, can actually distort or ignore the experiences of some persecuted people.

I wanted to know how a victim had to be constructed and represented in different kinds of gender-based asylum cases, *hypothesizing that different kinds of violence would elicit different kinds of "worthy victim" frames*. As I explain in chapter 2 when describing the asylum process in more detail, an asylum seeker's credibility is crucial to determining asylum outcomes.

Indeed, Bohmer and Shuman contend that *credibility is the most common reason asylum seekers' claims are denied.*[32]

A worthy victim frame reflects presumptions about who counts as a victim, and how someone is supposed to behave to be seen as credible. For example, rape survivors might not remember chronological details because the trauma of the violence impacts their memories. Without an understanding of this particular effect of violence, a judge might decide that if an asylum seeker fumbles over the exact order of a series of events, she is lying. However, she is likely to be experiencing a trauma response. Or, if a trafficking victim was or is a sex worker, because of the frame that trafficking victims must be innocent, a judge might doubt her credibility in claiming that she was coerced into having sex. Other judges might find gay and lesbian asylum seekers credible but think that transgender people do not exist and thus do not find anything a trans asylum seeker has to say as credible.

This is not to say that worthy victims frames emerge *only* for gender-based asylum cases. As I discuss in the last chapter, they can be relevant for other types of asylum cases. However, the necessity of framing gender violence as a form of persecution requires more explicit and consistent references to the worthiness of the victims.

How do frames emerge about victims? Asylum lawyers, feminist advocates, and the array of US governmental agencies involved in the asylum process draw upon *discursive climates* of ideas and concepts about gender, race, sexuality, nationality, immigration, and global politics.[33] As discussed earlier, gender is not a category in refugee law, so it makes sense that feminist and human rights advocates, particularly those working with asylum lawyers, would want to have readily available explanations of types of violence and what the experiences of violence are like for survivors. In other words, different types of gender-based violence have to be "framed."

Feminist advocates participate in carefully crafting frames to legitimize gender violence as a form of persecution. Sometimes these frames are attentive to the root causes of violence as well as the multitude of experiences of survivors. One can see examples of such complex framing by feminist scholars or asylum lawyers commenting on cases in law reviews; they collaborate with asylum seekers to integrate their stories. But sometimes these frames simplify understandings of violence so as to increase the chances of asylum seekers receiving immigration relief. Feminist advocates and asylum lawyers may distort or reduce the nuances of the survivor's story to make the asylum seeker seem more credible. The frames that emerge can inadvertently contribute to notions that there are

"good" victims of violence, the perfect, prototypical victim who is easy to rally behind.

The US governmental players in the asylum process also create, shape, utilize, and transform frames, as they are pressured to respond to issues of gender persecution. They do so through the adjudication of cases, legislation, the issuance of guidelines and briefs, and intervention in asylum decisions. Worthy victim frames ensure that the United States can comply with human rights norms but reject the unworthy victim and thus manage the number of non-citizens coming into the country.

The frames that construct "worthy victims" have the most resonance in courtrooms and thus gain the most strength, leaving those with more nuanced framings of gender violence battling to challenge ideas about who deserves protection. Sometimes frames of gender violence work in securing a grant of immigration relief, sometimes they do not, but the *effects* of the stories are far-ranging on how gender violence is understood, the chances of potential future victims to receive protection, and how the United States exercises power. *Indeed, I contend that we must pay attention to frames because they last long after they are used in a court case*. The asylum seeker remains nameless and forgotten, but what endures is the "worthy victim" frame she or her attorney uses or feels compelled to use, or that a judge articulates.

Distinctions between "Good" and "Bad" Non-citizens

I contend that the worthy victim frames with the most political currency are those that utilize an "us-them-over there" trope. In such a narrative, "we" have to save "them" from the egregious violence that only happens "over there," in uncivilized countries. To be sure, many asylum/immigration officials and judges do engage in nuanced analyses that are mindful of the survivors' experiences. Many asylum lawyers with whom I discussed this book or whose cases or analyses I examined are aware of the difficulties in navigating racial and cultural sensibilities. But the prevalence of worthy victim frames reveals the "racialization of gender violence." Gender violence is "raced," such that some groups of people, particularly in certain parts of the world, are differentiated from other groups of people in other parts of the world based on the construct of race. And that "differentiation" relates to whom we see as the perpetrators and victims of violence, and what we see as the causes of violence.

The racialization of gender violence operates at two levels. First, the "worthy victim" frames draw upon distinctions between "civilized"

countries, to which the asylum seeker has fled, and "backward" countries, from which the asylum seeker fled. Second, asylum seekers who do not fit the worthy victim frames are not only deported but also recategorized from potentially good migrant (vulnerable asylum seeker) to a bad migrant (illegal alien). Thus underlying the distinctions between worthy and unworthy asylum seekers is the second level: presumptions that undocumented immigrants are unacceptable for entry/life in the United States.

Consider two examples that briefly illustrate these two levels of racialization. In the first example about racialized differences between countries, I refer to a critical reflection piece by Bruce Einhorn, former US immigration judge. In one anecdote, he explains that in the 1990s, "as the brave but failed efforts of the US military to bring peace to Somalia became front-page news, I had in my courtroom an asylum seeker from that poor and war-torn country."[34] He then explains that he asked the Somali asylum seeker for a Xerox, but the woman did not know what this word meant. Einhorn comments:

> This young woman, intelligent but indigent and barely familiar with the gadget-goofy and technology-dependent ways of the West, illustrated better than I ever could the cultural disconnect between her background of desperation—of drought, famine, and internecine tribal warfare unrestrained by the anarchy of the state—and mine.[35]

Because Einhorn can only see this claimant as *different*, from a country the United States tried valiantly to save, he fails to recognize the United States' governmental and military role in *contributing* to conflict in Somalia.[36] The conditions of oppression, persecution, famine, and war are contained so neatly within that particular nation-state. Einhorn sees this example as a call for immigration judges to understand cultural differences. But actually, Judge Einhorn and his claimant are engaged in asymmetrical international relations, in terms of being connected as "insider" and "outsider" at a state's border. Underlying general asylum cases, but especially those with gender-based claims, is the *difference* between countries.

In a second example about the construction of undocumented immigrants, consider a thought exercise in which we juxtapose two seemingly different women. The first woman is not in the United States legally but expresses fear to a government official about being forced to undergo genital circumcision if she is returned to her country. The second woman is an undocumented domestic worker apprehended after returning to the United States after trying to visit her family. The former, fitting into the

category of "asylum seeker," gets access to the asylum system that, while deeply flawed and inconsistent, offers an opportunity to avoid deportation. Asylum/immigration officials determine that the woman seeking asylum should be protected from deportation because of the view that genital cutting is persecutory. Female genital *mutilation* is something that would never happen "here," and thus she must be brought into the folds of the enlightened United States, where women are allegedly free and autonomous. To see this woman's experiences entirely through the lens of a type of violence deemed backward and cultural, is rooted in racial, colonial understandings of "other" women. They are monolithically constructed as always at risk of death and oppression in their countries.[37]

The undocumented woman who entered the country unlawfully in order to work is racialized as criminal, one of a stream of lazy, illiterate migrants taking our jobs, having as many children as possible to abuse our welfare system, and breaking our laws. *This* perception is also racial, but in a different way. This racialization process is multifaceted and complex, as it is entangled with racist categorizations of nonwhites in the United States.[38] More precisely, the social value conferred on marginalized communities within the United States and non-citizens entering the United States is "assigned and denied on racial terms."[39] Undocumented freeloaders and black welfare queens are cast in the same category of repulsive, threatening behavior.[40] But "worthy" migrants, those who allegedly want and desire US protection and *civilization*, are often exempted from this particular kind of racialized demonization.

But this distinction between asylum seekers and undocumented immigrants is a false one. It is not immediately evident into which category a non-citizen falls. As I will explain further in chapter 2, asylum seekers are effectively undocumented, because they are often not authorized for entry into the United States and at high risk of deportation during the entire process of requesting asylum. Asylum seekers are also likely to have experienced the same kinds of economic violence as undocumented immigrants and may even see their persecution as related to class and socioeconomic issues. People who are considered to be voluntary migrants or "illegals" may have experienced various forms of exploitation and harm that government officials do not classify as persecutory. I challenge the idea that asylum process is about an alleged distinction between asylum seekers and undocumented immigrants, or between fraudulent and legitimate asylum seekers. *Asylum is about telling the right story.*

To better understand my claims about the racialization of gender violence, I turn to how feminist IR draws upon the specific field of postcolonial feminism. Agathangelou and Turcotte contend that postcolonial

theories can hold feminist IR accountable for assuming and relying upon as natural the "geographical separations of land, people and knowledge."[41] Geopolitical segregation, as they call it, "regulates, elides and spectacularizes bodies (people, land, knowledge) through gender, racial, ethnic, sexual, national and global orders."[42] Thus, different places are not seen as influencing and constituting each other but as only connected to each other through lopsided power relationships. [43]

Postcolonial feminist scholars illustrate the centrality of gender in asymmetrical power relationships between countries that benefited from slavery and colonialism, and countries that were once used for slave labor and access to resources. These scholars also demonstrate the colonial vestiges of "helping" and "saving" the most "vulnerable," such as women or minorities *from barbaric men and societies.* As Uma Narayan explains, Western feminists engage in problematic activism when they "travel" across borders, to look at gender-based violence elsewhere, disconnected from the violence "at home."[44] In other words, these feminists may rely upon skewed representations of cultures, religions, and ethnic/racial groups to explain the *cause* of violence. *So, at some general level, the perfect victim is "exotic"*; she represents difference, escaping her backward community, culture, and country to join and be saved by "us."

Thus the issue of gender-based violence resonates not only because of the familiarity that crosses all women's lives, as Keck and Sikkink mention, but also because of the *strangeness* of some forms of gender violence. Let us revisit one of the Keck and Sikkink quotes that opened the section: activists organize most effectively around "issues involving bodily harm to vulnerable individuals, especially when there is a short and clear causal chain (or story) responsibility."[45] I recast their claim, focusing on the words "bodily," "vulnerable," and "responsibility." The asylum process legitimizes various discursive understandings about *whose bodies* are being disfigured, maimed, and brutalized, about why people are *vulnerable*, and about the *type* of people, cultures, communities, states, and regions that are *responsible* for perpetrating violence.

To state it bluntly, the hegemonic perception in popular and human rights discourses is that gender violence happens *more* to those in the so-called non-Western world and to minority, indigenous, and immigrant communities within Western countries, in more violent, egregious, otherworldly, and barbaric ways than what happens to white or otherwise privileged women in the global North.[46] The violence is worse *there* because *they* are more backward, more traditional, less educated, less democratic. On the other hand, gender violence in "Western" countries happens not due to culture or oppressive/weak states but because of the pathology of

the individual perpetrator. Western countries, unlike non-Western countries, are allegedly capable of addressing and preventing gender violence. Indeed, this capacity is what makes those countries *Western*. The "strangeness" of the violence thus is also often rooted in how the government "over there" condones, sanctions, or ignores the violence, as it is unimaginable that "civilized countries" would do the same.

Feminists critical of the "racialization" of gender violence proffer that *all* forms of violence are manifestations of patriarchal power, particularly if one recognizes that domestic violence homicides in the United States and so-called dowry murders in India occur at comparable rates.[47] Or one might consider that "crimes of passion" in the United States and "honor killings" in Arab countries have been constructed as wholly different but play out in similar ways.[48] Another example is how female circumcision and cosmetic surgery in the West both can result in negative consequences to health for the sake of ideas of beauty and femininity.[49] These feminists ask how descriptions of specific forms of violence actually stand in for what "we" think we know about a country, a culture, or a community.[50]

How did gender violence become racialized in asylum law? In part, it is due to the necessity of critiquing a pattern of persecution in the asylum seeker's country. To receive any type of asylum, an applicant or her lawyer must illustrate the government's role in or lack of will in addressing persecution. The contemporary international asylum and refugee regime emerged with the end of World War II, as the United States negotiated the admission of Jewish refugees and addressed the growing tensions between "Western" countries and communist and socialist countries in the "East." Increasingly, the United States and western Europe saw "refugee regulation" as integral to their foreign policies in the context of the Cold War.[51] Refugees and asylum seekers described oppressive communist policies and anti-Semitic practices and laws. Asylum-granting states accordingly pointed to the advantages of "democracy," even as their acceptance of non-citizens varied greatly and pivoted upon xenophobic ideas and immigration laws.[52]

But "Third World" migrants found it difficult to claim persecution, even after the end of the Cold War, because they could not always frame their stories about conflict and violence as a form of totalitarian "communist" state persecution. As the United Nations increasingly acknowledged the historically ignored experiences of female refugees and asylum seekers, it helped shape the narrative of a "Third World female refugee" fleeing "cultural norms" and "harmful traditional practices" that non-Western countries were unwilling or incapable of stopping. While this recognition of persecution of women, particularly from non-Western countries, seems

like a victory for stretching the category of asylum seeker, it launched a focus on culture, thus excluding women's "political opinions, . . . religious interpretations, [and] material oppression" as well as the larger historical and political context of violence.[53]

As McKinley asserts, colonialism

> animates arguments and attitudes about culture that shape Western understandings of the [violence] long before the asylum cases brought by African women reach a U.S. court. These cases become part of the arsenal of geopolitical and ideological tools for perpetuating Western hegemony (and its attendant anxieties) in a polarized yet interdependent world.[54]

Razack observes how an asylum petition is "*inevitably* an encounter between the white First World and the racialized Third World."[55] This is because, she claims, women from the global South are forced to speak about their experiences with sexual violence "at the expense of their realities as colonized peoples."[56] Thus, she fears that through the asylum process,

> when people of the Third World come knocking on our doors, we are able to view them as supplicants asking to be relieved of the disorder of their world and to be admitted to the rational calm of ours. It is in this way that racialized distinctions underpin the deceptively ordinary and outwardly compassionate process of granting asylum.[57]

Akram argues that when misleading or simply inaccurate information about religious practices becomes written record through asylum cases, incorrect information then becomes "fact."[58] This makes it more difficult for those who are legitimately being persecuted by certain interpretations of religious practices or texts because if the judges do not accept varying interpretations of Islam, the asylum seeker's story has to be molded into preexisting narratives.[59] Indeed, by forcing the refugee into a position where she has to blame "Islam" as the source of her persecution, there is a "repeat in the country of intended refuge the very denial of self-expression that women in particular are fleeing . . . mak[ing] it impossible for the applicant to express her own religious beliefs."[60]

When feminists, US governmental officials, and other actors demonize particular countries, communities, and people, they deflect the violence condoned or perpetrated by or in the United States. The perceptions and discourses at play in a gender-based asylum court case build upon and strengthen more widespread, institutionalized discourses about "us

versus them." In effect, the kind of violence deemed to be horrifying and inspiring of *outrage* has less to do with the experiences and effects of the violence than with what such outrage *then* justifies: militarized intervention, self-importance, ideas of the Other as backward, racial profiling, and so on.

Through an examination of different types of gender-based asylum claims, I discovered that it is not specific enough to just examine the "exotic" victim of barbaric violence. Racialization manifests in multiple ways. As I explain in chapter 3, the "autonomous" victim frame entails racializing families from "over there" as backward and inhumane, such that the deserving asylum seeker had to flee and remake herself, shedding her otherness to be "independent" like US women. In chapter 4, we encounter expectations of "innocence." Innocence can be thought of as racialized and gendered if we consider the (neo)colonial tropes of infantilizing women as in need of protection from evil perpetrators, who are racialized as communist or terroristic Others.[61] Finally, in chapter 5, the "non-deviance" frame is also racialized because *constructions* of what it means to be normal/abnormal, straight/queer, good/deviant occur at the intersections of sexuality, gender, race, and nationalism.[62] In other words, colonial and racial classifications of "otherness" historically shaped perceptions of normalcy, as well as who and what was "unnatural," thus leading to the targeting of groups understood as "sexual minorities."[63] As I explain later in the book, these worthy victim frames do overlap, particularly in terms of the general experiences of non-citizens.

Ultimately, these insights will be useful in examining the perceived distinctions among asylum seekers as well as between asylum seekers and undocumented immigrants. Undocumented immigrants, inclusive of asylum seekers in the legal process, encounter and resist the United States in ways that illustrate the "gendered and racialized logics of foreign threat."[64] Feminist analyses demonstrate how gender, race, class, and sexuality interact in shaping the dehumanization and demonization of undocumented immigrants.[65] Feminist IR thus would do well to more thoroughly examine not only how countries use immigration restriction to *do* sovereign power but also how anti-immigrantism finds it roots in neocolonial, racialized ideas about who constitutes a threat to the state.

The point of this section is to conceptualize the potential negative effects of "worthy victim" frames. These frames can result in ignoring the experiences of other asylum seekers whose stories do not fit into such narratives. Second, they may deny agency to asylum seekers who might be critical of violence in their countries but also find strength, empowerment, and belonging in their communities. Third, their existence incentivizes

asylum seekers to lie because they know they have to show how severe the violence was and play into certain representations of their countries; and these exaggerated and fabricated claims then play into the perception that asylum seekers are potentially fraudsters and liars. Fourth, the frames fail to recognize the noncultural political and economic reasons as to why violence occurs. Finally, the frames fail to connect the stories of asylum seekers with those of undocumented immigrants, who may have similar experiences of violence before and after entering the United States.

Distinctions between "Better" and "Worse" Countries

Worthy victim frames also affect and play a role in global power relationships. The frames become useful in how the United States interacts with other countries. The need to identify what kind of asylum seeker is "good enough" is important because of two contradictory desires the United States must negotiate. First, it wants to "secure" its borders against non-citizens and "undesirable" outsiders. Second, it wants to show that it is a human rights leader and thus position itself as "better" and more "capable" than the oppressive countries from which asylum seekers flee. The frames do not unilaterally shape how the United States behaves but rather reflect and influence US relationships with other countries.

What does it mean for a state to "protect" if it is simultaneously invested in protecting *itself* from "outsiders" and threatening "insiders"?[66] Studying gender-based asylum reveals that "protection" is not always about complying with international human rights norms but also about a country's power relationships. The very countries offering gender-based asylum and other forms of "protection" are also deeply committed to anti-immigrantism. But letting in only worthy victims allows these countries to be more "civilized" than the countries from which the migrants hail while simultaneously being "strong and secure" by keeping out threatening outsiders and foreigners. The more we investigate and politicize gender-based asylum, the better we can understand how sovereign power works through the "protection" of only certain categories of migrants and the restriction/expulsion of other categories of migrants. As I illustrate throughout the book, US protection then becomes useful in justifying the right to influence other countries' policies regarding gender violence and gender norms.

Chapter 2 offers a much more detailed analysis of the worthy victim frames in the context of protection, immigration restriction, and US sovereign power. It sets up the argument in the rest of the chapters about

how the United States influences other countries. For example, the United States uses discursive ideas from the autonomous worthy victim frame to try to influence countries in which female genital cutting is practiced. Thus the impact of the frames is felt not only within the United States during the asylum process but also elsewhere when the US intervenes in other countries' policymaking. The discussion in chapter 2 is made possible by a feminist IR framework, which links the "marking" of bodies for inclusion/exclusion with how countries create and maintain their identities and social positions vis-à-vis global power relationships.[67] Shepherd, for example, explores the "types of bodies that are marked and made through violence that is specifically gendered—that is, violence that 'emerges from a profound desire to keep the binary order of gender natural or necessary.'"[68] She finds that the violence committed against bodies in order to keep "gender binaries" intact is very much linked to the violence on an international scale that is used to keep state sovereignty and global power intact. As Nayak puts it, hegemony works through gendered and racialized violence.[69]

Other feminist IR scholars are interested in how it is politically expedient for countries to cast sovereign power as the capacity to create and implement policies that are attentive to the rights of women and sexual minorities.[70] In doing so, these scholars identify the political salience of gender in distinguishing between "better" and "worse" countries. But there are several problems that result from these distinctions. First, global political economic structures and processes contribute to gender violence, so sometimes it is not even useful to compare countries without looking at intersecting phenomena. Second, drawing distinctions can potentially negatively impact relationships between the United States and other countries. Third, distinctions can contribute to decisions to try to "control" the behavior of "worse" countries, with harmful consequences. Fourth, distinctions lead to the hypocritical denial of violence committed by the allegedly "better" states. In gender-based asylum cases, we might thus ignore how asylees and refugees may experience racism, additional forms of gender violence, and isolation once they are in the United States. Fifth, we can fail to recognize how "better" countries *contribute* to violent conditions in "worse" states, particularly through militarization and a variety of economic and political policies.

In sum, gender-based asylum serves as a point of departure to understand more about how state practices as well as global, asymmetrical relationships between states can shape and are shaped by the production and expression of gender bias. Because gender-based asylum requires an investigation into specific categories of gender violence as well as the role of the

asylum seeker's state in being complicit with such violence, this legal process is uniquely situated to reveal how the United States uses immigration relief for survivors of gender violence as an opportunity to emphasize its own power. This power plays out in decision-making about non-citizens, in human rights "leadership," and in relationships to other countries from which asylum seekers flee.

Feminist Possibilities for Confronting Distinctions: Challenging the Worthy Victim Frames

My final point is that the worthy victim frame is contested and contestable. The feminist critiques of asylum advocacy and the racialization of gender violence are crucial in understanding the distinctions drawn between non-citizens. Feminist activists often successfully use, articulate, and circulate frames to make intelligible that a human rights violation exists. But these advocates can leave out and distort certain stories, or serve as a conduit to strengthen distinctions between us and them, good and bad, insider and outsider, powerful and powerless.

But I do not want to inadvertently downplay the important role of even flawed feminist and legal activism in changing people's lives, such as in preventing deportation. Part of discussing the political context of asylum is considering whether it is possible to change that context. Can the tension between protection and restriction be eased, or is it a constitutive part of what it means to be an asylum-granting country? Can flawed representations of victims be challenged? What kinds of interventions should be made? Could rethinking worthy victim frames help to humanize all non-citizens, including undocumented immigrants?

Those who might tentatively agree theoretically with the points raised in the previous sections could find them irrelevant on a pragmatic level. First, many asylum advocates are not interested in the negative effects of "representations" of culture precisely because they are attempting to show that culture systematically *causes* gender persecution. Countries often resist granting gender-related claims because they argue that gender persecution results from cultural rather than political harm. Thus, they see gender-related persecution as caused not by the government but by "private actors."[71] So, mindful of both the resistance to gender-based claims and the United Nations' framing of human rights violations in terms of "harmful cultural/traditional" practices, asylum advocates have responded by trying to get "culture" to be taken seriously, as a systematic problem sanctioned *by* the state. "Culture," then, is an important asylum

advocacy tool. Perhaps asylum advocates find it more prudent to speak about harmful cultures than to try to engage in fancy feminist footwork because judges need to see that stark *difference* between countries in order to grant asylum.

Second, asylum advocates might note that the client's desire to stay in the host country trumps any concern about representations. Karen Musalo, well-known US advocate for gender-based asylum claimants, notes that it is not she, the lawyer, but the claimant who is critical of the culture.[72] Asylum seekers themselves knowingly may participate in "racializing" and "othering" themselves or their countries and communities for the sake of immigration relief. Lawyers tell me that gender-based asylum claimants often purposely leverage and take advantage of such stories about their cultures and countries. They know that by being the "helpless" victim of their cultures, they are possibly more likely to receive asylum and then gain access to the opportunity to work and send remittances home, become empowered as sponsors for other family members, obtain access to HIV/AIDS medications, or create potentially better opportunities for their children. The familiar refrain by many lawyers: the representations of cultures and countries are what their *clients* want.

Third, asylum advocates argue that critics fail to recognize that the asylum system is not designed to do more than grant legal status. Deborah Anker, a prominent lawyer and law professor involved in gender-based asylum cases and director of the Harvard Immigration and Refugee Clinic, takes note of the criticism that asylum cases might propagate simplistic stereotypes about migrants from the global South. She asserts that gender violence is indeed everywhere, not just in the global South. But she claims that

> refugee law offers a particular structuring that confronts human rights questions . . . less contentiously than . . . the human rights regime's more ambitious framework. Refugee law does not seek to reform states and does not address root causes. Its role is palliative; it represents the interests of the individual in dissociating herself from her community and her State.[73]

Of course, postcolonial feminists might balk at the notion of an individual "dissociating herself from her community and her State" because it assumes a secular universalist understanding of migrant experiences, whereby some are "saved" by Western liberal democracy. But, as one lawyer told me, the granting of refugee status to an asylum seeker is not about capturing the complexities of international relations. It is indeed "simply" about the conferral of a legal status.

But it is worth seeing if there is a way to reconcile the requirements of the asylum system with the critiques, particularly given the aforementioned damaging effects of negative representations of asylum seekers and their countries. As Oxford notes,

> It is always in the best interest of an individual asylum seeker to conform to the hegemonic narrative of persecution. The reward for asylum seekers is considerable—protection against deportation and the frightening possibility of violence and death. However, this conformity has serious consequences for reproducing a structural dynamic of inequality through the subordination of subversive stories to hegemonic narratives of gender and persecution that may undermine gender justice.[74]

This "hegemonic narrative of persecution" is another way of saying taken-for-granted discourses about what persecution looks like, what its effects are, and why and how it happens. Ultimately, if we are not continuously vigilant about dominant discourses, then we may unwittingly collude in denying reprieve to a significant number of survivors of violence. In a recent book, *Gender in Refugee Law: From the Margins to the Centre*, the editors proclaim that "refugee law presents an opportunity for feminists to develop paradigms for advocacy that promote inclusion in new ways."[75] Contributors to this book include Karen Musalo, Deborah Anker, and Connie Oxford, already mentioned in this section. The variety and diversity of their perspectives lead me to believe that a "meeting point" between advocates and critics of asylum is possible. All contributing authors share a commitment to specifically making the asylum system work better and to generally understanding better the realities of gender persecution. The more feminists intervene in the discursive climates from which worthy victim frames emerge, the more that they can also bring more complexity to discussions about asylum seekers, undocumented immigrants, and non-citizens. I revisit this point, drawing particularly upon feminist IR, in chapter 6.

METHODOLOGICAL APPROACH

I first compiled cases and descriptions of different types of gender-based asylum claims.[76] As I started to interpret trends in gender-based asylum, I consulted decisions by "asylum decision-makers" in adversarial court proceedings, such as the US immigration courts and federal courts. I also examined articles analyzing and interpreting these decisions in legal and

academic journals as well as by law clinics, research centers, and immigration/asylum advocacy organizations.[77] Finally, I consulted additional material regarding relevant laws, policies, and guidelines published by a variety of US agencies including the Department of Justice, the Department of Homeland Security, the Executive Office for Immigration Review, US Citizenship and Immigration Services, and the Office of Refugee Resettlement. Chapter 2 details the asylum process and various players.

I identified the types of violence that asylum advocates, governmental agencies, and asylum seekers discuss: domestic violence, female genital cutting, rape, trafficking, honor killings, coercive sterilization/abortion, persecution due to sexual or gender identity, forced marriage, repressive social norms, and persecution due to women's rights activism. Then, by drawing on the methodology and work of Celeste Montoya, I looked for patterns and trends in how the violence was described; who was describing the violence; which parts of the asylum seekers' stories the asylum seekers, attorneys, judges, and advocates emphasized; reflections by asylum lawyers about how they framed the cases; and analyses by legal and academic scholars as well as expert witnesses. In addition to looking at the presumed causes and effects of the violence, I looked for descriptions of how the survivors experienced the violence.

Through textual, interpretive, and content analysis, I identified common phrases and descriptors about the victims of violence, paying careful attention to descriptions of their credibility. I looked for patterns and trends in these phrases and descriptors. The "worthy victim" frames are not "named" as such. For example, there are no guidelines that explicitly say "we need autonomous victims in female circumcision cases" or "try to fit the mold of an innocent victim if you are applying for coercive sterilization." Rather, I was able to compile consistent and persistent descriptions, phrases, and narratives that emerged in three distinct patterns: autonomy, innocence, and non-deviance.

Through this analysis, I asked: who is *not* included in the framing of victims? Who is left out? How do I know? What kind of story would not "fit"? To answer these questions, I looked particularly at judges' statements and reflections by asylum lawyers, advocates, and expert witnesses about how asylum seekers left out or fabricated particular parts of their stories. In researching the effects of each type of violence, I searched for examples of asylum cases regarding a wide variety of survivors. For example, since sex workers are trafficked, I looked for but did not find sex worker asylum cases.

Since I also researched laws and policies related to the asylum cases and generally related to the types of gender violence addressed in gender-based asylum cases, I discovered a variety of policy objectives, stances, and discourses that used the same type of descriptors and phrases I discovered while researching the framing of "victims." I analyzed the origin of these policy stances, finding that the United States often explicitly referenced the understandings that undergird the worthy victim frames. Thus, I was able to link the worthy victim frame to certain policies/positions/stances; and, in turn, when I researched how those policies shaped and enabled US actions toward other countries, I made a link between the worthy victim frame and US influence.

Figure 1.1 illustrates my methodological approach. The discursive climate indicates different ideas and discourses, including "us-them-over there" distinctions, from which worthy victim frames emerge. The frames, in turn, strengthen those particular discourses when they are repeatedly used in courtrooms and legal analysis. The discursive climate also contributes to US policies, as what the United States sees as possible and meaningful as an exercise of power draws from and strengthens discursive ideas about what the world is like and should look like. The worthy victim frames interact with the US policies as well.

The worthy victim frame is not a causal factor that will predict which cases will result in grants or denials. Rather, it is a significant factor in constructing the asylum seeker's credibility. Further, because the worthy victim frames are rooted in other presumptions about gender, race, distinctions between countries, and how the world works, they have far-ranging effects. The frames shape the kinds of obstacles and difficulties other asylum seekers with similar cases will face and thus can shape the strategies they or their attorneys will try to adopt. And judges repeatedly mention,

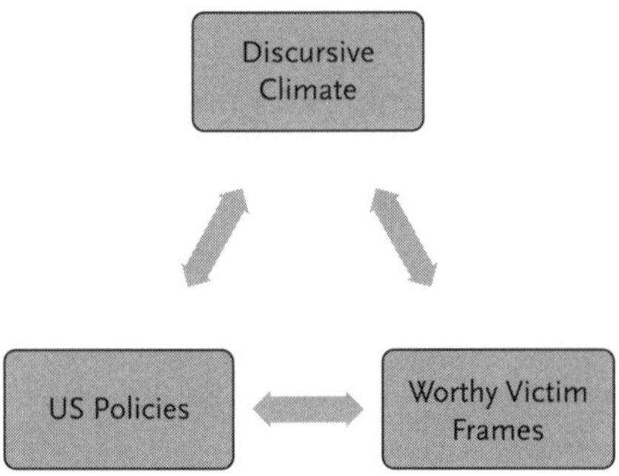

Figure 1.1 The Connection between Discursive Climate, Worthy Victim Frames, and US Policies

invoke, or reference frames when deciding cases. The frames also serve as entry points for US power politics. In the chapters that follow, we discover that the reason why certain frames prevail over others is precisely because of the traction they find in the context of US power relationships. Whether one judges US actions in the world as desirable or not, it is crucial to explore how the frames become useful for justifying US influence and power in global politics.

I offer the following qualifications about my methodology. Because I do not operationalize and "quantify" the frames, I do not know the relative weight of the frame vis-à-vis the other factors, such as which individual immigration judge is hearing the case or whether the asylum seeker has an attorney.[78] But my typology is valuable for future research that could code frames and potentially conduct quantitative studies that test the relative weight of identifiable factors that shape asylum outcomes. But such studies would be limited by access to case data.

Second, I limited my scope of cases. As I will explain more in chapter 2, in the asylum process, asylum officers conduct interviews of asylum seekers, and immigration judges assess claims through an adversarial court process. Information about court proceedings, while inconsistently available, is far more accessible and detailed, including amicus curiae briefs and written arguments by lawyers and asylum seekers, than information about the asylum officer interviews.[79] This is a methodological problem that confronts many researchers trying to analyze not only gender-based asylum cases but the immigration and asylum process as a whole.

Third, the frames I identified are not necessarily mutually exclusive; rather, I look at what kinds of frames seemed the most salient in different types of asylum cases. Finally, this book does not look in detail at cases involving forced marriage, repressive social norms, or feminism as political opinion (or women's rights activism). These three types of persecution were often enfolded within or considered secondary to the other forms of violence discussed in the chapters to come.[80]

PLAN OF THE BOOK

Chapter 2 dives deeper into the tension between immigration restriction and asylum protection. It does so by first explaining how the asylum system works, examining immigration laws as well as the key political players in the US government involved in making decisions about whether to grant asylum. While I often say "the United States" in this book, as we dig deeper, we see that there are multiple agencies acting on behalf of the

country, often with contradictory interpretations and interests regarding "whom to protect." Any reader interested in but confused by asylum and immigration laws will find clarity in that chapter. Chapter 2 also explains that the "worthy victim" frame is more pertinent in gender-based asylum cases because of the lack of gender as a ground of persecution. I provide data on general asylum trends and patterns in gender-based asylum grants and denials. I show that the movement to address gender-based asylum predominantly focuses on women, and more recently, sexual minorities.

all figures here

Chapters 3, 4, and 5 discuss three main "worthy victim" frames or classifications through empirical studies of different types of gender-based asylum claims. Table 1.1, "Overview of 'Worthy Victim' Frames," provides a comparative summary of the frames, which asylum seekers are left out of these frames, and how the frames are useful for US policymaking.

As I discuss in chapter 3, I found an unexpected commonality in the construction of the "worthy victim" in domestic violence and female genital cutting cases. The "good" asylum seeker is expected to demonstrate *autonomy*. She must "stand apart" as an individual seeking freedom in the United States. But many asylum seekers still love their family members and are forced to describe them in ways that may be abhorrent to them. Or they are able to prove that they suffered harm but not that they rejected their families. People in these situations are "left out" of the autonomy frame. The United States links these autonomy frames to distinctions between itself and other countries, opening space to deflect from its own domestic violence problems, to attempt to shape how other countries address domestic violence, and to financially pressure and influence countries in which genital cutting occurs. Because of the idea that "good" migrants are autonomous, rejecting their countries, cultures, and families, the United States can justify targeting and influencing those "rejected" countries that are allegedly too "weak" to control "violent families."

Another unexpected similarity occurs in the construction of worthy victims for trafficking and coercive sterilization or abortion cases. In both of these types of cases, I discovered an expectation that the deserving victim is *innocent*. As I explain in chapter 4, the trafficking survivors most likely to receive immigration relief tell stories of finding themselves trapped in a world of endless rape and sexual slavery, from which they must be rescued. Thus, those who escaped their traffickers might confront a perception that they are not truly vulnerable by virtue of their ability to flee. Also left out of this frame are sex workers and migrants who were smuggled into the country and ended up in situations that exploited their labor or bodies. They are not seen as innocent because they engaged in criminal activity. I found here too that the United States uses the

Table 1.1 OVERVIEW OF "WORTHY VICTIM" FRAMES

Type of violence	Worthy victim frame	Effect of frame on asylum seekers (who is left out?)	Effects of frame on US policies and power relationships
Domestic violence	Autonomous	Survivors left out include those unwilling to prove "rejection" and disconnection from "culture" as well as from family/kin responsible for violence.	United States distracts attention from its own problems with domestic violence. United States makes a case for influencing domestic violence responses in other countries that it perceives as too "weak" to control "violent families."
Female genital cutting	Autonomous	Same as above	United States financially pressures countries that do not address female genital cutting in the same way the United States does. United States shapes immigration policy to frame FGC as an immigrant problem.
Trafficking	Innocent	Sex workers and smuggled migrants not included because of alleged "criminal activity." Sex-trafficking victims prioritized over labor-trafficking victims. Trafficking victims who were rescued are prioritized over those who escaped.	United States ranks and sanctions countries according to not only how well they control trafficking but also whether they take an anti-prostitution pledge. United States links smuggling and trafficking with terrorism, focusing more on criminal activity than on harm done to survivors.

Coercive sterilization/ abortion	Innocent	Unmarried victims not included. Less severe forms of population control such as forced gynecological exams and birth control insertion not included. Victims of forced pregnancy and maternity (particularly due to lack of access to abortion) not included. Focus on loss of "innocent unborn children" rather than on harm to women or on their reproductive choices.	United States draws distinction between itself as a protector of women's rights and China (and its coercive population control practices) as an oppressor of women's rights. United States strengthens commitment to deny use of funding to global organizations that provide access to abortion services/counseling.
Persecution based on sexual orientation and gender identity	Non-deviant	Gender conformity in contradictory, paradoxical ways expected of sexual minorities. Sexual minorities more likely to be detained/ penalized due to perception they commit "moral turpitude" crimes. Sexual minorities discouraged from applying for asylum.	United States proclaims distinction between itself as protector of sexual minorities and other countries as oppressors of sexual minorities, while distracting attention from homophobia/transphobia that is part of the US immigration/asylum system.

innocence frame to influence and possibly sanction or limit aid to countries that are not engaged in anti-trafficking efforts in ways the United States judges to be adequate. In particular, since the innocence frame leaves out sex workers, it justifies US sanctions of countries that do not commit to anti-prostitution as part of their anti-trafficking efforts. The United States also links smuggling and trafficking with counterterrorism efforts.

The second type of violence I discuss in chapter 3 concerns victims who are coerced to have abortions or undergo sterilization primarily as a result of China's one-child policy. In 1996, Congress amended the Immigration and Nationality Act to explicitly mention this type of persecution as a possible claim for asylum seekers. But the concern for victims of coercive reproductive practices does not extend to unmarried women who experience these practices. It also does not include women who are forced to undergo "less severe" forced practices, such as gynecological exams against their will, because the United States is primarily concerned with the loss of "unborn children" that deprive married women of their ability to be mothers. This frame is useful for the United States to draw a distinction between itself as a protector of women's rights and China as an oppressor of women's rights. In addition, if the innocence frame articulates who is worthy, then it creates space for the United States to influence or respond to the choices of the unworthy. The US pro-life movement that was behind the congressional amendment for victims of coercive sterilization and abortion also plays a role in US governmental denial of funding to nongovernmental organizations that provide access to abortion services and counseling, particularly to rape victims in conflict zones. Lack of this access then creates the conditions for forced pregnancy and maternity, which I name as a persecutory form of gender violence that is left out of the discussion of coercive reproductive practices.

LGBT *

In cases about the persecution of gay, lesbian, bisexual, and transgender migrants, the "worthy" victims are supposed to be *non-deviant*.[81] As I discuss in chapter 5, the legal system is biased against sexual minorities, with legislation, policies, and practices that presume that people with non-conforming sexual orientation and gender identities are *not normal*. As a result, LGBTQ migrants are incentivized not to apply for asylum. Or they find that they face in the courtroom convoluted and contradictory expectations about how sexual minorities supposedly behave. They encounter the intransigence of homophobia and transphobia in asylum law and how the US government operates. For example, laws that demand incarceration of asylum seekers and undocumented migrants who have committed "crimes of moral turpitude" disproportionately target sexual

minorities who are more likely to be perceived as immoral. In effect, while sexual minorities flee countries due to persecution because of perceptions of their "deviance," they confront variations of those same perceptions in the US asylum system. The United States uses the non-deviant frame to manage how many migrants are let into the country while also drawing distinctions between itself as protective of sexual minorities and other countries as oppressive of sexual minorities.

Given the range of effects and uses of these worthy victim frames, in chapter 6 I explore possibilities for pragmatic advocacy to challenge the damaging and dehumanizing distinctions made among non-citizens and victims of violence. I explicitly challenge the worthy victim frames. I examine alternative constructions of "family" and the role of socially meaningful relationships to challenge the autonomous worthy victim frame. By considering "forced maternity or pregnancy" as a possible additional category in gender-based asylum, I challenge the innocent worthy victim frame, particularly regarding coercive reproductive practices. By elucidating and challenging the concept of "moral turpitude," which targets sex workers and sexual minorities, I take on the innocent worthy victim frame operating in trafficking cases as well as the non-deviant frame in sexual orientation and gender identity cases. In this way, I go beyond critique to sketch out possibilities of future dialogue, advocacy, and scholarship that can be relevant in general strategies to address gender violence. Thus, in chapter 6, I create a dialogue between academics, advocates, and lawyers because of the contributions we can make collaboratively to articulate new political and legal understandings about asylum, immigration, and gender violence. I also create mutual accountability for those of us researching and advocating in the realm of asylum and immigration.

I conclude the book with chapter 7, which forgoes the typical summary of arguments for the use of a "question and answer" format to engage with potential critiques or concerns about future research or advocacy. In that chapter, the questions I pose and answer are the following: Is gender-based asylum only for women and sexual minorities? Are the worthy victim frames relevant in asylum cases (in general) that do *not* focus on gender-related persecution? Are the worthy victim frames relevant in the cases of the undocumented children discussed in the first lines of the book? This book seems to demonstrate that asylum seekers lie or misrepresent themselves; given that tendency, is it not appropriate to protect the United States from fraudulent non-citizens seeking to abuse the asylum system? Is this book arguing that the United States should not control its borders? Doesn't the United States have the right to determine who enters the country? The distinctions drawn between "better" and "worse"

countries are not necessarily problematic; wouldn't the asylees living safely in the United States agree that the United States is "better"? What are specific contributions feminist IR can make to address the human rights of non-citizens?

In sum, this book offers *four significant contributions* that build upon the rich literature on gender-based asylum.[82] First, while the existing scholarship examines different types of gender-based asylum, often exploring the politics of how we categorize violence as "exotic," I illustrate unexpected commonalities between types of gender violence that force us to reconsider unexamined dimensions of how gender violence operates. I would not have discovered these surprising elements of violence had I not studied gender-based asylum. It is also not enough to critique distinctions between "worthy" and "unworthy" migrants, as some scholars do. As I demonstrate, we must explore the specific typologies of worthiness, as they have different kinds of effects.

Second, other scholars note that many of the issues asylum seekers face are rooted in flawed immigration policies.[83] I draw attention to how discussions about the rights of refugees or asylum seekers to flee persecution can reinforce the gendered and racialized distinction between "desired" and "undesired" non-citizens. Thus I challenge the arbitrary distinctions made not only among asylum claims but also between asylum seekers and undocumented immigrants.

Third, we cannot look at asylum, a discretionary *sovereign* grant of protection to *non*-citizens, without situating such a process in the context of how global power works. The United States is able to draw upon and strengthen these "worthy victim" frames to enhance distinctions between itself and others, to justify shaping other countries' policies, and to walk the line between protection and restriction. Worthy victim frames become *useful* in shaping, strengthening, or legitimizing US actions in the world. My approach thus questions the very "politics of protection." We might ask, what is the point of protection offered by asylum if it is only offered to those who fit preconceived notions of what it means to be a worthy victim? The hypocrisy of this type of protection is that the United States does not desire to provide safe haven to the persecuted as much as it wants to claim the ability and capacity to protect them.

Fourth, while I came across excellent critiques of the asylum system, it is important to engage with those tasked with representing asylum seekers or serving as advocates in other capacities. What are the intersections of theory and praxis? I contend we can create new possibilities in the asylum system and immigration rights advocacy.

CHAPTER 2

Understanding the Tension between the Protection and the Restriction of Non-citizens

In 1980, the US Congress passed the Refugee Act,[1] inspired in part by a large mid- to late 1970s refugee influx of Soviet Jews and migrants from Cambodia, Vietnam, and Laos.[2] This act brought the United States into compliance with the 1951 United Nations Convention Relating to the Status of Refugees and the 1967 United Nations Protocol Relating to the Status of Refugees.[3] Refugee law is one of the few "human rights" areas in which the United States has incorporated international legal standards and norms into domestic law.

The Refugee Act adopted the 1951 United Nations Convention's definition of *refugee*:

> someone who owing to a well-founded fear of being persecuted for reasons of race, religion, nationality, membership of a particular social group or political opinion, is outside of the country of his nationality, and is unable to, or owing to such fear, is unwilling to avail himself of the protection of that country.[4]

The passage of this legislation means that the United States upholds the principle of *non-refoulement:*

> No country should return a refugee to a country where his life or freedom would be threatened on account of race, religion, nationality, membership in a particular social group or political opinion.[5]

Soon after the passage of the Refugee Act, politicians voiced worries about the potential exploitation of the asylum/refugee process by fraudulent, undocumented immigrants. Thus intensified the tension between the obligation to protect migrants fleeing persecution and a desire to restrict immigrants.

In 1995, the United States started to more explicitly recognize gender-based asylum claims when the Immigration and Naturalization Service (INS) issued the "Asylum Gender Guidelines," which described how to adjudicate claims based on gender persecution.[6] The Harvard Immigration and Law Clinic drafted the guidelines in collaboration with feminist advocates.[7] The final document referenced the United Nations Convention on the Elimination of Discrimination Against Women, the United Nations Declaration on the Elimination of Violence Against Women, the United Nations High Commissioner for Refugees statements on the plight of refugee women, and the Canadian Gender Guidelines issued in 1993. To asylum/refugee advocates, even though the United States never published the guidelines, it was moving in the right direction in acknowledging gender-based persecution.

At the same time, in the aftermath of the 1993 bombing of the World Trade Center in New York City along with several publicized incidents of asylum seekers and asylees who had committed crimes, Congress started to pass immigration laws to crack down on undocumented immigration as well as on potential asylum seekers who might abuse the system. Asylum advocates and lawyers have been justifiably concerned about the negative effects of these immigration restrictionist laws on legitimate asylum claims. If we look at table 2.1 and table 2.2, we might wonder how two opposing trends, in protection and restriction of non-citizens, could occur concurrently. But I argue in this chapter that the two tendencies are intimately intertwined. Ultimately, I challenge the idea of finding the "worthy victim" of violence by interrogating the distinction between asylum seekers and undocumented immigrants.

In this chapter, I first explain the asylum system and process. I then demonstrate the effects of restrictionist immigration laws on the asylum system and asylum seekers, arguing that the only way to ensure fair, transparent, and just assessment of asylum claims is to comprehensively examine immigration restriction and how the United States responds to non-citizens in general. I conclude with an analysis of how "protection" and "restrictionism" help to reinforce each other, particularly since protection is not necessarily benign and humanitarian but also politically expedient.

Table 2.1 KEY DEVELOPMENTS IN THE CREATION OF THE REFUGEE AND ASYLEE PROTECTION REGIME, PARTICULARLY REGARDING GENDER AND SEXUALITY

Year	Document	Purpose
1951	United Nations Convention Relating to the Status of Refugees	States religion, race, nationality, political opinion, and social group are grounds for persecution; notes refugees should not be returned to face persecution
1967	United Nations Protocol Relating to the Status of Refugees (United States ratifies in 1968)	Removes the geographical and temporal restrictions of the 1951 Convention
1975	First United Nations World Conference on Women in Mexico City	World Plan of Action focuses attention on refugee women in particular
1981	US Refugee Convention	Aligns US law with international law
1985	United Nations High Commissioner on Refugees (UNHCR) Conclusion No. 39	Notes that women may constitute a "social group" for which they are persecuted
1991	UNHCR Guidelines on the Protection of Refugee Women	Identifies the particular issues that refugee women face and how to create better assistance and protection
1993	Canadian Gender Guidelines	Provides guidance to asylum adjudicators for deciding claims by women and based on gender-related violence and persecution.
1995	US Gender Guidelines (cites relevant United Nations documents)	With influence of feminist and human rights advocates, United States follows Canada's pioneering step and issues gender guidelines
2002	UNHCR Guidelines on International Protection No. 1: Gender-Related Persecution (cited by US asylum training manuals)	Examines what kinds of violence and crimes comprise gender-based persecution; notes that claims based on non-conforming sexual orientation "contain a gender element"
2008	UNHCR Guidance Note on Refugee Claims Relating to Sexual Orientation and Gender identity (cited by US asylum training manuals)	Provides analysis of forms of persecution and specific obstacles in proving credibility
2012	UNHCR guidelines on international protection No. 9 regarding claims to refugee status based on sexual orientation and/or gender identity	Provides more specific legal interpretive guidance for claims based on sexual orientation or gender identity

Table 2.2 RESTRICTIONIST IMMIGRATION LAWS AND POLICIES

Year	Law	Provisions
1996	Illegal Immigration Reform and Immigrant Responsibility Act (IIRIRA)	Creates one-year filing deadline for applying for asylum; creation of 287(g) program through which local police can act as immigration officials; 3- or 10-year ban on undocumented immigrants apprehended without appropriate documents from re-entering the United States; enforcement and patrolling practices established; expands list of deportable crimes; creates expedited removal of those arriving in or living in the United States without proper documentation, severely limiting opportunities for administrative and judicial review of people in deportation proceedings; mandatory detention for those without proper documentation awaiting credible fear interviews and asylum hearings
1996	Personal Responsibility and Work Opportunity Reconciliation Act	Restricts non-citizens from accessing most public benefits
1996	Anti-Terrorism and Effective Death Penalty Act (AEDPA)	Prohibits international terrorist (individuals, organizations, and states) financing and fundraising; narrows asylum procedure to prevent potential terrorists from using asylum laws to enter the United States; makes it easier to deport someone who has committed a crime of "moral turpitude" even if he or she has not been imprisoned for the crime; expands list of deportable crimes
2001	Uniting and Strengthening America by Providing Appropriate Tools Required to Intercept and Obstruct Terrorism Act (USA PATRIOT)	Expands upon financial prohibitions detailed in AEDPA; limits immigration relief for undocumented immigrants harmed by the September 11, 2001, attacks; authorizes indefinite detention of immigrants and non-citizens.

2002	Homeland Security Act	Creates the Department of Homeland Security, which subsequently takes on significant duties previously performed by Immigration and Naturalization Services, while the Executive Office for Immigration Review and the immigration court system are retained in Department of Justice
2002	Enhanced Border Security and Visa Entry Reform Act	Provides more Border Patrol agents.
2004	Intelligence Reform and Terrorism Prevention Act	Section on border protection, immigration, and visa matters makes immigration process more difficult and steps up border protection attempts by increasing border patrol agents by 20%; builds more immigration detention centers; increases penalties for those who transport undocumented immigrants; creates committee to ensure that asylum system is not being exploited by terrorists
2005	REAL ID Act	National standards for identification; higher standards for proving credibility for asylum seekers; clears path for building barriers for border between United States and Mexico
2005	US Border Patrol National Plan for Prevention Through Deterrence	Increase of personnel, fencing and surveillance technology. Aim is to disrupt migrant smuggling and stop recidivism.
2006	Secure Fence Act	Approval of creation of 700 miles of barriers erected along United States–Mexico border

THE US ASYLUM SYSTEM AND PROCESS

For the next several pages, I take the reader through the different components of the asylum system. I point to figure 2.1, "Key Asylum Players" and table 2.3, "Roles and Responsibilities of Key Asylum Players" as references. I generally use the term "migrant" or "non-citizen" to indicate anyone with foreign nationality who has entered the United States, regardless of the reason. I also use the term "immigrant" to indicate that migrants and non-citizens are not in the United States for specific reasons, such as tourism or to study, but rather to live and stay. Undocumented immigrants are any non-citizens who do not have authorization to live, work, or reside in the United States.

"Refugee" is a general term that is often used to reference migrants who flee their countries or cross borders in the context of war, crisis, or repressive conditions. But in refugee law, refugee applicants are those who petition the United Nations from *outside* of the United States (or other countries) for legal protection. Applicants interested in migrating to the United States go to US embassies in their country or a transit country. The applications are reviewed by US State Department employees, who consult with the US Department of Homeland Security procedures and requirements. The United Nations High Commissioner for Refugees (UNHCR) is also involved in reviewing the applicants' claims through a consultative body that works with governments.[8] Those who receive referrals from the US Refugee Admissions Program move to the United States and transition to life in the country through the "Refugee Resettlement Program," facilitated by the Office of Refugee Resettlement. Each fiscal year, the president of the United States issues the proposed caps on the number of allowable refugee admissions.

Asylum applications, on the other hand, are submitted once the person, the "asylum seeker," is *already inside* the United States. Once an asylum application is granted, the petitioner is called an "asylee." But *before* the asylum seeker receives a decision, he or she is in legal limbo; this person is at risk of a denial of asylum, which would result in removal proceedings, or leaving the country. *The asylum seeker and the undocumented immigrant both have unsettled statuses; the only difference is that asylum seekers are protected from deportation if they have applied for asylum.* Asylum seekers cannot work for at least six months once they have filed.

This book focuses entirely on asylum applications made inside the United States, as I am primarily interested in the distinctions made among non-citizens who have entered the country. Both refugees and asylees have access to assistance from the Office of Refugee Resettlement,

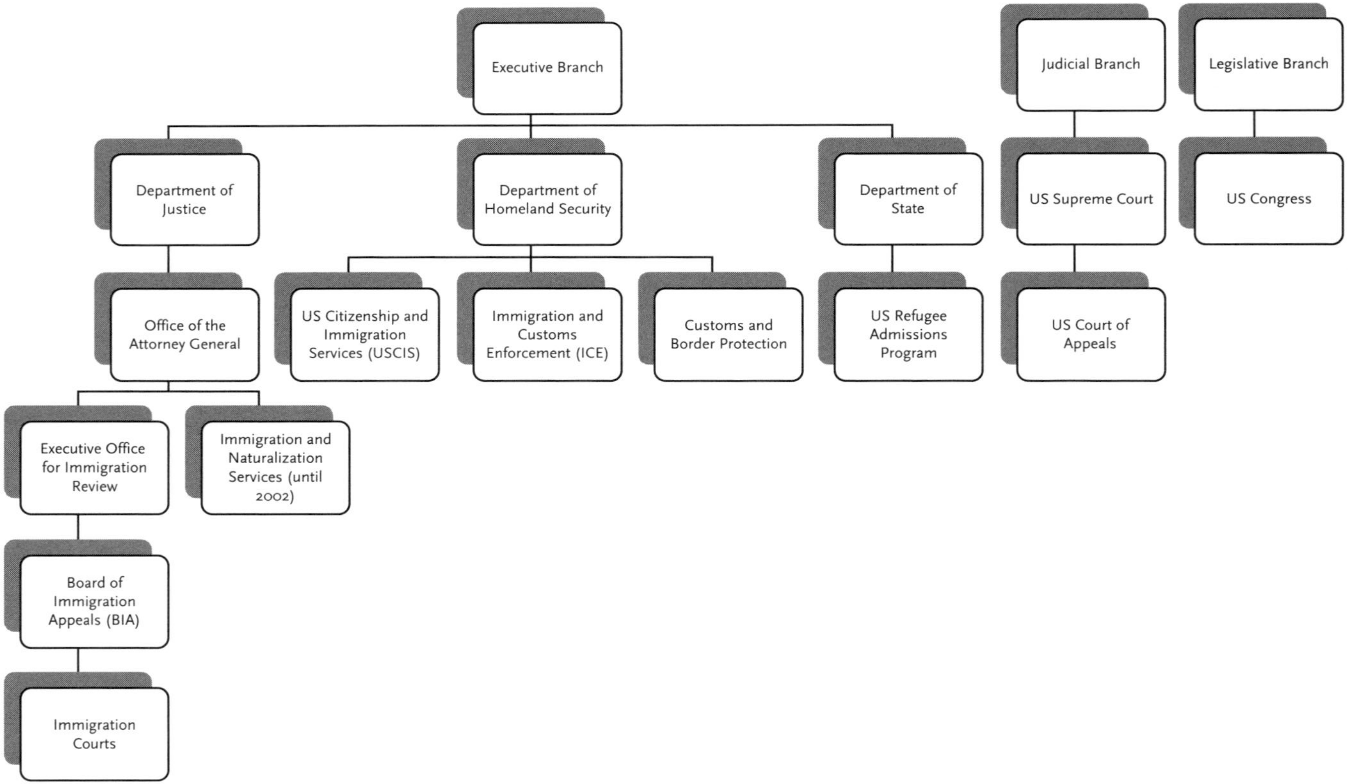

Figure 2.1 Key Asylum Players

Table 2.3 ROLES AND RESPONSIBILITIES OF KEY ASYLUM PLAYERS

Agency	Role/Responsibility
Department of Justice: Office of Attorney General	Head of the Department of Justice and chief law enforcement officer; represents the US government in legal issues and matters
Department of Justice: Executive Office of Immigration Review	Adjudication of immigration cases and interpretation of immigration law
Department of Justice: Board of Immigration Appeals	15-member body interprets and applies the law, hears appeals from immigration judges' decisions. Decisions are binding on Department of Homeland Security officers and immigration judges.
Department of Justice: Immigration Courts	52 courts, 224 immigration judges selected by the attorney general. Not considered to be a part of the judicial branch.
Department of Justice: Immigration and Naturalization Service	Dissolved after 2002; all duties performed by newly created Department of Homeland Security
Department of Homeland Security: US Citizenship and Immigration Services	Asylum Officers assess asylum claims. Assistance with administration of immigration services and benefits
Department of Homeland Security: Immigration and Customs Enforcement	Addresses and investigates border "vulnerabilities." Runs/contracts immigration detention centers.
Department of Homeland Security: Customs and Border Protection	Serves as federal law enforcement of the Department of Homeland Security
Department of State: US Refugee Admissions Program	In coordination with Department of Health and Human Services, and Department of Homeland Security, manages refugee applications, resettlement of refugees, and related processing issues
Judicial Branch: US Supreme Court	Hears a limited number of cases at its discretion that start in state or federal courts and deal with questions and interpretations of the US Constitution and federal law
Judicial Branch: US Court of Appeals	12 regional circuits throughout the country hear appeals from federal administrative agencies, including the Board of Immigration Appeals
Legislative Branch: US Congress	Bicameral legislature of the US federal government tasked with making financial, budgetary, security, and immigration policies

including temporary cash assistance, medical and social services, and the ability to adjust their status to "legal permanent resident" after one year of continuously living in the United States. It is crucial to note that asylum seekers have *one year* from the date of entry to apply for asylum; I discuss the hardships and obstacles posed by this rule below.

Three Paths to Asylum

Asylum seekers applying within the United States do so in three main ways. The first possibility is "affirmative asylum." In these cases, the asylum seeker presents himself or herself as a petitioner for immigration relief. Generally speaking, these particular asylum seekers are not detained in the immigration detention centers described below, but if their petition is denied, they might be held, even during the appeal process, which could last weeks, months, or even longer.

Applicants must go to an office of US Citizenship and Immigration Services (USCIS) for fingerprinting and security checks. They then receive a notice to be interviewed by an asylum officer along with a request to provide their own interpreters. This process occurs within the jurisdiction of the Department of Homeland Security (DHS). The asylum officer may grant or deny asylum. If the claim is denied, then the asylum seeker may explain in writing, providing new evidence if available, within 16 days why the claim should be granted. The asylum officer will then grant asylum or provide a final denial letter. Asylum officers' final decisions cannot be appealed.

If the case needs further review, the asylum officer will refer the asylum seeker to the jurisdiction of the Department of Justice (DOJ), in which case the applicant must appear before an immigration judge for the asylum hearing. About 30%–35% of cases adjudicated by asylum officers are granted asylum;[9] 60%–65% of asylum seekers are referred to immigration courts.[10] Denials can occur only in cases where asylum seekers have legal immigration status; just a fraction of cases result in denials by asylum officers because only 7% of asylum seekers apply with legal status.[11] Someone without legal status who is not granted asylum would not be denied asylum by the asylum officer but rather referred to the immigration court.

While immigration courts provide interpreters, they do not conduct interviews, and the proceedings are conducted in a courtroom. These cases are usually titled "In the Matter of ——" with the initials of the claimant. If the immigration judge decides to deny asylum, the applicant may then appeal the denial to the Board of Immigration Appeals (BIA), which will

uphold the denial or overturn the judge's decision and remand the case to the judge to issue a new decision. BIA cases are also usually titled with the "In the Matter of ——" format, with information about the respondent (asylum seeker's attorney or legal counsel), the Department of Homeland Security attorneys, who represent the US government in upholding the denial of asylum, and any amicus curiae, or "friends of the court," ranging from expert witnesses to nongovernmental organizations that offer their perspectives in briefs submitted to the court.

If the BIA denies the appeal, another appeal can be sent to the appropriate federal court of appeals, in one of the twelve regional circuits. These court cases are labeled "Asylum seeker's name v. last name of the presiding US Attorney General," or "Cordoba v. Holder," for example. Before the Immigration and Naturalization Service agency was dissolved (see table 2.3), federal court cases were titled "Asylum seeker's last name v. INS." The federal court will either remand to the BIA to examine the case again, with instructions on correcting interpretive errors, or recommend upholding the BIA's decision. An applicant can appeal a federal court's ruling to the Supreme Court; if the court decides to hear the case, its decisions will be binding for all asylum adjudicators and judges at all levels.

The second way an asylum seeker petitions the government for asylum is through "defensive asylum." These applicants are in removal proceedings (to be deported from the United States) after apprehension in the United States or at a port of entry because they do not have legal documents or are violating the terms of their immigration status. If a person is apprehended by Customs and Border Protection (while crossing into the United States) or through Immigration and Customs Enforcement action (such as in a raid), he or she is detained and put into removal proceedings to be deported. If the apprehended person proclaims that he or she is seeking asylum and fears persecution, then US Citizenship and Immigration Services will conduct a "credible fear" interview to determine whether an asylum application can be submitted.

Credible fear is a lower standard than the "well-founded fear" standard in asylum cases. If credible fear is not found, the applicant may appeal for an immigration judge to make that determination. If credible fear is found, there is a hearing before an immigration judge. Even if the judge grants asylum, the US government has the right to appeal the decision. If the US government contests the decision, or if the immigration judge denies asylum, the asylum seeker follows the same path of appeal options as described above, to the BIA and then the US federal courts system. The final way to apply for asylum is derivative asylum, when someone who

has received asylum applies for asylum for his or her spouse or unmarried child under the age of 21. In addition, asylum seekers during any step of the process will be denied asylum if they have committed crimes, including "nonpolitical" crimes committed before arriving in the United States, are thought to pose a danger to the United States, have participated in or funded terrorism, have resettled in other countries or could be resettled in a safe "third country," or have committed persecution.[12]

The Components of the Asylum Case

In all asylum cases, there are several components to prove:

1. Well-founded fear of persecution, meaning it is likely the applicant will suffer if returned or deported to the country of origin
2. Belonging to or having characteristics of one of the accepted grounds of persecution in refugee law (political opinion; social group; race; nationality; religion)
3. Persecution having occurred due to this characteristic
4. Participation by the government of the country from which the applicant fled in the persecution, or an unwillingness or inability to prevent the persecution
5. Credibility and believability of the asylum seeker

To prove "well-founded fear of persecution," an asylum seeker must prove legitimate fear based on past or potential future experiences as well as that the harm, suffering, or violence feared is "persecutory." While there is no statutory definition of persecution, in *Kovac v. INS* (1969) the Ninth Circuit Court of Appeals first broadly defined it as "the infliction of suffering or harm upon those who differ . . . in a way regarded as offensive."[13] The kinds of harms that amount to persecution could include "serious physical harm; coercive medical or psychological treatment; invidious prosecution or disproportionate punishment for a criminal offense; severe discrimination and economic persecution; and severe criminal extortion or robbery."[14] The persecution can include discrimination or harassment but must be deemed offensive and systematic, not arbitrary or random.[15]

The asylum must also prove "well-founded fear," by pointing to evidence of past persecution she or he has experienced, to patterns of persecution against "similarly situated" people, or to expectations of future persecution. Well-founded fear means that there is a reasonable possibility of

suffering. The asylum seeker also needs to show that relocating within the country will not help avoid persecution. The applicant must demonstrate a "subjective" element of fear that he or she experiences, and an "objective" element, showing that any "reasonable" person in a similar situation would also be fearful.

For fear of future persecution, the Board of Immigration Appeals notes in *Matter of Mogharrabi* (1987) that the asylum seeker must demonstrate that

> the applicant possesses a belief or characteristic a persecutor seeks to overcome in others by means of punishment of some sort; the persecutor is already aware, or could become aware, that the applicant possesses this belief or characteristic; the persecutor has the capability of punishing the applicant; and the persecutor has the inclination to punish the applicant.[16]

The federal courts are split on whether it is required to prove "punitive intent," or the desire and motivation of the persecutor to cause harm based on the possession of the belief or characteristic. In order to prove "well-founded fear," an asylum seeker has to ultimately prove the *second* and *third* requirements of asylum eligibility: "possessing a belief/characteristic protected in the Refugee Convention"; "being persecuted because of this belief/characteristic."

Asylum seekers wishing to put forward gender-based asylum claims have limited options to prove persecution based on possession of characteristics. First, they can emphasize another aspect of persecution, such as religion, and include the gendered aspects of the harm. Many asylum seekers in general apply based on the racial and ethnicity/nationality grounds, which pose their own difficulties given that these categories can shift or have very different, sometimes contradictory meanings.[17] Thus, combining gender with one of these categories could be particularly difficult since understandings of gender persecution can also greatly differ or be context-specific. Second, asylum seekers can claim that they were persecuted due to political opinion. Historically, asylum applicants in general have most frequently cited persecution due to political opinion.[18] Gender-based examples include persecution against feminist activists, women transgressing local gender norms of behavior, or women holding beliefs that one should not be viewed as property of men, particularly if they are harmed by someone who does believe men should dominate and control women. However, asylum adjudicators are more likely to take seriously claims of persecution due to political opinions held by men than by women.[19]

The final category is persecution based on membership in a particular social group; members of the group "share a common, immutable characteristic the members either cannot change or should not be required to change because it is so fundamental to their individual identities or consciences."[20] It is particularly difficult to prove that a particular targeted gender, gender identity, or sexual orientation constitutes a social group, since asylum judges misunderstand or deny the existence of gender violence. Or they fear the group would be too broad. But at the same time, the social group ground is quite flexible, leading asylum lawyers to use this category for gender persecution claims. Social group claims often overlap with political opinion claims; for example, consider the targeted group of "lesbian women who protest the government".

The claim that gender is a social *group* is not equivalent to the claim that gender is a social *construct*. To reference gender as a *social construct* means that social structures, institutions, and people participate in creating, performing, and perpetuating ideas about gender. There is a "purposefulness" in making gender what it is, rather than some inherently "true" qualities based on biology. A *social group* is based on being a member due to something that one cannot change or should not be required to change because it is so fundamental to one's identity or conscience.[21] Thus, in the "asylum world," gender is not always seen as constructed but as an "innate" characteristic targeted by persecutors. Courts and judges vary on how flexible they are when they interpret social group characteristics. The Ninth Circuit, for example, has noted that the characteristic can be immutable *or* based on voluntary associational relationships.[22]

In the *Matter of C-A-* (2006) the BIA decided that social groups should also have a visibility component, meaning that social groups must be cognizable as such in society, which can be problematic to prove.[23] In the *Matter of S-E-G-* (2008), the BIA added particularity, which means that the group should be distinct from other groups.[24] The BIA effectively added much higher standards for arguing for persecution based on social group. Some federal courts have used the BIA guidelines, whereas others have contested them.

Asylum decision-makers tend not to understand that gender violence is *political* and a form of persecution that targets people systematically because of gendered expectations, ideas, constructs, and norms. Thus, gender-based violence is often ignored or downplayed. Judges and officials, per my review of cases, might dismiss the violence as a "personal or psychological problem" of the perpetrator, as a "one-time occurrence" that was an unfortunate "byproduct" of an event or encounter, or as a "personal issue." As I will demonstrate throughout the book, sometimes the

social group ground is successful, but it can contribute to ideas about worthy victims. *This is because membership in a social group is proven by noting which people are persecuted, and how they are* <u>*distinct*</u> *from others.* "Worthy victims" are often created in many types of asylum cases, because of the immigration protection-restriction tension, but I argue these frames are much more prevalent in gender-based asylum cases because of the additional burden posed by the lack of gender as a category in refugee law.

The fourth requirement is that the asylum seeker must prove that the government participated in or was complicit with the persecution. The asylum seeker could also prove that persecution occurred at the hands of a group the government is unable or unwilling to control, such as a paramilitary organization or other nonstate actor. If gender violence is not seen as "political," then asylum decision-makers are not likely to understand how a government might be complicit or participate in gender violence.

Finally, the asylum seeker must prove "believability," which is determined based on the claimant's consistency of claims, ability to corroborate the claims, and character/credibility. Like the other requirements of proving an asylum case, this component is also left to the subjective interpretation of asylum judges. To assess credibility, judges and asylum officials may ask questions that try to get at the asylum seeker's character. Questions could include the following: What kind of mother is the asylum seeker? Why did she choose to leave her children behind? Why did she not immediately report the violence she suffered? Why did she cry so much in court (was it an act)? Why did she not cry at all (is she lying)? Why did she mix up the details in the chronology of what she did before, during, and after the violent acts? Did she make any decisions that could have provoked her attacker? Why was she living with a man who was not her husband? Why does she not seem very "masculine" even though she claims she is a lesbian? The list goes on. This kind of scrutiny does not happen in every case, but because asylum eligibility requires an evaluation of credibility and character, asylum seekers are often subject to a "victim-blaming" line of questioning. It is not far-fetched, then, that "worthy victim" frames would emerge and gain traction in the context of the legal wrangling required to make an asylum seeker seem believable.

Other Considerations: Forms of Relief and Decision-Making

The last two issues to cover are (1) the different forms of asylum/immigration relief available; and (2) how asylum decisions are made. As to the first area of concern, throughout the book, I use the general terms "asylum"

or "immigration relief," but there are different types of protection. If an asylum seeker is denied asylum, his or her case is automatically considered for withholding (which can also be granted if someone applies for asylum after the one-year deadline). Asylum seekers may also apply for, or judges may recommend, consideration of protection under the United Nations Convention Against Torture and humanitarian asylum. Asylum and humanitarian asylum provide the most benefits, while withholding and protection under the Torture Convention offer fewer benefits. Asylum means that the applicant is allowed to remain within the country with an option to adjust the status to legal permanent resident at a later date. Someone who receives withholding of removal is simply able to stay in the United States; she cannot adjust her legal status, leaving her in legal limbo. Spouses and children also cannot receive derivative asylum through someone who receives withholding status. Someone who wants withholding does not have to show fear of persecution but only that his or her life or freedom would be threatened. The evidentiary burden is much higher for asylum than for withholding.

Humanitarian asylum functions like asylum, but it focuses on past persecution. This type of asylum is reserved for those who might not be persecuted today in their country of origin but can demonstrate reasons for being unwilling or unable to return to a country due to the severity of the past persecution. Protection under the Convention Against Torture addresses a smaller category of crimes than asylum and withholding, as it only deals with torture, but the applicant does not need to prove that the torture occurred due to a protected ground. Also, the burden is lighter, as the applicant just has to show that it is more likely than not that there is a probability of torture.

The last relevant form of immigration relief is a special visa. The Victims of Trafficking and Violence Protection Act provides access to 5,000 T visas for survivors of trafficking, as well as for their family members. This act also allows for 10,000 annual U visas. U visa applicants must be victims, indirect victims, or bystanders who suffer substantial physical and mental abuse due to crimes such as rape, domestic violence, female genital cutting, slavery, blackmail, or torture. Applicants must be willing to cooperate with criminal investigation and must receive law enforcement certification of helpfulness to the investigation or prosecution of the crime. They should also be admissible to the United States, meaning they do not have any immigration violations or criminal convictions. The U visa recipients may adjust to permanent legal status after three years, but criminal cooperation is a significant and necessary element. The Violence Against Women Act (VAWA) allows migrants experiencing forms of domestic violence to

self-petition for immigration relief. While there are no caps for VAWA petitioners, the abuser must be a US citizen or legal permanent resident. The applicant must prove that he or she was or is married to the abuser, entered the marriage in "good faith," and if divorced, show a connection between the divorce and the violence experienced. VAWA petitioners must also demonstrate "good moral character."[25]

While I discuss domestic violence and female genital cutting in chapter 3, I do not include an analysis of the U visa, because it encompasses a wide array of violent crimes, or the VAWA self-petition, because it is relevant only when the persecutor is a US citizen/permanent legal resident. Thus neither option lends itself to the comparative analysis in this book of specific categories of violence when the perpetrator is outside of the United States. Chapter 4, however, examines more extensively the dynamics of the T visa to comparatively highlight the difficulties with trafficking asylum cases, particularly given US governmental resistance in offering guidelines in such asylum cases. It should be noted that special visas are granted when the violence occurs *in* the United States, but the T visa process usually involves the international element given that victims are trafficked from elsewhere into the United States.

Second, I turn to how asylum/immigration judges and officials make their decisions. I refer the reader again to figure 2.1 and table 2.3 as a reminder of the key players. The Department of Homeland Security issues guidelines and memos that help guide the behavior of immigration inspection officers and asylum officers but are not binding on those, such as immigration judges, under the jurisdiction of the Department of Justice. Department of Justice regulations and guidelines similarly are applicable to immigration judges but not to those employed under the auspices of the DHS.

Asylum decision-makers are able to draw upon international law, the UNHCR guidelines, case law including from other countries or international criminal tribunals, expert knowledge, amici curiae briefs, law review articles about the type of violence or country in the asylum application, and country condition reports created by the US State Department. But judges and asylum officers often rule on a case-by-case basis, sometimes ignoring or taking out of context the various sources of information and analyses named. Decision-making might also depend on the political inclinations of the immigration judges, who are appointed by the attorney general, who in turn is nominated by the president of the United States and confirmed by the US Senate.[26]

Asylum officers' (under the Department of Homeland Security) decisions are not published or documented; thus one can only access them

by permission or through interviews with asylum officers. Immigration judges' decisions are accessible, but they are not required to explain why they made a particular decision. Decisions made by the Board of Immigration Appeals (Department of Justice) and the federal courts (judicial branch) are accessible, and are also potentially "published" and made "precedent." As a note, most of the Board of Immigration Appeals' decisions are "unpublished," meaning they are not binding. Precedent-setting published decisions are supposed to, as a matter of law, guide future asylum decisions. Decisions by the federal courts are binding only for asylum adjudicators within their jurisdiction. The attorney general also has the power to declare a decision as precedent-setting.

Sometimes, "quiet" precedent-setting occurs, in which a federal court of appeals might issue a different interpretation of the law or explain how to define a particular social group, but there is no "declaration," as might occur with an attorney general decision. But immigration judges have been known to misinterpret or flat out ignore even precedent decisions. If asylum cases were uniformly accessible, or the DOJ and DHS created joint rules and guidelines,[27] it would be helpful to asylum lawyers preparing cases and researchers attempting to find trends and patterns.

THE US PROTECTION REGIME

Even though the US refugee/asylum system is complex, significant numbers of non-citizens are granted asylum and receive refugee status. Thus, we see evidence of trends and patterns of the *protection* of migrants fleeing persecution. Table 2.4 illustrates the number of refugee admissions as well as affirmative and defensive asylum grants.

The average rate of grants of asylum cases varies depending on which immigration court and which asylum officer hears the case. The national average of denials by immigration courts was a staggering 85%–90% in 1986 and between 75%–85% thereafter. Between 1995 and 2001, the rate dropped from 80% to 60%. There was a slight dip in 2004, and the rate has been about 40%–50% in recent years.[28] That does not mean that everyone else receives a grant of asylum; they may receive withholding status, or their cases may be pending. According to data by US Citizenship and Immigration Services, Justice Department, and Department of Homeland Security, the average asylum grant rate for both asylum officers and immigration judges is about 30%–35%. Female immigration judges also grant asylum at a rate of 53.8%, as compared to male judges, whose average rate is 37.3%.[29] As noted earlier, asylum officer grant rates are 30%–35%, they

Table 2.4 REFUGEE AND ASYLUM DATA

Year	Refugee cap	Admitted refugees	Top countries	Number of asylum applications	Affirmative asylum grants	Top countries	Defensive asylum grants	Top countries
2003	70,000	28,286	Ukraine	73,780	15,367	Colombia	13,376	China
			Liberia			China		Colombia
			Iran			Haiti		Albania
			Somalia			Cameroon		India
			Ethiopia			Ethiopia		Haiti
2004	70,000	52,840	Somalia	52,630	14,340	Colombia	13,022	China
			Liberia			Haiti		Colombia
			Laos			Venezuela		Albania
			Ukraine			China		Haiti
			Sudan			Ethiopia		India
2005	70,000	53,738	Somalia	48,800	13,491	Haiti	11,757	China
			Laos			Colombia		Colombia
			Cuba			China		Haiti
			Russia			Venezuela		Albania
			Liberia			Ethiopia		Indonesia
2006	70,000	41,094	Somalia	51,500	12,955	Haiti	13,304	China
			Cuba			Colombia		Colombia
			Iran			China		Haiti
			Ukraine			Venezuela		Albania
			Liberia			Guatemala		India

2007	70,000	48,218	Burma	49,200	12,360	China	12,859	China
			Somalia			Colombia		Colombia
			Iran			Haiti		Haiti
			Burundi			Venezuela		Albania
			Cuba			Indonesia		India
2008	80,000	60,107	Burma	49,600	12,081	China	10,982	China
			Iraq			Colombia		Colombia
			Bhutan			Venezuela		Haiti
			Iran			Haiti		Iraq
			Cuba			Iraq		Albania
2009	80,000	74,602	Iraq	49,020	11,925	China	10,300	China
			Burma			Ethiopia		Ethiopia
			Bhutan			Colombia		Colombia
			Iran			Haiti		India
			Cuba			Nepal		Venezuela
			Somalia					
2010	80,000	73,293	Iraq	55,530	11,178	China	9,906	China
			Burma			Ethiopia		Ethiopia
			Bhutan			Haiti		Colombia
			Somalia			Venezuela		India
			Cuba			Nepal		Nepal
			Iran			Iran		

(*continued*)

Table 2.4 CONTINUED

Year	Refugee cap	Admitted refugees	Top countries	Number of asylum applications	Affirmative asylum grants	Top countries	Defensive asylum grants	Top countries
2011	80,000	56,384	Burma	74,000	13,369	China	11,504	China
			Bhutan			Venezuela		Ethiopia
			Iraq			Haiti		Eritrea
			Somalia			Egypt		Nepal
			Cuba			Ethiopia		Egypt
2012	76,000	58,179	Bhutan	88,400	17,506	China	11,978	China
			Burma			Egypt		Ethiopia
			Iraq			Venezuela		Nepal
			Somalia			Ethiopia		Eritrea
			Cuba			Haiti		Egypt

Source: Data are from the United Nations High Commissioner for Refugees, US Department of State Bureau of Population, Refugees, and Migration, Worldwide Refugee Admissions Processing System, US Department of State Proposed Refugee Ceilings to Congress, US Citizenship and Immigration Services Refugee, Asylum, and Parole System, and the Executive Office of Immigration Review to provide general information about asylum admissions. In particular, I looked at the Department of Homeland Security's statistics on Refugee and Asylum Flows. Figures for 2013 were not released at the time that this book was completed and data were not available before 2003 since the Department of Homeland Security was created in 2002. The table does not include pending asylum applications and withholding grants.

refer 60%–65% to immigration judges, and less than 7% of applications are denied. There is a negligible gender difference in the grant rates of male and female asylum officers. Refugee status is comparatively easier to get than asylee status, with the rates hovering between 58%–93% of the allotted refugee cap.

The average gender breakdown for refugee claims is 51.75% male, 48.24% female. The average affirmative asylum gender breakdown is 52.46% male, 47.54% female. The data for defensive asylum claims are harder to access, as are data on the proportion of female asylum seekers. Finally, governmental agencies do not provide data on the grounds upon which asylum decisions were filed, so we do not know the percentage of claims that deal with gender-based persecution, including by sexual minorities.

Bohmer and Shuman note that while women do not apply for asylum as much as men, they are often more successful than men, in part because they might be perceived as less likely to put forward fraudulent claims; at the same time, decision-makers often do not take women seriously when it comes to recognizing their experiences and also operate on presumptions about how women should react when telling their stories.[30] Gerard points out that while women have more disadvantages than men in crossing borders and learning about asylum due to sexual violence, limited resources, and caretaking responsibilities, women may at times benefit from "victimology," of being more believable than men as victims of violence.[31] While this might be the case generally speaking, I find that "victimology" operates in more complex ways when it comes to gender-based asylum claims in particular.

When people apply for gender-based asylum claims, they are making claims not just as women, but as women with particular claims about *gender violence*, which, as noted in chapter 1, requires asylum adjudicators to consider and draw upon their political opinions about the causes, content, and effects of this type of violence. Gender-related persecution is also infrequently recognized, with gender-based claims constituting a small percentage of overall claims.[32] Gerard notes that gender guidelines do not seem to have much impact on actually shaping asylum decision-making. Her case studies do not include the United States,[33] but empirical evidence indicates that US immigration officials and judges frequently dismiss or ignore guidelines on gender-based asylum claims.

To learn more about gender-based asylum cases, I obtained data from the Center for Gender and Refugee Studies (CGRS) at the University of California–Hastings, which provided information on 1,868 completed cases between 1996 and 2013 regarding several types of gender-based violence.

I received information on grants and denials, organized by country. The top five countries from which asylum seekers received gender-based grants were El Salvador (rape, gang violence, domestic violence); Guatemala (domestic violence and rape); Guinea (domestic violence, female genital cutting, forced marriage); Honduras (domestic violence, rape); and Mexico (domestic violence, rape, LGBT-based persecution). Interestingly, while immigration restrictionists name four of those countries (all except Guinea) as the biggest source countries of undocumented immigration, courts are granting asylum claims from these countries. The greatest numbers of denials were for Guatemala, Mexico, China, El Salvador, and Nigeria, but the number of grants far surpassed the number of denials for Guatemala, Mexico, and El Salvador. Table 2.5 shows a breakdown of grants and denials according to the type of violence.

The CGRS data are incomplete in some ways because the Center depends on information that attorneys provide and does not include pending cases. CGRS staff members note that the picture is skewed toward the positive, as attorneys who report outcomes might be more likely to only report grants, or might be more likely to receive grants when receiving assistance from CGRS. Further, while CGRS has data on over 7,000 cases that are

Table 2.5 GENDER-BASED ASYLUM TRENDS

Type of violence	Number of grants	Number of denials
Domestic violence	747 (El Salvador, Guatemala, Honduras)	129
Rape	374	78
Female genital cutting	365	47
Repressive social norms	271 (Afghanistan, Iran)	40
Forced marriage	171	20
LGBT-related claims	121 (El Salvador, Guatemala, Honduras, Mexico)	6
Honor killings	84 (Pakistan)	13
Child abuse	74	6
Gang violence	59	15
Trafficking	52 (Albania, Guatemala, China, Honduras)	19
Women's rights activist	32	2
Sex slavery	29	6
Coercive population control	25 (China)	18

Note: This categorization of types of violence is according to the Center for Gender and Refugee Studies. The numbers indicate all cases in which claims based on the type of violence are present. Where there is a preponderance of claims from a particular country, I have indicated as such in parentheses. See chapter 1, note 80 for a detailed explanation of case selection and categorization.

accessible via its database, this table only includes cases with final decisions. I will discuss these findings and the case data throughout the book.

Even with the relatively small number of cases and with all of the obstacles in both applying for and researching gender-based asylum, there is an intriguing worldwide momentum when it comes to the recognition of gender-based asylum claims and gender-related persecution. Canada was the first country to issue gender guidelines in 1993. The United States issued them in 1995. Australia, Panama, South Africa, the United Kingdom, and Switzerland soon did as well. By 2014, 32 additional countries had recognized the existence of gender-based persecution through national legislation.[34] This acknowledgment illustrates the success of feminist social movements in drawing attention to this type of violence. Gender-based violence exists. It is politically motivated, has harmful effects, and is fundamentally related to gendered power relationships particularly as they intersect with race, class, and other constructs. For countries to formally recognize gender-based asylum cases is no small feat.

Brysk and others note that gender-based asylum cases are evidence of the power of "bottom up" advocacy, prompted and shaped by the stories of asylum seekers.[35] Indeed, asylum advocates have made significant progress in getting various governments and administrations to legitimize gender-based asylum cases and advocacy. For example, in the United States the Women's Refugee Project, a collaborative partnership of legal and human rights advocates, started in the late 1980s to bring gender analysis to refugee law.[36] CGRS and prominent asylum lawyers involved in gender-based asylum cases, such as Karen Musalo and Deborah Anker, have helped draft guidelines and served as expert consultants to Congress for various issues. Further, CGRS and various immigration law clinics regularly provide guidance on how to navigate the asylum system, working on ways to empower lawyers and asylum seekers to understand how to maximize chances of winning an asylum grant.

Gender-based asylum is a part of the US "protection regime," meaning a set of norms, rules, and practices that focus on extending legal protection to those who are eligible under domestic and international law. I remind the reader of table 2.1, listing key developments in legitimizing gender-based asylum, including United Nations documents the United States has ratified, cited, or drawn upon. While it might be easy to completely dismiss gender-based asylum as an ill-fated option, there is (albeit spotty) "buy-in" by some players in the asylum process, such as many individual asylum adjudicators, governmental agencies that issue guidelines and training manuals, and some of the federal courts.[37] Asylees, not just refugees, receive benefits through the refugee resettlement program,

which the US State Department lauds as a "model" for the rest of the world and a reflection of the country's "highest values and aspirations to compassion, generosity and leadership."[38] Many legal commentators even seem to think that because the United States already has a reputation for being a world leader in providing safe haven, based on the consistently high rates of refugee admissions and the highest number of asylum claims as compared to other Western countries, the country is obligated to increasingly pay attention to gender-based asylum to "live up" to its own standards.

But we also need to politicize protection. How is the grant of protection for asylum seekers a political act for countries? To answer, I turn to the concept of international hierarchy. How countries support norms plays a role in their position in "international hierarchy."[39] As Ann Towns points out, "Social hierarchy, a term [that can be used] synonymously with social inequality, stratification or rank, concerns *the ordering of actors as superior or inferior to one another in socially important respects*."[40] Hierarchies position countries as more or less "superior" or "advanced." For example, treating women and sexual minorities well (or appearing to do so) matters in making states look "good," and "better" than states that do not, illustrating that international relations is "social."

When activists pressure countries to make decisions or to create policies that uphold norms, they "need to make clear why that state *as a being of a certain kind and rank* should [change a behavior]."[41] Specifically, Towns examines norms regarding the status of women, in terms of their inclusion in the state via equal voting rights, whether/how national policy bureaus focus on advancing women's rights, and sex quotas for national legislatures. In each case, both activists and politicians set up states as more or less superior in terms of their accomplishments in each area.

States are increasingly engaging in "gender-correct" behavior. Gender-correct behavior means acting in ways that take seriously norms that emphasize the appropriate treatment of women and sexual minorities, and that challenge and eradicate norms that reinforce unfair and unequal gendered expectations. In the context of the production of international hierarchy, the perceived presence of gender-correct behavior determines whether countries are constructed as gender-equal or gender-oppressive. Gender-equal states incorporate and advance norms of equality and rights for women and sexual minorities. Gender-oppressive states condone or strengthen practices that dehumanize, degrade, or render as unequal, women and sexual minorities. Gender-oppressive states reject human rights norms. I contend that part of what it means to be constructed as gender-correct is to uphold internationally agreed-upon norms regarding

the prohibition of gender-related violence and persecution. So if we consider that violence against a group is also a way to measure that group's status in society, then we can, using Towns's theoretical framework, presume that norms prohibiting gender violence and persecution could theoretically serve to rank which states are better and worse.

The unique component of gender-based asylum is it addresses a normative prohibition of gender persecution that is implemented through the treatment not just of one's own citizens *but of foreign nationals.* To prohibit gender persecution means to use gender-based asylum to offer redress to those who suffer from it in other countries. I argue that the country that is perceived as gender-equal protects citizens from countries that are gender-oppressive in part to demonstrate *capacity and capability.* This capacity is a sign of strength and leadership, engendering the right to influence those countries that are *not* capable. The country that can protect not only its most vulnerable but also those from other countries is seen as or sees itself as "better" than the country *from which* people must be protected. Asylum, a "discretionary grant of sovereign power,"[42] highlights drastically the lower "rank" of the country from which the citizens need protection.

Countries in the global South, including the ones from which migrants flee, accept refugees and grant asylum. As mentioned before, an increasing number of countries around the world are recognizing gender-based persecution: 25 countries in the global West/North, and 13 countries in the global South.[43] But while the flow of asylum seekers might occur between countries in the global South, or from the global South to the global North, we usually do not see examples of people fleeing gender-based persecution from Canada, the United States, Australia, and the European Union *to* countries in Africa, Central and South America, the Middle East, South Asia, and East Asia. A simplistic explanation of this phenomenon would be to state that an asylum seeker is leaving a low-ranking country, in terms of treatment of women and sexual minorities, to enjoy rights in a high-ranking country. But this explanation does not elucidate why gender violence occurs or the complex factors that determine flows of migration.

Countries in the global North do not necessarily take gender violence more seriously than countries in the global South but rather find it politically expedient to participate in gender-correct behavior. In order to understand this claim, we have to first understand *why* gender-correct behavior contributes to the generating of social rankings, or the discursive ways countries and activists position countries in relation to each other. Why is the "situation of women" increasingly considered a "standard of assessment" of how "civilized" a country is?[44] Why has there been

an emergence of a norm that "better states exhibit appropriate practices towards women?"[45] And, why, more recently, is the treatment of sexual minorities a concern of countries as well?

Towns traces the changes from the inclusion of women in political life during the era of absolutism (late sixteenth to eighteen centuries) to *new* notions during European colonialism (commencing in the nineteenth century) that the exclusion of women from political life was actually crucial for civilized states.[46] In turn, European societies viewed women's political agency in non-European countries as indicative of being "primitive." Towns then discusses the shift to construct women as a "unified sex" in the context of liberal secularism, or the creation of constitutional states. Women were to be seen as a "civilizing" force (particularly through their roles as wife and mother), yet they were to be kept out of the political, public sphere for their "protection."[47]

But it was this very construction of women as a group, as a civilizing force, that created space for women's rights movements around the world to eventually frame women's participation in political life *as* an indicator of a civilized state.[48] Women's rights activists subverted and leveraged the idea of civilized states to push countries to adopt changes that would advance women's rights.[49] For example, they put forward the narrative that *civilized* and superior states include women in political life. Towns's study compels us to look at the deliberations around the world in various countries about how the status of women means something about countries and their position in the world. Women are *useful*, because their inclusion is perceived to lead to more cooperation and to the increased injection of "female traits," however constructed, that can allegedly lead to certain positive outcomes such as the countering of aggression or the expansion of the role of states in making lives better for all citizens.[50] Crucially, Towns illustrates that Western countries may or may not fare better than non-Western states in the treatment of women, nor have European or North American countries always led initiatives for the better implementation of women's rights.[51]

Both feminist movements and lesbian, gay, bisexual, and transgender (LGBT) organizations started to stretch gender norms to include the rights of sexual minorities.[52] So these groups began to pressure countries to see sexual minorities as important political and economic constituencies and to frame the treatment of sexual minorities as a human rights issue that also indicates the "progressive" nature of states. A series of resolutions and commitments by the international community helped to reinforce the idea that it was socially important for countries to be more inclusive of sexual minorities. Examples include the Yogyakarta Principles on the

Application of International Human Rights Law in Relation to Sexual Orientation and Gender Identity in 2006 and the United Nations Human Rights Council's 2011 Resolution on Human Rights Violations Based on Sexual Orientation and Gender Identity. Just as journalists writing about women's rights have ranked countries as the "best" and the "worst" places to be a woman,[53] so too are they starting to rate the best and worst places to be a sexual minority.[54] Countries are also increasingly tying foreign aid to how countries treat sexual minorities or calling out leaders for condoning or ignoring violence and discrimination.

Rankings of how well countries do in upholding norms seem to be rooted in empirical realities. Organizations and agencies, such as the Freedom House Survey Team, various bodies of the United Nations, and the World Economic Forum, actually order/rank countries based on various empirically assessed indices. For example, the Freedom House Survey Team gives the United Kingdom of Great Britain and Northern Island (UK) a status of "free" with the highest possible scores on "political rights" and "civil liberties."[55] The United Nations Development Programme ranks it number 35 in the world in terms of gender equality.[56] Bangladesh has a status of "partly free" with midlevel scores on political rights and civil liberties, and it is ranked number 115 in gender equality. The UK, then, is presumed to be "better" than Bangladesh in upholding rights. But I contend that because the UK is ranked higher, it is also presumed to be more *capable* in shaping global trends and making decisions that affect other countries, not just regarding "gender" issues but a whole host of other concerns.

Even without such statistical rankings, global discourses about and by countries that are more "gender-correct" than others help to legitimize those "better" countries as more capable of making decisions about and intervening in the countries that are "inferior." This is not to say that there are no differences between countries but to ask how those differences get translated into *socially* recognized rankings that then shape the interactions between "better" and "worse" states. The very distinction between "better" and "worse" states has shaped, and is shaped by, how we make sense of international relations, who is imagined to have agency, who or what is the "other," and ideas about how countries should behave.[57]

The distinction is particularly rooted in discursive ideas about the differences between "here" and "there," between Western and non-Western, between civilized and backward. As mentioned in chapter 1, these distinctions form the "discursive climate" from which worthy victim frames arise. Towns's study provides empirical evidence that challenges these racialized discursive ideas, showing how marginalized groups from non-Western countries can use the concept of social rankings to their

advantage. However, as noted in chapter 1, the enduring hegemonic premise in human rights discourse is that Western countries are better than non-Western countries in addressing the rights of women and sexual minorities, particularly regarding gender violence.

Through this book's case studies, I highlight how the United States draws upon and strengthens international hierarchical relationships via the worthy victim frames. I thus create space to explore how an approach that assumes Western countries are better at addressing gender violence can backfire. For example, women's rights groups and LGBT organizations find they are "squeezed" between Western pressure and their governments' resistance to Western influence. They must simultaneously defend themselves from claims that they, as citizens of a particular country, are categorically backward, while also trying to hold their countries accountable. Further, they may face accusations from their governments that they have been corrupted by Western propaganda. Evaluations of countries also can be *ahistorical*, because they fail to consider the role of colonialism and conflict in creating the conditions of discrimination and violence against certain communities. Rankings are also *apolitical*, by ignoring how the very countries critiquing others have variations of the same problem "at home" or contribute to violence in the "lowest ranked" countries.

I am not contesting the mere *act* of evaluating laws, norms, and treatment of various groups of people. It is indeed useful and powerful to be able to assess how far countries have come in complying with human rights norms. Compliance can create legislative and infrastructural changes, strengthen domestic movements, hold leaders accountable, and legitimize marginalized communities in significant ways. Rather, I am concerned about *how* these evaluations are created and appropriated to justify power relationships and actions including foreign aid conditionality, sanctions, and militarized intervention. Human rights advocates often pressure powerful countries to, in turn, influence other countries to comply with human rights standards. But we should ask at what cost and whether this pressure results in real qualitative changes for the people most impacted by human rights violations. Collaborative, solidarity-based work to end violence and discrimination is often more successful and less costly than strong-arming countries to "behave."

Sally Engle Merry, noted feminist anthropologist and scholar of gender violence, is currently working on a research project that examines the impact of creating human rights indicators.[58] She looks at committees monitoring human rights treaties, violence-against-women surveys, and the US State Department Trafficking in Persons Report (discussed in chapter 4) to ask about which perspectives and knowledge claims shape

these methods of ranking and monitoring countries' compliance with human rights standards. She is also concerned about whether those who are "studied" have a voice in the creation of these ratings. Given a more complex view of protection, it is now worth examining the *politics of restriction*.

THE IMMIGRATION RESTRICTION REGIME

The Department of Homeland Security estimates that there were about 11.4 million "unauthorized" or undocumented immigrants living in the United States as of January 2012, with 42% having entered after 2000, and 14% after 2005.[59] Almost 60% of undocumented immigrants are from Mexico. The next highest rates are from El Salvador (6%), Guatemala (4%), Honduras (3%), and the Philippines, India, South Korea, China, Ecuador, and Vietnam each at 2% of undocumented immigrants. Unfortunately, there is no information on whether asylum seekers who are in the middle of the legal process of affirmatively or defensively applying for asylum count as unauthorized immigrants.

As mentioned earlier and indicated in table 2.2, 1996 heralded a new era of attempts to curb immigration flows into the United States. There are immigration opportunities, such as the diversity-lottery visa programs. But I focus primarily on immigration restriction so as to trace whether and to what extent the United States is contradicting its overall commitment to protect migrants fleeing persecution. Organizations such as Amnesty International, the Lawyers Committee for Human Rights, Human Rights Watch, the US Conference on Catholic Bishops, and the Harvard Immigration and Refugee Clinic note that immigration laws have a deleterious impact not only on undocumented and unauthorized immigrants but also asylum seekers.[60] The three main elements that affect asylum seekers are the *one-year filing deadline, expedited removals*, and *mandatory detention practices*.

First, the Illegal Immigration Reform and Immigrant Responsibility Act (IIRIRA) of 1996 created a law that asylum seekers must apply within *one year* of their entry into the United States. Exceptions apply if the asylum seeker can prove extraordinary circumstances, such as illness, trauma related to the persecutory harm, and a change in conditions in the country of origin that prompted a new asylum claim.[61] Critics argue that this deadline is prejudicial against potential asylum seekers who may not have the legal resources or knowledge to know about the asylum option. It also causes unnecessary hardship to asylum seekers with ineffective or

no attorneys. And despite the exceptions clauses, asylum seekers are often denied without much investigation into the circumstances that caused a delayed filing. A significant percentage of asylum decisions simply state that asylum was denied only because of missing the one-year deadline.[62]

Second, *expedited removals* eliminated the previously guaranteed "automatic" evidentiary hearings for people who were apprehended when trying to enter the country without proper legal documentation/authorization.[63] Higher-level asylum and immigration officials conducted those previous hearings. However, with expedited removals, even if an asylum seeker knows to request a credible fear interview due to fear of persecution, hearings are regularly conducted by "lower-level" officials who may not be trained to comprehensively assess asylum claims, particularly gender-related ones. These officials rely on inappropriate or insufficiently trained translators, sometimes even a traveler the immigration official finds in an airport. One misunderstanding could lead to deportation proceedings.

The power of removal is now unprecedented, particularly since the Anti-Terrorism and Effective Death Penalty Act (AEDPA) and IIRIRA also dramatically expand the definition of "deportable crimes" and reduce opportunities to seek waivers of deportation if one is convicted of "crimes of turpitude,"[64] such as drug possession, drunken behavior, prostitution, and other crimes. The AEDPA allows deportation for long-term US residents with any type of drug offense and removes the right to judicial review of deportation cases. The IIRIRA limits the power of federal courts to review deportation decisions. Before the passage of these laws, immigration inspectors could at their discretion refer those using fraudulent documentation or convicted or accused of crimes to an immigration judge to assess asylum claims. But the emphasis on expedited removal and the accompanying stripping of due process for migrants means higher rates of deportation and removal.

Mandatory detention is the third and probably most controversial provision that impacts asylum seekers. There are currently three types of migrant prisoners.[65] First are "deportable aliens," who lawfully enter the country but overstayed a visa or violated the terms of entry. The second category includes "criminal aliens," who lose legal status because they were convicted of a crime. The final category comprises "excludable aliens," who are apprehended at a port of entry without legal documentation; they are subjected to detention during expedited removals.

Incarceration of migrants certainly existed before the restrictionist laws of 1996. After a large influx of Haitian immigrants in the 1980s as well as the entry of almost 100,000 Cubans during the Mariel boatlift in

1980, the United States started to increasingly use detention to "manage" migrants.[66] *Incarceration thus became an acceptable and legitimate tactic shortly after the United States changed its domestic laws to protect refugees with the Refugee Act.* Part of this discrepancy could be attributed to two different administrations: President Carter signed the Refugee Act, and the Reagan administration inaugurated more widespread detention.[67]

From the Reagan administration's perspective, refugees were not brave heroes fleeing Communist regimes but rather potential "welfare recipients or criminals."[68] Increasingly since the 1980s, the United States has articulated that it is within its scope and sovereign right to determine why, how, and for how long non-citizens can enter or live in the United States.[69] As the INS Commissioner Gene McNary noted in 1990, detention in correctional facilities and processing centers would be a "deterrent."[70] In his view, potential asylum seekers in countries south of the United States would know that they could not just "drop in on our doorstep without a just cause and a provable cause of fear of persecution," because they would be living under conditions that would not be like the "Ritz Carlton."

By the early-1990s, a series of events prompted the 1996 immigration restriction laws and the increased desire to institutionalize the use of immigration detention. Those events included increasing waves of immigration, growing concerns that the asylum/immigration system could not handle the changing migration patterns after the end of the Cold War, and economic recession. When the 1996 laws made detention mandatory for a significant proportion of those waiting for the results of defensive asylum claims and credible fear interviews, the already fuzzy line between asylum seekers and undocumented immigrants became even fuzzier. A claim of fear of persecution did not protect asylum seekers from being detained. Further, the American Civil Liberties Union points out that the 1996 laws sanction indefinite detention for those that the government has not been able to deport, because their countries refuse to accept them, or those from countries with which the United States does not have diplomatic relationships.[71]

After the September 11, 2001, attacks on the United States, Congress expressed the fear that potential terrorists would use the asylum system to stay "indefinitely" in the country, either by obtaining legal protection or by failing to appear at asylum hearings/interviews and disappearing into the country.[72] Before the US war on Iraq began in 2003, the Department of Homeland Security launched Operation Liberty Shield, which required the detention of asylum seekers from 33 countries in which al-Qaeda was operating or thought to operate, without being able to appeal for parole. The program was disbanded after one month, due to an outcry from

human rights organizations.[73] But people from these countries are still subjected to detention and expedited removals.

And also in 2003, Attorney General Ashcroft issued a blanket detention order that undocumented immigrants, including asylum seekers, could be held indefinitely without bond if they posed "national security concerns." Ashcroft's decision was a result of the DHS asking for his response after the Board of Immigration Appeals sought to release on bond a detained Haitian asylum seeker. Ashcroft noted that "national security would be threatened if the release triggered a huge wave of immigrants to attempt to reach US shores. That would overtax the already-strained Coast Guard, Border Patrol and other agencies that are busy trying to thwart terror attacks."[74] After 2004, the DHS also gave the Border Patrol (part of Customs and Border Protection) authority to exercise expedited removals for undocumented migrants within two weeks of entry into the United States if they were apprehended within 100 miles of the border between the United States and Mexico. Immigration and Customs Enforcement (ICE) also *requires* apprehended asylum seekers to be detained unless they receive "parole" or waivers.[75] Asylum seekers are eligible for parole if they establish the validity of their identity and community ties and prove that they are not security risks. But ICE does not consistently apply these criteria and has issued stricter policies over time. Indeed, parole rates dropped from 41.3% in 2004 to 4.2% in 2007, remaining at around this rate as of recently.[76]

The detention of asylum seekers is a violation of their human rights, particularly if they have fled persecution, did not know how to affirmatively apply or to apply for refugee status from abroad, and have no idea why they are being fingerprinted, handcuffed, and put in correctional facilities. The DHS's takeover of immigration issues has ensured a priority on immigration *control* rather than adherence to international legal obligations to assess whether people have been persecuted. Immigration detention has thus increased rapidly in the past decade and a half.[77] There are over 300 detention centers and facilities across the country, holding at least 300,000 non-citizens per year, that include undocumented immigrants who have never sought asylum, asylum seekers still in proceedings, and asylum seekers whose claims have been denied.[78] The vast majority of defensive asylum applicants or those requesting credible fear interviews upon apprehension are detained; less than 10% of affirmative asylum applicants are detained.[79]

But the detention of "genuine" asylum seekers with "real" fear is not my only concern. The deeper problem is "crimmigration," a term used to designate the merging between criminal law and immigration law.[80] The

attempt to criminalize *any* non-citizen effectively means punishment for the "crime of arrival."[81]

Whether undocumented or potential asylum seekers, no distinctions are made in the treatment of immigrants, even if they are administrative rather than criminal detainees, once they are in the facilities. They are all integrated into the prison-industrial complex. [82] Private jails and security corporations benefit as they fill prison beds with immigrants.[83] Congress actually mandates immigration detention quotas, requiring ICE hold an average of 34,000 individuals on a daily basis, primarily to ensure profits for Corrections Corporation and the Geo Group, which run correctional facilities and have a strong lobbying presence.[84]

With increased attention to and criticism of mistreatment, abuse, and violence in the detention system, in 2009, DHS secretary Janet Napolitano admitted the problem with the "paradigm" of detention centers operating like correctional institutions/prisons. At that time, the Obama administration also pledged to comprehensively address the detention system.[85] And ICE started to use an "automated risk assessment" instrument to guide its officers in considering sexual orientation and gender identity when they make custody decisions to ensure that sexual minorities are protected from violence within detention centers.[86] However, these various responses only address excessive conditions of confinement. Issues still remain with privatization, the untracked transferring of detainees, prolonged detention, unnecessary detention, and substituting overly intrusive "supervision" for detention.[87]

Large-scale enforcement, deterrence, and restriction of immigration rely on detention. Immigration detention is a part of the larger story of US mass incarceration as a way to manage, surveil, and control what are perceived as society's ills.[88] The decision to "manage" migration through punitive and deterrence measures increases the violence against migrants, particularly by increasing the likelihood of even riskier attempts to cross the border and in turn strengthening smuggling networks. Further, the militarization of the US-Mexico border as another form of deterrence leads to more violence, particularly against women, as they are raped as they cross, almost as a "toll," or have to pay in order to avoid being raped. Many women are pulled into sex work to pay their way into the country, which subjects them to criminalization and potential detention.[89]

Just as I put the "protection" regime in the context of global power politics, I also analyze the "restriction" regime in terms of how the United States constructs its identity vis-à-vis its relationship with other countries. Protection, as I noted earlier, needs to be understood in the context of the social meaning it confers to political actors doing the protecting.

So too restriction contributes to how countries understand themselves and become known as certain kinds of states. In the case of immigration restriction, states use immigration policies of exclusion to reassert sovereign power and to indicate that boundary-making and boundary fortification are crucial for territorial integrity.[90] Thus, sovereignty is a social construct that must be continuously reproduced and negotiated so that states are socially recognized by others as authoritative sources of power. Asylum is a "discretionary act of sovereignty" because of normative expectations that sovereignty entails stabilized boundaries, the power to enforce laws, and the power to admit or exclude people.[91]

Critical and feminist IR scholars argue that the very existence of the "state" thrives on the constant creation of "threats."[92] For example, Doty poses the troubling but key question: who is the outsider, the stranger, the one "who do not belong, but whose constitution is inherent in the construction of the included, and the society of which they are part?"[93] In other words, who "belongs" and is a part of a country is determined in part by putting them in opposition with those who definitely do *not* belong. "We" are not like those illegal aliens, terrorists, traffickers, border kids.

Doty situates immigration in the context of "desire," which she argues "underlies so many practices that aim to create order, to banish ambiguity, to create stability and fixedness."[94] She notes that "the movement of human beings across territorialized and coded geographic, cultural, and political space is itself a flow understood as threatening to order, security, and identity."[95] Thus, she is pointing out that the non-citizen has everything to do with what the state is, and how the state "defines" itself as an entity. The state exists because of insiders *and* outsiders. The state cannot have a border and thus have a position in the world without knowing who or what needs to remain on the "other" side of that border, who "within" the borders should not really be there, and who will always be questioned and interrogated as really belonging.

The basis of fear around immigration can be captured in the following statistic: "Until the 1960s, 80 percent of immigrants to the United States, Canada, and Australia came from other industrialized countries. By the end of the 1980s, 82 percent came from developing countries."[96] These outsiders are from particular places, the so called Third World or developing world, migrating to a select few: the United States, Canada, Germany, France, Australia. In reality, migration occurs within "Third World" regions as well, but in immigration restriction discourse, countries in the global North/West are concerned about particular kinds of Others who could allegedly destroy the essence and integrity of the Western state.[97]

How does the state decide which outsider to let in? What is the difference between the threatening outsider, and the one who is worthy of protection? How do we sort through the tension between protection and restriction?

RESOLVING THE TENSION?

Think about refugees and asylees who have found safe haven in the United States, or the number of people admitted into the country, protected from being returned to countries where they might face persecution.[98] Then think of undocumented migrants, including potential asylum seekers, who risk violence and death as they cross the border into the United States, sometimes targeted by vigilantes, only to be turned away by immigration officials. Protection and restriction seem impossible to reconcile because they can result in such drastically opposite outcomes.[99]

As Gerard points out, there are very real tensions between protection and restriction when it comes to decisions that impact people's lives.[100] She asks, will refugees/migrants be able to cross borders or be prevented from doing so? Will they have access to options to resettle in other countries or languish in holding centers? Will they have access to full or diluted rights and entitlements? Will they penalized for illegal entry or not? Will they be deported before being given an opportunity to express fear of persecution?

Salehyan and Rosenblum note that asylum exemplifies the long-standing conflict between "humanitarian norms" and "traditional state interests."[101] In other words, on the one hand, states have an international legal obligation to acknowledge crimes against and extend protection to those who are the most "vulnerable." Asylum advocates thus engage in pressuring states to comply with norms, such as those upheld in Article 14 of the United Nations Declaration of Human Rights, which articulates the right to seek and to enjoy asylum, and the United Nations Refugee Convention of 1951 and its 1967 Protocol. On the other hand, states are committed to national security, protection of their borders, and the elevation of their political and economic interests over "altruistic" obligations.

I offer a different way to think about this tension. *First, protection/humanitarianism and security are actually not antithetical to each other.* The state is not "giving up" sovereignty by protecting asylum seekers or by granting refugee/asylee status. Rather the abilities *both* to protect *and* to secure are pivotal to the production of masculinist state identity, as impenetrable yet protective. *Second, and relatedly, <u>both</u> protection and*

security allow countries to be in certain "superior" positions in international hierarchy. The country that can *simultaneously* protect citizens from other countries *and* keep out undesired foreigners is one that accomplishes "civilizational security."[102] Persaud uses this term to discuss the racialization of national security, in terms of who are considered insiders and outsiders. I assert that the protection of *certain* outsiders actually strengthens the superiority of the racialized "US civilization" by signaling the very ability and right of the United States to extend membership to certain foreigners who "qualify." These migrants "earn" this qualification by *agreeing* through certain asylum narratives that they, too, prefer US "civilization."

The state is not "giving up" security and committing to a "preference" of humanitarianism. Put another way, there is not a "choice," per se, between masculinized national security and feminized gender-correct protection. That is because *to offer gender-correct protection is a masculinist act.* Masculinity is expressed and performed in different ways, but hegemonic masculinity is, per Tickner, "sustained through its opposition to various subordinated and devalued masculinities, such as homosexuality, and more important, through its relation to various devalued femininities."[103] To protect is to actually perform a particular kind of sovereignty, to be the *kind* of state that is better than others, to be the kind of state that can protect . . . unlike weak states that are not *masculine or civilized* enough to do so.

As scholars of gender, war, and militarization have argued, the very idea of protection pivots on gendered ideas. Men are warriors defending the homeland; women are vulnerable, the defense of whom is apparently a noble cause. But protection is not truly possible in the context of conflict, war, and militarization, given the general climate of violence and insecurity.[104] The gendered binaries that dictate who is to be protected are the same that demand that states engage in organized violence and militarization. In other words, the protection of (some) innocent people, primarily women, constructed as vulnerable and worthy of saving, is a site for states to assert hegemonic masculinity.

What does this discussion have to do with the experiences of asylum seekers and undocumented immigrants? First, it is important to be aware of how protection and restriction are intertwined so as to better grasp what asylum implies. It is *one level* of protection, which may come with benefits but may also come with restrictions, loss, and potential violence. Asylum seekers and asylees do not experience *either* protection or restriction; they likely experience both. As Bohmer and Shuman put it, there are possibilities of *belonging* and *loss of belonging* for asylum seekers, particularly when

one considers the experiences of exile, dislocation, detention, and the difficulties of explaining their stories to government officials.[105]

There are many asylum seekers waiting to hear their fates and many undocumented immigrants who have created lives and communities in the United States. These people are living in-between lives, simultaneously experiencing the promise of state protection and the reminders of not being wanted. "Worthy victims" do not necessarily have any more value than those who are deported, forgotten, turned away; rather, they exemplify the "best" kind of migrants, who receive some measure of protection because through them, *the state can remain firmly committed to immigrant restriction by emphasizing that not just anybody gets to be protected*. As Bhabha puts it, "Asylum . . . keeps migration exclusion morally defensible."[106]

Second, in attempts to make asylum work better or to make comprehensive immigration reform more humane, it is worth unpacking the state as comprising many different components that are accountable and responsible in different ways for decisions impacting non-citizens. As Wendy Brown notes, the state is "a significantly unbounded terrain of powers and techniques, an ensemble of discourses, rules, and practices, cohabiting in limited, tension-ridden, often contradictory relation with one another."[107]

Doty points out:

> There is no such thing as "the state," only a powerful desire for "the state" that pervades the social realm. Of course, there are governmental bureaucracies and institutions, and human subjects engaging in practices. But these, neither individually nor collectively are "the state." "The state" is nothing but a desire that is manifested in *practices of statecraft*, practices that can originate in government bureaucracies and institutions, churches, schools, corporations, theaters, novels, art museums, our backyards, our front yards, our kitchens, and living rooms and bedrooms. Practices of statecraft can come from anywhere and from anyone; from Madeline Albright to Colin Powell to young skin-heads in Germany to San Diego teenagers who take sport in beating up migrant workers to vigilante ranchers on the US/Mexican border to the clerk in the local passport office.[108]

Biswas and Nair also claim that sovereign power is dispersed "first, by investing local agents with the discretionary power to 'decide' and second, by entangling itself in various kinds of complex configurations that make it difficult to locate, and be held accountable."[109] Think, for example, of all the different players in the asylum/immigration system. Who, really, is responsible when non-citizens come in contact with so many

different governmental agencies and officials? Biswas and Nair are concerned with what happens to those "out of reach" of accountability, who should "legally expect state protection . . . but are *routinely and systematically* denied it—some minority citizens, 'voluntary' economic migrants, poor sweatshop workers, indigenous populations, etc."[110]

So the more we learn about the diffuse nature in which the state operates, the more the question shifts from "who is worthy of protection" to one about who is responsible and accountable for the treatment and rights of non-citizens. Why did two different judges reach two different conclusions on similar asylum cases? Why is one person detained and another person paroled? Who decides the distinction between a so-called economic migrant and a political refugee/asylum seeker? As to the latter, as Bohmer and Shuman point out, political persecution is deeply intertwined with the economic conditions and class-based persecution that prompt people to migrate to other countries.[111] However, in practice, political persecution is often constructed as different and distinct from economic deprivation and discrimination.

This book reveals how the United States relies upon the protection of outsiders as crucial to its construction of its identity and position in international hierarchy. Doing so shows the *fragility* of US power. Asylum seekers, undocumented migrants, and countless people and organizations invested in immigration rights have found ways to hold these multiple state agencies and actors accountable. They do so through amici curiae briefs, lawsuits, testimonials, street protests, press conferences, social media campaigns, and congressional briefings. And, as I discuss in chapter 6, there are multiple ways to intervene in the restriction-protection relationship by challenging the worthy victim frames that emerge in the context of US immigration politics.

CHAPTER 3
The Autonomous Worthy Victim Frame
Comparing Female Genital Cutting and Domestic Violence

This chapter compares domestic violence (DV) and female genital cutting (FGC). Feminists, human rights activists, asylum advocates, and survivors of DV and forced FGC have mobilized around both types of violence as two *separate* issues.[1] However, I discovered an unexpected, similar "autonomous worthy victim" frame operating in both types of gender-based asylum cases.

Domestic violence generally comprises interpersonal violence committed by intimate partners in relationships, whether legally married or not. DV often occurs in conjunction with other types of violence such as abuse by other family members, rape, forced marriage, and economic deprivation and isolation. Through the 1979 United Nations Convention on the Elimination of Discrimination Against Women, the 1993 United Nations Declaration on the Elimination of Violence Against Women, and the 2004 General Assembly Resolution 58/147 "Elimination of domestic violence against women," the United Nations has named domestic violence as a human rights violation that is particularly insidious because it can be dismissed as a "private" matter. Accordingly, a key feminist contribution is to name *state* responsibility for preventing and addressing domestic violence. According to feminist activists, states should recognize DV as a political issue, as well as actively use other tools such as legislation and criminalization, police accountability and training, preventative education and counseling, and resources and social services for survivors.[2]

Female genital cutting is the removal or alteration of parts of female genitalia involving varying degrees of coercion and consent, often expected as an appropriate and necessary ritual for young girls entering puberty and many adult women. The practice occurs in close to 30 African and Middle Eastern countries.[3] FGC can be a condition of or accompany forced marriage. Feminists and human rights advocates from various regions have rallied against the practice altogether, arguing that there is little choice in the matter due to social conventions about sexuality and femininity, the economic structure of female "status" and "marriageability," and the societal pressure to sustain the livelihoods of the women who perform the procedure.[4] Those who see FGC as a form of violence explain that even women who voluntarily undergo the practice experience harmful health consequences, depending to some extent on whether sterilized equipment and anesthesia were used. The United Nations and many feminists use the terminology female genital *mutilation* to denote the harmful consequences of this practice and to designate it as a human rights violation. In 2012, the United Nations General Assembly passed a resolution (A/RES/67/146) condemning and calling for an end to female cutting.

Other feminists, often from African countries, argue for more nuance and complexity in addressing this practice, calling it female circumcision or female genital cutting/surgery. These feminists argue that a ban silences the women who either support the practice or understand why cutting and circumcision exist. They also note that while several countries in Africa have criminalized FGC, legal prohibition has mixed results, such as poor enforcement and driving the practice underground.[5] They also assert that a Western obsession with FGC can be confounding to women who have experienced it, or who might cite poverty, rape, access to healthcare and clean water, inheritance/property rights, or state violence as their biggest concerns.[6] But many of these same activists see FGC as a human rights violation particularly when forced upon children.

Two of the most prominent grants in US gender-based asylum history were of DV and FGC. Fauziya Kassindja[7] fled Togo due to fear of future, forced FGC. She arrived in the United States in late 1994. In 1996, the Board of Immigration Appeals (BIA), the administrative body that hears appeals of immigration judges' decisions and is the country's highest immigration court, declared the Kassindja decision "precedent," meaning that fear of future FGC became a legitimate basis for a claim of asylum.

Rody Alvarado left Guatemala in 1995 after years of domestic violence at the hands of her husband. The Alvarado case took significantly longer to be resolved, as she was not granted asylum until 2009, and it was not a precedent-setting decision. It was not until August 2014 that the BIA

ruled in a separate published, precedent decision that domestic violence victims, specifically from Guatemala, are eligible for asylum.[8]

Because Kassindja's case was the first asylum grant in the United States for violence against women and Alvarado's case languished in the legal system for 14 years, feminist scholars claimed that FGC cases were easier than DV cases because FGC is perceived as more "foreign" and "barbaric," thus compelling asylum judges to respond more urgently. But the increasing US acceptance of DV cases and coding of some DV cases as "cultural" can complicate the claim that FGC asylum is easier to get. Further, I discovered evidence that FGC asylum grants are also difficult to receive.

In the pages that follow, I complicate and add nuance to the claim that I discussed in chapter 1 about worthy victims as "exotic." I put forward the argument that *both* FGC and DV cases invoke a similar "worthy victim" frame, that of an autonomous woman.[9] Asylum seekers in both types of cases usually have to demonstrate that they attempted to escape and resist their family/relatives and were punished by their families for refusing to conform to certain gender norms, such as undergoing FGC or staying with an abusive partner. *In this frame, the family is seen as the key vehicle for reflecting and propagating "cultural," patriarchal expectations, roles, and relationships.* Autonomy in the context of the asylum cases means *individual expression of independence through the rejection of the family.* Key descriptors are "autonomy," "freedom," "individuality," and "assertion of rights," as well as descriptions of how family members brutalized and repressed them or condoned the violence.

The autonomy frame emerged from a *discursive climate* in which feminists tried to get states to take seriously and be accountable for violence at the hands of private actors *known* to the victims. As US judges and governmental agencies increasingly intervened and issued decisions in "private violence" cases, they specified that family relationships are *immutable.* Immutability, as I discussed in chapter 2, means that a circumstance or belief cannot change or be expected to change. On the face of it, immutability claims help survivors demonstrate that they could not leave a relationship in which they faced harm. However, precisely because the relationship with a parent or partner is immutable, the asylum seeker has to demonstrate a *desire* or *attempt* to reject that family association. A person's autonomy is exercised by the act of wanting to end one's involvement in a relationship that cannot be changed. The asylum seeker also has to illustrate that the state is too weak, incapable, or unwilling to stop her oppressive family.

After illustrating how the autonomy frame operates, I show the harmful effects of this frame on asylum seekers because it can potentially

circumscribe what kind of agency they must demonstrate when fleeing persecution at the hands of a parent, spouse, or extended family member. As I explained in chapter 1, I am interested not only in the successful asylum cases but also in the people who are potentially left out of understandings of what a successful asylum seeker looks like. Feminists have successfully drawn attention to "nonstate" and "private" abusers, thus politicizing types of violence that have previously been dismissed as "personal matters." However, I explore the possibility of describing family violence in more nuanced ways, so as not to play into exoticizing stereotypes of "bad families" propagating "barbaric" cultural practices. To deny the humanity of families "over there," who are depicted as monsters incapable of basic human emotions such as love, is to also deny the complex emotions of the asylum seeker who flee but may still love or feel attached to her family members. I then illustrate that the autonomy frame, by strengthening the *discursive climate* of ideas about strong/weak states and good/bad families, enables the United States to more easily justify certain policy practices and stances that attempt to influence other countries' policies on FGC and DV and to avoid addressing gender violence within its own borders. Table 3.1 summarizes the effects of the autonomous frame.

THEORIZING AUTONOMY: COMPLICATING THE EXOTIC WORTHY VICTIM FRAME

Feminist critics claim that in the case of FGC, US asylum adjudicators and advocates perceive this practice to be "weird and barbaric." Thus, the asylum system constructs the United States, through a grant of asylum, as a savior of people suffering from crimes that seem otherworldly, that could not possibly be committed by westerners.[10] These same critics argue that those suffering from crimes more "prevalent" in the West, such as domestic violence, will be ignored. There is, in other words, a strange/familiar dichotomy that explains why FGC cases will allegedly be more likely to receive grants of asylum than DV cases.

When we compare the trajectories of the two most famous gender-based asylum cases in the United States, it certainly seems as if the "exoticism" of FGC makes for a more "worthy" victim. Fauziya Kassindja arrived in the United States from Togo by way of Germany in 1994 on someone else's passport.[11] She fled Togo to avoid forced FGC. Kassindja's family, including her father, did not support this practice, but after her father passed away, her aunt forbade her from continuing her education and ordered her to

Table 3.1 THE AUTONOMOUS WORTHY VICTIM FRAME

Type of violence	Worthy victim frame	Effects of frame on asylum seekers	Effects of frame on US policies and power relationships
Domestic violence	Autonomous	Survivors left out include those unwilling to prove "rejection" and disconnection from "culture" as well as from family/kin responsible for violence	United States distracts attention from its own problems with domestic violence. United States makes a case for influencing domestic violence responses in other countries that it perceives as too "weak" to control "violent families."
Female genital cutting	Autonomous	Same as above	United States financially pressures countries that do not address female genital cutting in the same way the United States does. United States shapes immigration policy to frame FGC as an immigrant problem.

be circumcised before a forced arranged marriage. Kassindja was able to leave with the assistance of her mother and sister. She was subsequently detained for 16 months in the United States before her case was eventually resolved, thanks to a nationwide letter-writing campaign organized by asylum advocates and feminists.

The immigration judge who first heard Kassindja's appeal questioned her credibility. The judge argued that the claim was "irrational and incredible," she would likely not be circumcised if returned to Togo, and forced circumcision was not persecutory. In 1996, the Board of Immigration Appeals reversed the decision. The BIA found FGC to be persecutory, in terms of "sexual oppression," based on her "ethnic identity" and "gender identity."[12] The BIA declared its decision to be precedent, and Kassindja eventually received asylum in 1996.

This case was no doubt monumental. First, it ushered in the possibility that asylum seekers could apply for asylum based on persecution

due to or on account of "gender." The BIA noted that "gender-based, or gender-related, asylum claims within the 'membership in a particular social group' construct . . . [are] entirely appropriate and consistent with the developing trend of jurisprudence in the United States and Canada as well as with international norms."[13]

Second, gender-based asylum advocacy increased and became "professionalized." For example, Layli Miller-Muro, a law student involved in the Kassindja case, founded the Tahirih Justice Center to provide legal advocacy for female asylum seekers fleeing gender-based persecution. Karen Musalo, the attorney for Kassindja during the BIA reversal, founded the Center for Gender and Refugee Studies (CGRS) at the University of California–Hastings, which provides a formidable database of resources and research about gender-based asylum. And Kassindja became a member of the CGRS Honorary Board.[14] Frankly, this book and many other scholarly pieces on gender-based asylum would not have been possible without the work of the CGRS.

But Gunning asks why Kassindja's case was successful during a "virulently anti-immigrant moment in U.S. history,"[15] the same year of the passage of the 1996 immigration restrictionist legislation discussed in chapter 2. Many feminists answered that it had to do with the perceived "sensational" nature of FGC as an egregious example of patriarchal cultural violence.[16] For example, even if FGC was not the primary trauma or an issue at all in the lives of some asylum seekers, some lawyers press women to emphasize that part of their narrative or to lie about it to get an easier grant of asylum.[17] In a 2005 decision by the US Court of Appeals, *Mohammed v. Gonzales*, the judge even refused to the use the oft-used acronym FGM (female genital mutilation), stating: "The use of initials, if it has any effect, serves only to dull the senses and minimizes the barbaric nature of the practice."[18]

I turn next to the case of Rody Alvarado,[19] who is also on the CGRS Honorary Board. In 1995, Rody Alvarado left Guatemala for the United States after a decade of torture, abuse, and violence perpetrated by her husband. Guatemalan police did not respond to her complaints, nor would courts grant her a divorce without her husband's consent. An immigration judge granted her asylum, noting that domestic violence was a form of persecution. The judge argued that Alvarado belonged to the "social group" of "Guatemalan women, who have been involved intimately with Guatemalan male companions, who believe that women are to live under male domination" and had the political opinion of "opposition to male domination."

But shortly after this grant, the Immigration and Naturalization Service (INS), on behalf of the US government, appealed the immigration judge's decision to the BIA, contesting both the social group and the "political" nature of the violence. Importantly, the INS argued that framing domestic violence as persecution would "open the floodgates" to women around the world in domestic violence situations.[20] In 1999, the BIA reversed the immigration judge's decision, arguing that Guatemala did not encourage or condone the violence.

The BIA claimed that "when action is directed toward but one individual, or toward a small number of close family members it calls into question both the propriety of the group definition and the alleged group motivation of the persecutor." In other words, it argued that the DV targeted just Alvarado and was not indicative of patterns of violence that targeted many women. The BIA concluded by invoking the Kassindja case, claiming that domestic violence in Guatemala was not as pervasive as FGC was in Togo. While cutting was "expected" in Togo, domestic violence in Guatemala was not. In other cases, judges have cited domestic violence as too "ordinary" or a part of "everyday life" to count as persecutory, but in this particular case the BIA mentioned that DV was not very pervasive or significant.[21] The BIA failed to understand the "political" nature of domestic violence or how states are complicit with its occurrence when there is lack of support for women attempting to leave or address abusive relationships.

After the BIA reversal, Alvarado's attorneys appealed and publicized the decision. Feminist scholars and legal analysts started to debate the difference between Kassindja and Alvarado, an expected reaction given that Alvarado's case seemed to undo what many hoped would be new opportunities for gender-based asylum claims post-Kassindja.[22] Sinha, for example, writing in 2001, pointed to the BIA's reversal in Kassindja and congressional legislation a few months after that decision outlawing FGC in the United States. She argued that the outrage was due to "direct[ing] the gaze towards particularized cultural practices instead of the overall problem of violence against women."[23] In her view, Alvarado did not offer a convincing "cultural" reason for her violence.

Alvarado did eventually receive asylum, after a very long battle. Soon after the BIA's reversal of asylum, Alvarado's lawyers appealed the decision. During the Clinton administration, Attorney General Janet Reno, on behalf of the Department of Justice (DOJ), vacated the decision, remanded the case to the BIA, and provided suggestions to proceed so that Alvarado could gain asylum. But then newly elected president

George W. Bush appointed John Ashcroft as attorney general, who proclaimed that he would make the final decision about this case. However, he never did and finally sent the case back to the BIA in 2005 when he left office. The passage of REAL ID in 2005 (see chapter 2) arguably raised the bar of how to establish credibility for asylum seekers.[24] The next two attorneys general, Alberto Gonzales and Michael Mukasey, also avoided the case.

Finally, in 2008, under the Obama administration, Attorney General Mukasey remanded the case to the BIA once again. Department of Homeland Security (DHS) attorneys submitted a brief for the *Matter of L-R-*, another domestic violence case being heard at the time.[25] In the *L-R-* case, the DHS attorneys offered the following social group memberships: "Mexican women in domestic relationships who are unable to leave," or "Mexican women who are viewed as property by virtue of their positions within a domestic relationship." The DHS thus emphasized that domestic violence victims were persecuted on account of their "status" in their marriages. In 2009, a DHS brief explicitly acknowledged that domestic violence should be considered as a form of gender persecution.[26] That same year, Alvarado was finally granted asylum, about *14 years* after her arrival in the United States.

The long road for Alvarado certainly demonstrates the dispersal of state power discussed in chapter 2. More importantly, it did not change many feminists' opinions about the "exotic victim" frame because of the length of time it took for Alvarado to receive immigration relief. But I offer some qualifications to the exotic/familiar binary. First, FGC cases are not always as straightforward as one might imagine they would be after the Kassindja case. Second, through the process of the Alvarado case, the United States did eventually explicitly and directly recognize domestic violence as a potential form of persecutory violence. And the United States can and does see the "cultural" element of DV when it happens "elsewhere."

First, regarding FGC, a precedent case does not "guarantee" that another asylum seeker claiming persecution based on circumcision will necessarily receive asylum but just that fear of this kind of violence *can* be the basis of a grant of asylum. In Kassindja, the BIA noted the following:

> Nevertheless, the parties disagree about . . . the parameters of [female genital cutting] as a ground for asylum in future cases . . . In deciding this case, we decline to speculate on, or establish rules for, cases that are not before us.[27]

Through this disclaimer, the BIA also failed to clarify whether past persecution carries the same weight as fear of future persecution. In the *Matter of A-T-* (2008), an asylum seeker from Mali experienced forced FGC and fears of forced marriage and potential domestic violence at the hands of her future husband. But she initially did not receive immigration relief. The BIA asserted that FGC was a "one time" occurrence that she already suffered; so there was no fear of harm if she returned to Mali.

Asylum advocates protested the decision because it created a much more difficult legal standard for applying for asylum.[28] Other asylum seekers who experienced forms of persecution other than FGC were not being required to prove that the *same* harm that they had experienced in the past *had* to happen again in the future. Nor did the experience of one type of violence in the past preclude them from fearing *another* type of violence in the future. The BIA's decision had negative effects on other cases with prior occurrence of FGC, resulting in the denial of claims and even governmental attempts to "rescind protection already granted."[29]

Eventually, thanks to the mobilization of activists and the CGRS's amicus curiae brief filed with the Fourth Circuit Court of Appeals, in September 2008, Attorney General Mukasey vacated the BIA's decision and remanded the case back to the BIA. The BIA issued a new decision in June 2009 that adopted a new legal framework recognizing that past forced FGC should not rule out consideration of fear of various forms of harm. The immigration court reheard the case and reversed the previous decision, granting A. T. asylum.[30] This case history belies the assumption that FGC cases are easier, or that adjudicators consistently understand the dimensions of this form of violence post-Kassindja.

Second, despite the "familiarity" of domestic violence the United States has a track record of approving DV cases. According to CGRS data from 1996 to 2013, successful DV grants (747 cases) outnumbered successful FGC grants (365). Even when one looks solely at "single persecution" cases, meaning that DV and FGC claims were not combined with other types of violence, such as forced marriage or rape, there were 385 DV and 148 FGC grants. Further, as mentioned above, in August 2014, the BIA finally declared in a precedent decision that women fleeing severe domestic violence are eligible for asylum when states have failed or are unwilling to address or prevent the harm.

DV cases are certainly not easy, as indicated by the BIA's own description in this 2014 case of the rocky and convoluted history of domestic violence cases.[31] In a study that analyzed domestic violence asylum claims in the United States between 1994 and 2012, Bookey argues that

the lack of clear and binding norms and of guidance from the DHS and DOJ about domestic violence is what led to inconsistent outcomes.[32] Any emerging norms were not consistently and clearly articulated or strengthened. Asylum adjudicators struggled to consistently and fairly assess DV claims until 2008, when the DHS and DOJ started to increasingly provide direction.[33]

Returning to the Kassindja–Alvarado comparison, feminist and human rights advocates mobilized comparable levels of publicity and advocacy for both women, so other factors must have played a role in the different asylum journeys.[34] McKinnon thus looks at the role of global power politics in explaining why Kassindja was initially more "appropriate for incorporation into US belonging" than Alvarado.[35] She notes that during the initial stages of Alvarado's legal journey, Guatemala was still relying on the United States as a military ally during the end of its civil war (1960 to 1996) and was facing accusations of human rights violations. Indeed, feminists note that domestic violence increased dramatically during the Guatemalan civil war. For example, Alvarado's husband "gloated" over his "civil war exploits," illustrating in at least one small way the intersection between militarization, hypermasculinity, and violence against women.[36] Then after the end of the war, the United States changed the way it viewed Guatemala, from a country with which it was entangled to yet another country incapable of preventing its citizens from migrating illegally to the United States. The end of the war allowed the United States to construct enough "distance" between itself and Guatemala. McKinnon thus concludes that Alvarado's high profile as an activist made her an *exceptional* migrant, particularly at a time when the Obama administration promised to overhaul the immigration system and could no longer justify holding off or rejecting the case.[37]

Alvarado's journey was less about the familiarity of DV and more about a combination of the US relationship with Guatemala and the inability of the DHS and DOJ to consistently guide DV cases in the context of changes in presidential administrations. There is also a general tendency of judges to see DV as a "private" matter and the perpetrators as motivated by "personal" rather than political/systematic reasons.[38] As we will see in chapter 4, trafficking asylum cases are similarly depoliticized.

But as I explain later in the chapter, I also see evidence that judges are often swayed by "sensationalistic" descriptions of intimate partner violence as not private but *culturally sanctioned*.[39] The difference between successful and unsuccessful DV cases often pivots upon whether the adjudicator thinks of the perpetrator as an *individual*, or as a *family member*.

If it is the former, adjudicators pathologize the abuser; if it is the latter, the abuser represents a propagation of a patriarchal and violent culture. Further, *within* the United States, hegemonic perceptions of domestic violence frame the cause as culture or religion when it occurs within immigrant, indigenous, or nonwhite communities, thus coding DV in those communities as not familiar but *different*.[40]

So while distinctions might be drawn between FGC and DV, asylum judges are influenced by ideas of strangeness/cultural difference when it comes to DV. The *difference* between DV and FGC cases, as I discuss below, has more to do with how it is easier to prove state responsibility and accountability for FGC cases than for DV cases. The *similarity* between DV and FGC cases is in the comparable construction of *culture* in cases of *family violence*.[41] We should explore *how the family is constructed as perpetrator in both instances*. Regardless of how FGC and DV are differently described, or the different types of activism involved, in both instances, the country of origin is blamed for being unable and unwilling to protect its own citizens from what their *loved ones* do to them. This frame pivots on constructing not just the victims but families "elsewhere" as exotic, in terms of their strange, unloving, oppressive ways.

As we see in the next section, the development of both FGC and DV cases occurs via the positioning of the *survivors' status within their families*. It is indeed important to ensure that government and immigration officials and judges take violence seriously, precisely by demonstrating how family violence is not just "personal" but part of larger systematic political and economic conditions that engender, and enable to emerge, such violence. Thus, it is necessary to explain a dynamic of overwhelming state- and society-sanctioned family oppression to prove persecutory harm. For example, family units often pressure women to stay with their abusers, to withstand violence to punish perceived transgressions, or to undergo FGC for the purpose of family reputation or to ensure "marriageability." As asylum lawyer and Harvard law professor Deborah Anker notes, the social group "married women in Guatemala who are unable to leave their relationship," created in the precedent BIA August 2014 decision, can profoundly increase the abilities of Central American women to seek asylum rather than be deported; the decision legitimizes their claims that violence at the hands of family members is persecutory.[42]

The problem is not *that* family perpetrators are named, as certainly attention to nonstate violence is a crucial dimension of raising awareness about gender violence. Rather, I am concerned about *how* families are constructed because of potential unintended negative consequences for

asylum seekers. I am interested in the asylum narratives that implicitly or explicitly draw upon the autonomous victim frame to prove an asylum seeker's credibility.

THE DEVELOPMENT OF FAMILY AS PERSECUTOR AND THE "AUTONOMOUS VICTIM" IN FGC AND DV CASES

FGC Cases

Recall that one of the grounds of basis of persecution is membership in a particular social group. As the BIA articulated in the 1985 case *Matter of Acosta*,

> The members of a particular social group must share a common, immutable characteristic, which may be an innate one, such as sex, color, or kinship ties, or a shared past experience, such as former military leadership or land ownership, but it must be one that members of the group either cannot change, or should not be required to change, because it is fundamental to their individual identities or consciences.[43]

Most scholars commenting on gender persecution highlight "sex" in this definition of social group. But it is the "kinship ties" that catch my attention.

Indeed, in *Sanchez-Trujillo v. INS* (1986), the Ninth Circuit Court of Appeals noted that "perhaps a prototypical example of a 'particular social group' would consist of the immediate members of a certain family, the family being a focus of fundamental affiliational concerns and common interests for most people."[44] Courts since then have frequently (although inconsistently) ruled in favor of petitioners if they can prove that they were persecuted because they belong to a particular family (such as a politically active family targeted by the government) *or* if they can prove that they are a member of a family that targets them.[45] Kinship ties are allegedly "immutable"; one cannot be expected to change one's mother or husband, often because the "blood relations," the history of the relationship, or legal or societal constraints prevent severing all ties. So it could be argued that someone should not be expected to continue to be subjected to violence because of the immutability of the family connection.

In the asylum context, "immutable" family connections usually include a spouse, as will be discussed in the next section, or any "blood" relative,

but kinship ties can also reference one's "tribe." As Coffman points out, "tribe" can be a problematic term especially when treated in an ahistorical manner. But asylum adjudicators tend to see tribes as familial because the "membership" cannot be changed, and they may use family, tribe, and clan interchangeably.[46] Per my review of FGC cases, there is a slippage between family and tribe throughout the cases, sometimes on the part of the asylum seeker or advocate/lawyer as a way to point out the complexity of defining family and community, and sometimes on the part of the judge, who may or may not be thinking carefully about the terms used.

The Kassindja social group had to do not only with gender and FGC but also with family, interpreted as both immediate family members and one's tribe. When the BIA issued its disagreement with the immigrant judge's denial of Kassindja's claim, it noted the following:

> First, the record before us reflects that the applicant is a credible witness. Second, FGM [female genital mutilation], as practiced by the Tchamba-Kunsuntu Tribe of Togo and documented in the record, constitutes persecution. Third, the applicant is a member of a social group consisting of young women of the Tchamba-Kunsuntu Tribe who have not had FGM, as practiced by the tribe, and who oppose the practice. Fourth, the applicant has a well-founded fear of persecution. Fifth, the persecution the applicant fears is "on account of" her social group. Sixth, the applicant's fear of persecution is country-wide. Seventh, and finally, the applicant is eligible for and should be granted asylum in the exercise of discretion.[47]

The BIA found that Kassindja could not change being a young woman or her membership in the tribe. The BIA added that "FGM is practiced, at least in some significant part, to overcome sexual characteristics of young women of the tribe who have not been, and do not wish to be, subjected to FGM. We therefore find that the persecution the applicant fears in Togo is 'on account of' her status as a member of the defined social group."[48] They noted that the "characteristic of having intact genitalia is one that is so fundamental to the individual identity of a young woman that she should not be required to change it."[49] Finally, the BIA addressed Togo's "minimal effort" to protect women.

Chapter 5 will challenge the idea that there are characteristics that are "immutable" and "cannot change." But we see here that the BIA contended that women should be able to have an identity that is not subjected to norms of their "tribe," their "kin." The BIA claimed that this particular construction of this particular kind of familial unit, the tribe,

does not have sexual control over women who are a part of that tribe, as women have a right to have "intact genitalia." *This precedent case, in other words, not only legitimized gender violence as a form of persecution but also proclaimed that women have a right to be separate from their family members/kin.*

Certain feminists have certainly rallied against the opposition of the "liberal individual" and her "oppressive society/community/religion/culture," arguing that such a dichotomy is simplistic and fails to capture the multiple ways in which people identify themselves and find belonging.[50] We can build on this argument by looking at how women as individuals are pitted against not just community/society but their family and kin who are the primary *agents* for perpetuating the allegedly harmful practices and beliefs held in the institutions, structures, and communities around them. For example, the *New York Times* covered the aftermath of Kassindja's asylum grant, in a piece curiously titled "A Refugee's Body Is Intact but Her Family Is Torn."[51] Interestingly, US Citizenship and Immigration Services includes this article in its Asylum Officer Basic Training module on gender-related claims.[52]

The article describes the rift within Kassindja's family over her asylum case. While an uncle expressed his disapproval of the decision to grant Kassindja asylum, and Kassindja's mother had to redeem herself through a contrition ceremony, other family members debated the legitimacy of FGC and supported Kassindja. But the author, Dugger, does not focus on these events as indicative of the complexity of understanding FGC. Instead, she presents Kassindja's story as one about genitals being "cut off" as has happened "for millennia [to] girls across Africa." And Dugger describes family disagreements about FGC as an *effect* of the asylum case, of "America seeping in," forcing challenges to the "tradition," despite evidence of debates within the family *before* Kassindja even left Togo. Recall that Kassindja's father was *against* FGC prior to his death but that her aunt was not; Kassindja's lawyers also specified the different positions of her family members. But Dugger describes Kassindja's parents' decision to "resist the traditions of their people" as "extraordinary," rather than as evidence of the existence of internal debates about FGC.

Further, the notion of "American" influence in a presumably positive manner stands in contrast with Kassindja's strong critique of the *American* immigration system, as she was so traumatized during her incarceration that she wanted to request deportation.[53] The relevance of this article is in contributing to the perception that women *elsewhere* are not only being

oppressed by their cultures, but they also have to *choose* between their families and ownership over their bodies. It is *this* choice, that women must make "there" but never "here." *Over there, families are dangerous for women with autonomy.*

So both the Kassindja case and the discussion around it set the stage for taking seriously violence committed by family members, whether understood as tribal members or parents. In the FGC case, *Matter of A-T-*, discussed above, the immigration judge who eventually reheard the case found that A. T. had suffered past persecution in the form of forced circumcision as a member of a social group comprised of "Bambaran women in families that practice the Wahabi religion."[54] In addition, *Matter of A-T-* was eventually successful for a withholding claim because the judge looked not only at the act of violence itself but also at the "status" of the claimant vis-à-vis family members. In other words, the judge reached the conclusion that the claimant was choosing to leave her family, and that the violence occurred to the asylum seeker because Bambaran women are part of families that practice a persecutory religion.

In 2005, the Tenth Circuit Court of Appeals ruled in *Niang v. Gonzales* that the social group definition in FGC cases could include just gender and tribal membership.[55] Simply stating that one was a woman who was part of a kinship affiliation that practices FGC would be sufficient for imputing that FGC would be a requirement of membership.[56] As the Ninth Circuit noted in *Mohammed v. Gonzales* and as the Tenth Circuit stated in *Niang*: "The shared characteristic that motivates the persecution is not opposition, but the fact that the victims are females in a culture that mutilates the genitalia of its females."[57] Even though both courts cited culture, they specifically discussed how *family* members propagate cultural practices. The Tenth Circuit Court included the testimony that Niang "'wanted to live in a country where [she] could be free,' [because] she still feared her family."[58]

The court described Niang, the petitioner, as follows:

> She was born into the Tukulor Fulani tribe in Senegal in 1970. Her family is Muslim and believes in rigid adherence to certain gender roles and expectations. There was a strict separation between the men and women in her household, which included [extended family]. Her family believed that women should not look at men, that family members should not display affection toward one another, and that women should obey their husbands. According to tribal custom, when Ms. Niang was born she was promised in marriage to her cousin Daud, a man her father's age who had three other wives. Because

> she was considered married to Daud, she was not allowed to date other men. Although most Tukulor Fulani girls were subjected to FGM and consummated their marriages when they were 10 to 12 years old, Ms. Niang refused to do so and her family acquiesced in her wishes, believing she would eventually change her mind. . . . [When] Ms. Niang was nearly 25, her family had a meeting in which they decided that she must consummate her marriage with Daud that evening. She again refused, and her family threw themselves on her, stripping her of her clothes, beating her, and burning her with a hot iron. Some then performed FGM on her "[s]o that [she] wouldn't be able to commit adultery and so that no one would want to have anything to do with [her]. And then she would be ashamed to show [her] body in front of another man." Testimony of Ms. Niang, R. at 188. She left her house the next morning. For the next four years . . . [s]he had no contact with her family.[59]

I quote this description at length because Niang's story is not just about being a woman in a particular tribe; there are also particular familial dynamics that are abusive and violent. Thus, it is not just that one's identity as a woman (the gender part of the social group) would *necessarily* come in conflict with one's identity in the tribe/kin (which allegedly requires FGC for membership in the tribe). Rather, I interpret this case in the context of how this particular family interacts. On the one hand, arguing that "female members of a tribe that practices FGC constitute a social group" can create more space for certain asylum seekers to make a case for asylum. Descriptions of debates and complex positions among family/tribe members about FGC could imperil the social group claim. On the other hand, Niang's story *is* complex and should not be imputed to mean that all cases of forced FGC are about a simplified conflict between an individual and the family unit/tribe. These cases could also be about pressure from *individual* family members or certain societal/economic expectations.

McKinnon notes that any discussion of "internal debates that occur in African societies and communities . . . would imperil the claim that African people are cultural automatons incapable of rational reflection on their actions."[60] The success of FGC cases does not necessarily depend on the autonomy victim frame, particularly since it is relatively easy for applicants to prove the lack of willingness/ability of their governments to protect them. Even in cases where the government has criminalized FGC, asylum seekers often can point to their membership in their tribe, and judges assume that the government has failed to intervene when the outlawed practice continues. But the autonomous woman / bad family construction is prevalent and persistent in the cases as well as in the analysis

by many asylum advocates trying to pave a way for higher grant rates for FGC cases. So while it might not matter to an individual asylum seeker how her family is constructed, it matters for the larger discursive ideas that circulate about what people "over there" are allegedly like.

In a survey of legal and feminist analyses in academic journals and law reviews of FGC cases since Kassindja as well as accessible written decisions of FGC cases, I found consistent reference to how women wish to enjoy "sexual freedom," "sexual autonomy," "autonomous decision-making," and "individual agency," and usually in reference to descriptions of betrayal, coercion, and intimidation by family members. Again, I am not denying the validity of women's negative emotions and experiences; the Tenth Circuit was in part quoting Niang's own words. Rather, I am drawing attention to a persistent framing of the asylum seeker as rejecting, condemning, or calling out her family. Is the asylum seeker willfully describing her family as such, or is she feeling pressure to do so in order to receive asylum? If one asylum seeker repudiates her family, is it assumed that all asylum seekers who fear FGC also reject their families?

DV Cases

A domestic violence claim could certainly rely upon the Kassindja case's formulation of kinship ties to argue that DV victims are also fleeing their families.[61] But DV cases and reactions to them have shaped the autonomous victim framing in their own right. The first social group proposed in the Alvarado case was "women who have been involved intimately with male companions who believe that women are to live under male domination." Because of mounting pressure from asylum advocacy groups and lawyers, at the end of 2000, President Clinton directed the Department of Justice to create new regulations recognizing marital status as "immutable." This meant that marriage could be recognized as a circumstance that was not easy or preferable to change, much like other "innate" characteristics. So while DV cases and FGC cases *seem* different, *the US government sees spousal, parental, and tribal relationships alike as "immutable."*

In 2004, the Department of Homeland Security proposed that the social group "married women in Guatemala who are unable to leave the relationship" would be relevant in the Alvarado case. Further, the DHS argued that "the applicant's marital status is immutable because it is an integral part of one's religious and moral identity." The DHS also said: "Even accepting the premise that one should be required to change marital status to avoid persecution, there may be circumstances in which it would be impossible

to do so, such that the characteristic would be immutable for that reason."[62] As a note, while the term "marital status" is used, in practice the US courts accept some DV claims about long-term intimate relationships between people who are not married. The United States has also heard DV cases for same-sex relationships. While the United States would ostensibly hear DV cases by heterosexual men, the case data I consulted did not include such examples.

During the period of time that the Alvarado case was pending, the domestic violence case of *L-R-* came before an immigration judge. That judge found "Mexican women in an abusive relationship who are unable to leave" as too circular, meaning the group was defined by the harm she suffered. The DHS submitted a 2009 brief supporting L. R.'s grant of asylum. It suggested these social groups: "Mexican women in domestic relationships who are unable to leave" or "Mexican women who are viewed as property by virtue of their positions within a domestic relationship." The DHS also noted that "a primary animus for violence arises from the abuser's perception of the subordinate status his wife occupies within the domestic relationship."

Thus, the DHS persisted with the notion that asylum seekers "trapped" in relationships that they could not change constituted a social group. The *L-R-* case won asylum, and the DHS reasoning helped to win Alvarado asylum as well. The evolution of these social groups captured the idea that the "status" as a wife/partner is "unchangeable" because of systematic legal or societal constraints. In line with DHS statements on DV, asylum seekers fleeing domestic violence can indicate societal beliefs about familial arrangements with statements such as "Guatemalan society still tends to view domestic violence as a family matter."[63] In other words, the "family unit," whether a couple or other relatives (such as extended family members), is a proxy for what society at large believes: domestic violence is a personal, not political, problem. Thus, the abusive family can harm with impunity.

Examples of social groups linking gender, marital status, and nationality in successful asylum cases include the following examples.[64]

- "Jordanian women who espouse western values and who are unwilling to live their lives at the mercy of their husbands, their society, and their government and/or women who are challenging the traditions of Jordanian society and government."[65]
- "Young, Westernized, Muslim wives in Bangladesh with a feminist political opinion and women of Bangladesh who have been victims of spousal abuse, especially by spouses who were in significant positions with the government of that particular country."[66]

- "Mexican women who hold beliefs contrary to established social norms; women who seek to divorce their abusive spouses; women who seek protection from the government from their abusive spouses; and female member of her own family, headed by a man whose goal is to control and dominate its members."[67]
- "Ivorian Muslim women who have suffered spousal abuse at the hands of their husbands and who are perceived as having disgraced their husbands by obtaining a divorce and failing to conform to the subservient role of women in the Ivory Coast."[68]
- "Women in Guatemalan society who resist male domination by living independently and self-sufficiently."[69]
- "Honduran women who believe that marriage is an equal partnership, and whose husbands are Honduran men who believe they have a right to dominate their wives through any means, including violence."[70]
- Women in Cambodia who have been raped and abused domestically and whose governments are unable or unwilling to protect them.[71]
- "Guatemalan women in an intimate relationship who have been subjected to violence and who assert through their actions their right to be free of violence."[72]
- Woman who "attempts to assert her individual autonomy and [refuses] to act in a subservient manner as is expected of women in Guatemala's male dominated society where women do not generally enjoy a social status equal to men."[73]

In each of these statements, as per my review of the cases, the female asylum seeker is constructed as an "individual" up against something larger than just the perpetrator, because the perpetrator is not just an individual but part of a family unit enacting gender norms embedded in the culture and condoned by the state. DV, in the context of immutable relationships, is coded as cultural, particularly when juxtaposed with the survivor as *westernized*.

Furthermore, the "immutability" of the marital relationship pivots upon painting marriage as a religious, cultural, or legal institution that trumps women's rights to choose their partners. When US adjudicators and officials do take seriously DV as a political harm, they pinpoint other countries' cultural, religious, and societal norms, inclusive of oppressive laws, as the reason women stay in abusive relationships. Thus, while DV is a "familiar" problem in the United States, unless it is occurring in an immigrant community or community of color, adjudicators do not understand it a systematic *cultural* problem in the United States, but they do see it as such in other countries.

The abuser as a "family member" rather than as an "individual" is a more appealing way to frame a DV perpetrator in order to avoid claims that DV is just a "personal matter," or committed by, as one judge once asserted, an "abusive individual who was an alcoholic and for whatever reasons that only God knows he was abusive of her and violent with her and other people."[74] Law professor Laura Adams shifts the focus from the motivations of an individual abusing a family member to how and why the state fails to protect survivors of DV.[75] DV is "more than a private harm because the state fails to protect victims of violence within families for the reason that these victims are members of a particular social group—the family—which the state treats as self-governing."[76] In other words, states are making a political choice to "defer" to family "governance" rather than to commit to eliminate the root causes of DV.[77] Thus, one could argue that it is a good move to reference family relationships as immutable so as to *recognize* and challenge countries' deference to family governance.

However, there is significant pressure on DV asylum seekers to *prove* that their governments protect family governance. In FGC cases, it is sufficient to illustrate membership in the tribe and identity as a woman, as it is presumed that families, tribes, and governments are clearly colluding in the oppression of women. Asylum seekers still need to prove the governmental role, but it is often presumed in FGC cases, even when the government has criminalized the practice. In a DV case, the asylum seeker must demonstrate government complicity with or lack of will regarding family violence by showing that the government could not help or intervene when she *tried to seek help*. In other words, asylum seekers have to demonstrate autonomy by rejecting the self-governance of the family and reporting the abusive family members to the government. Indeed, judges who deny asylum petitions in DV cases often proclaim that *had* the petitioner actually sought the government's help, *then* she could have pointed to government inaction as proof of her well-founded fear.[78]

How does an asylum seeker prove governmental inaction or unwillingness? To answer, the Department of Justice in 2000 proposed a way to evaluate government complicity/action by exploring whether the country in question took "reasonable steps" to control violence and whether applicants had "reasonable access" to government protection.[79] These guidelines, while unclear and insufficient, were never adopted. Accordingly, asylum adjudicators continue to assess government willingness/ability by seeing if the victim exercised autonomy by appealing for help in naming the family abuser as a perpetrator. But these actions can often put victims of DV at great risk. An asylum lawyer can certainly collect data and expert witness affidavits about patterns of sexist family arrangements or

systematic governmental denial of or complicity with patriarchal practices. These efforts can remove the responsibility out of the hands of the asylum seeker, but not everyone has access to a lawyer, much less a competent, informed one.

THE EFFECTS OF THE AUTONOMOUS WORTHY VICTIM FRAME ON ASYLUM SEEKERS

What we see in the FGC and DV cases is a persistent reference to autonomy in connection with an "immutable" family relationship. I offer a few possible effects of the autonomous victim frame on potential asylum seekers. First, examining the family as an institution of power is an important way to analyze gender violence, but family relationships are far more complicated than what one might gather from asylum cases and analysis. Certainly women experience feelings of betrayal or explicitly say they are rejecting their families' beliefs. But Connie Oxford interviewed several asylees, finding that all the women who were granted asylum based on domestic violence and FGC claims were effectively *still in contact* with their "persecutors" because they maintained their family relationships.[80]

Oxford claims that it is not possible to understand why this continued contact happens if violence and persecution are only understood in the context of "public" harm, where the oppressor and victim would not continue a relationship, or would not have one in the first place.[81] People may continue relationships to speak about children they have with the perpetrator, out of feelings of loyalty and affection, or because of economic support. But would a mention of continued contact in an asylum application or interview endanger credibility as an "autonomous" victim? Further, given that "community ties," or local contacts who can house or assist the asylum seeker, are a crucial part of assessing an asylum case, the petitioner may not know how to address the fact that she is still in contact with a perpetrator who also moved to the US.

Lawyers encourage many women from certain countries in Africa to highlight their experiences of FGC, even if the women did not leave their countries for that reason or see FGC as traumatizing; indeed, based on interviews Oxford conducted, women left their countries (Eritrea, Sudan, Nigeria) due to experiences or threats of detention or torture targeting them or their loved ones, particularly as punishment of political activism.[82] Despite these claimants' descriptions of political violence, asylum advocates and adjudicators asked these women about FGC, with asylum seekers eventually naming family members who condoned or participated

in the practice. The focus on the persecutory family inadvertently shifts the focus from the extent and nature of the actual suffering to what kind of relationship the alleged perpetrator and victim have. This shift in focus prompts unnecessary scrutiny of what the victim thinks of her family members' actions, what they mean to her, and to what extent she rejects their behavior and beliefs.

Second, this autonomy frame requires asylum seekers to exercise agency in particular ways. Gender-based asylum cases involve narratives that might make sense for how a *particular person* sees her own agency and her own relationships with her family and kin. But judges' decisions often generalize those experiences to what *anyone* would feel or think in similar circumstances. What about women who do not demonstrate a desire to escape the family yet did not want to undergo FGC? In DV cases, even though the "immutability" of marital relationships assumes that women may not be able to leave their relationships, asylum seekers are still expected to document the desire to leave and attempts to prove government unwillingness to intervene. But often it might be safer *not* to involve the police or to demonstrate any kind of rejection of a family member. For example, in the DV case of *Matter of A-R-C-G et al.* (2014), the BIA found that the claimant tried to contact the police in her home country of Guatemala several times, but they would not intervene; as a result of the claimant calling the police and moving into her father's house, her husband threatened even more abuse.[83] Yet the BIA was involved in this case because of an appeal of the immigration judge's finding that the husband abused his wife "arbitrarily" and "without reason." Thus, even proving attempts at resistance and governmental lack of intervention may not be enough.

When autonomy is measured in terms of "escape" and "resistance," it not only leaves a judge to decide the amount of *courage* an asylum seeker displayed in these cases, but it also sets the parameters for agency. Asylum advocates should consider the impact on an asylum seeker who must categorically denigrate her family members. Chitra Aiyar, the gender-based asylum lawyer I discussed in chapter 1, notes that some of her clients tell her that they understand the choices their family member made and are not comfortable with writing or saying, "My mother terrorized me, and I reject her beliefs."[84] Her approach is to try to support her clients in being able to say, "I love my mother, but I am making a difficult choice not to go back." But she can only create space for a client to make such a statement if she feels very confident in the case evidence she has collected.

Chitra has a point in trying to lend some integrity to the process as the fabrication of claims, often encouraged by legal counsel, can backfire.

Jennifer Coffman, an anthropologist, served as an expert witness in the case of Mary Gachumi, who arrived from Kenya in the United States in 1999. Coffmann found that Gachumi, likely influenced by what she heard about successful FGC asylum cases in the United States, distorted her story and facts about her country and community to claim that she feared FGC. Gachumi claimed that she was a member of the social group of Masai women and girls who oppose FGC and was careful to note that her family "strictly follows" Masai customs. The petitioner also vilified her father.[85] Coffman reluctantly realized that the inconsistencies and lack of evidence for claims Gachumi made about Masai practices meant that the client might not be telling the truth, or might not even be Masai. This asylum seeker was very likely crafting her statements based on what she had read about the Kassindja case.[86] Coffman notes that the asylum system set up Gachumi to fabricate her claims. In effect, limiting how asylum seekers are to speak about their autonomy and their families can put them in the position to distort their own stories.

THE EFFECTS OF THE AUTONOMOUS WORTHY VICTIM FRAME ON US POWER RELATIONSHIPS

The autonomous worthy victim frame is useful for the United States to draw distinctions between itself and other countries, particularly because presumably the asylum seeker *chose* to flee to the United States rather than to other countries. Enfolded in the assumption that the worthy victim is an autonomous victim who rejects her family is the idea that the asylum seeker came from a *bad, weak state* that not only failed in protecting individuals but specifically in protecting individuals *from* their own family members. In weak states, one sees "the [constructed] opposition of the enlightened female individual with an alien and premodern culture, which the state of origin was unable or unwilling to control."[87]

Noll points out that the labeling of a "weak state" is a crucial asylum strategy. This is because in prototypical asylum cases, one is dealing with a *strong*, totalitarian state that tortures an individual or denies another religious freedom. If "political opinion" is easy to prove, in other words, then "culture" is irrelevant and one just points to the overpowering persecutory government. However, there are many types of violence, particularly forms of gender violence, in which one cannot point to a government that publicly targets and goes after a group of people. So then "culture" is put "*en par* with that of the state, yet diffusely located, removed from volition and unaffected by calls for institutional intervention."[88] "Culture"

becomes the easily invoked reason for why violence is occurring; "culture" becomes as powerful as the government in its reach into people's lives, as immune to change as a dictatorial regime, and as such becomes an "acceptable" reason for violence.

Because of the alleged weakness of the state and the relative strength of cultural norms, presumably "nothing can be done" to prevent the oppression of women. Accordingly, an asylum lawyer can argue that her client deserves asylum, to receive protection from the perpetually persecutory culture in the weak state. As Noll notes, the consequences are multiple. First, making culture as a "cause" of persecution creates a false divide between "civilized countries of asylum and uncivilized countries of origin."[89] Second, a distinction is drawn between strong and weak states. "The strong state is associated with negative obligations, that is, obligations to not violate human rights, while the weak state is associated with positive obligations to prevent the violation through the private agents carrying out a repressive culture."[90]

Allegedly in non-Western states, the private sphere is supposedly "leaky"; religious and cultural norms seep out in ways the state cannot and will not control. Further, the family in Western states is *good*; families are invested in each other's well-being. The family in non-Western states is *bad*; it propagates always already backward and oppressive cultural and religious norms. The way this plays out in the asylum process is that while some cases (DV) may reference private harms and others (FGC) might reference cultural harms, they both can construct the family as a pathological social group, where *relatives*, whether parents, siblings, or spouses, are hurting their own, which the state is *unwilling and unable* to stop because it clearly is not secular, liberal, or strong enough to do so. The weak state is too incapable or too undemocratic to do anything but condone the violence or helplessly stand by. Since these weak states cannot protect *or control* their citizens, then it sets up asylum-granting states to point to *their* capacity to protect not only their own citizens but also foreign nationals.

But this leaves little room to recognize that in Western, asylum-granting countries, families might be violent or loving, or a combination of both, as much as they might be anywhere else. Western states are also guilty of being unwilling to take seriously, prevent, or "control" violence and oppression "in the home." Wendy Brown points out that states that identify themselves as secular with liberal universal "values" actually set aside a separate "depoliticized" sphere for the family and the household.[91] The family/household then becomes "sacralized," meaning attaining a special sacrosanct status where "holiness" resides. Patriarchal religious norms will be celebrated and protected from state authority. The family is so

holy that the state acknowledges, prioritizes, and desires certain kinds of "family life" and "family values" to legitimize statecraft, such as discriminatory policies toward sexual minorities. Thus, "strong," Western states *also* set it up such that families "get to do what they want," so to speak. Even if one presumes that strong states are democratic ones where women have political and legal equality, women

> still make less money than men, do more unpaid reproductive and household labor than men, and in part as a result of this structural inequality, suffer from oppressive and violent gender norms and practices in both work and family spaces. Non-conforming men, women, couples, and families constitute a threat to the state's vision of itself as egalitarian and liberal. In effect, the "private sphere" is simultaneously cast out from public debates and a site for state control.[92]

Yet legal commentators analyzing DV cases often draw upon distinctions between the United States and other countries. For example, Bullard argues that asylum adjudicators should recognize how much more difficult it is "elsewhere" than in the United States for domestic violence victims to receive government protection or acknowledgment. In other words, she is trying to create space for DV survivors *not* to have to demonstrate government complicity, because governmental lack of will and ability should be presumed elsewhere.

> Domestic abuse, by its very name, occurs primarily in the home. In most countries, the home is a private sphere where governmental influence is muted. Due to this lack of government influence, the likelihood of the government discovering domestic violence is very low unless the victim reports it. . . . This expectation of privacy in the home exists in the United States, and it would be hypocritical for the United States to require governments of other countries to breach privacy of their citizens to ensure protection from domestic violence when the home is given special consideration in the United States.[93]
>
> The United States combats the problem of private domestic violence through public education, the availability of victim support programs, and responsive law enforcement and courts. Even in the United States, however, there are areas of the country where these support programs do not function and women remain in abusive relationships. This implies that it is unrealistic to expect a foreign government to have a 100 percent success rate in protecting domestic violence victims. . . . Thus, the private nature of domestic violence crimes makes it difficult for an applicant to demonstrate a pattern of failure by her native country in responding to these crimes.[94]

Bullard agrees that the family is essentially left to its own devices in the United States because it is, as Wendy Brown would note, "set aside" in a sense. But she conflates the private sphere with *privacy*, coming dangerously close to inadvertently supporting anachronistic arguments that domestic violence is a "private" matter between family members. Second, the phrasing "*even* in the United States" implies that the standards in other countries would not possibly be the same as in the United States.

While the United States has a relatively visible infrastructure and strong network of organizations addressing domestic violence, as Uma Narayan points out, there are structural, not "cultural," reasons for lack of infrastructure in other countries to address forms of domestic violence.[95] Further, in Narayan's comparative study of domestic violence in India and the United States, the presence of "better" legal and political infrastructure does not always translate into "protection" or "help" for survivors of violence in the United States or mean that grassroots forms of assistance *do not* exist in India. Thus, assumptions about which countries are better at addressing forms of violence do not always match the experiences of *all* the survivors.

How specifically, then, does the autonomous victim frame play out in policy decisions and power relationships? The first way is in how the United States deflects from its own problems with domestic violence. The domestic violence situation in the United States may or may not be "better" than elsewhere, but it is still at tragic proportions deserving of concern. The United Nations Human Rights Committee in 2013 recently requested information from the United States about the prevention and combating of domestic violence. In its response to the committee, the United States noted its various measures, including the Violence Against Women Act and the Family Violence Prevention and Services Act.[96] But the United States did not address the disproportionate rates of domestic violence among women of color, immigrant women, and indigenous women within the country.

Consider also the case of *Jessica Lenahan (Gonzales) v. United States* (2011), in which Lenahan, a US citizen, claimed before the Inter-American Commission on Human Rights (IACHR) that the United States violated her human rights. Lenahan argued that police in her city in Colorado repeatedly failed to uphold a restraining order against her estranged husband; he then kidnapped their three children and eventually drove to the police department. After an exchange of fire between her husband and the police, her children's deceased bodies were discovered in the car. To this day, she still does not know exactly how her children were killed. In 2005, the Supreme Court ruled that the police department could not be sued for

its failures. Soon after, Lenahan took her case to the IACHR. The IACHR ruled that United States had failed to uphold the human rights of Lenahan and her children and issued recommendations for an investigation into the deaths as well as for overarching legislation, resources, and training to eradicate and address domestic violence.[97] In 2014, the American Civil Liberties Union and human rights organizations argued in front of the IACHR that the United States had failed to implement these reforms; the IACHR has not yet issued a response. For many DV advocates, this case is unique and more extreme than most DV cases. At the same time, the case is *representative* of US failures to comprehensively address DV survivors' rights. And it has spurred a discussion on how to address US international legal obligations toward domestic violence victims.[98]

But the United States is able to selectively ignore its inadequate responses by repeatedly referencing its capacity to protect its own citizens and foreign nationals.[99] The discursive climate underlying governmental statements about US commitment, willingness, and ability to eradicate gender violence is the same that underscores comments in asylum cases about the comparative lack of governmental capacity in other countries. The use of the autonomy frame draws upon and strengthens this distinction between better and worse countries.

Feminist advocates also reinforce the better-worse distinction, as evidenced by Bullard's comments earlier. More specifically, some scholars and advocates pressure the government to recognize more DV asylum claims by arguing that the United States, by virtue of its "better" practices, can and should influence other countries to adopt policies and stances about DV. Podkul notes that "the United States' reluctance to recognize domestic violence as a basis of asylum stands in striking contrast to the strong position it has taken against domestic violence within its borders."[100] Rodriguez argues that "the United States is in a much better position to provide these women [immigration] assistance compared to other countries. . . . The United States' failure to take adequate steps to protect these women could be interpreted as supporting the practices of these countries, or at the least, as passive in the fight against domestic abuse."[101]

When the Center for Gender and Refugee Studies put together reports on violence against women in Guatemala, it noted that if the United States were indeed concerned about "floodgates" of DV victims, then it could "address the root cause of refugee flows and use its considerable influence to pressure the Guatemalan government to implement concrete reforms in its legal code and criminal justice system to protect the human rights of women."[102] After the publication of the CGRS reports, the US Congress recommended in May 2006 to increase "technical assistance" from the

United States to Guatemala that would include strengthening "forensic teams," provision of "investigative tools," and help with "harmoniz[ing] data collection" with regards to violence against women.[103] The CGRS strategy was to influence the United States to pressure other countries to comply with human rights norms. But as Berger notes, the United States used the CGRS work as a way to shape Guatemala's policies without much reflection on its own domestic violence problems. Unfortunately the focus on how to influence another country elided the importance of the communication, networking, and interaction between Guatemalan women's rights activists and the CGRS, with both groups traveling to each other's countries.[104]

How should feminists speak to the tragic gaps and flaws in how other countries handle DV without playing into perceptions of backwardness that could ultimately silence feminists in those countries? How can feminists advocate for DV cases without reinforcing the better-worse distinction underlying the autonomy frame? It is possible to use gender-based asylum guidelines on DV as a way to pressure the United States to hold *itself* accountable for complying with human rights norms regarding gender violence. However, feminists have expressed concern about how states co-opt DV to increase the policing of and surveillance against marginalized men and communities.[105] In effect, the autonomy frame sidelines the variety of experiences of those who do not encounter the US state as helpful or protective.

The second way the autonomy frame is related to US global power is in the treatment of FGC. Prompted by information members of Congress members received about the Kassindja case as well as anecdotal evidence of FGC occurring among some immigrant communities in the United States,[106] Congress ensured that the 1996 Illegal Immigration Reform and Immigration Responsibility Act (IIRIRA) discussed in the previous chapter amended the Crimes and Criminal Procedure, 18 U.S.C. section 116, to outlaw FGC. The IIRIRA's Section 644 notes that the government must provide to all "aliens" issued visas for entry education about the harmful effects of FGC and the legal consequences of performing or allowing one's child to undergo FGC. This "educational initiative" is usually limited to immigrants arriving from countries where FGC is practiced.[107]

This inclusion of FGC in an act about immigration explicitly frames the practice as something that people "over there" do.[108] Legal commentators note that the IIRIRA addresses how "immigrants . . . bring the traditional practice of female genital mutilation to the United States."[109] But Abu-Lughod and Volpp argue that fears of immigrant communities "bringing their bad culture" with them has more to do with panic around

immigration than concerns about immigrants' human rights.[110] This fear makes sense in the context of a discursive climate in which US governmental actors believe that families elsewhere are presumably persecuting their daughters.

But the practice proved to be so infrequent within the United States that the governmental focus shifted to how the laws criminalizing FGC in the United States could send an important "signal" to countries where it was practiced.[111] And as part of the 1997 Foreign Operations, Export Financing, and Related Programs Appropriation Act, Congress required US executive directors of international financial institutions, such as the International Monetary Fund and the World Bank, to oppose any "non-humanitarian" loans to countries where FGC is practiced and where no anti-FGC education programs existed. [112] By 2000, the US Agency for International Development (USAID) incorporated elimination of FGC in its agenda. This tied foreign aid practices to the attempts of countries to regulate and prevent FGC.

I echo other scholars' concern that these changes were not just about strengthening norms that frame FGC as a human rights violation.[113] Rather, it was a way to demonstrate influence over the activities of FGC-practicing countries, not limited to how they address FGC. This is precisely why FGC asylum cases are useful—they indicate that asylum seekers are fleeing their families and countries for safe haven in the United States, where "American" families do not engage in such practices.[114] The autonomy frame helps to shape and undergird *why* the United States started to influence FGC practices within its borders and in other countries.

In effect, FGC and DV asylum frames do not unilaterally cause, nor are they solely caused by, US interactions with other countries or responses to violence within its borders. Rather, patterns of narrating FGC and DV in the context of the persecutory family find strength from and draw upon trends in how the United States uses gender violence as a site to engage with other countries. These trends intensify a discursive climate that understands gender violence in the context of bad families and weak states.

CONCLUSIONS

In this chapter, I argued that it is the autonomous asylum seeker who is constructed as worthy of protection. DV and FGC are different from other types of violence because the perpetrators are intimately known to the survivors. The independent survivor has fled the persecutory attempts of

family members to limit her autonomy. While DV and FGC are distinct from each other in terms of the specificities of the violence, I challenge the idea that FGC is more "exotic" than DV by illustrating how both types of violence are constructed as caused by "bad families" propagating bad cultural norms. The "bad family, weak state" construction props up the image of "good" migrants who exercise agency and autonomy to escape the people who could not love them as they deserved. It also strengthens the discursive climate that justifies the construction of the United States as a good and strong state that can and should, in turn, shape the policies of the weak states.

A possible critique of this analysis is that the asylum system is set up to support precisely those who exercise bravery and agency by rejecting certain norms and seeking freedom from persecution. One could argue that all asylum petitions reveal autonomy due to the asylum seekers' ability to be able to make the journey and apply for asylum in the first place. But I am challenging the *kind* of autonomy that is expected and "rewarded." Not all asylum seekers can or want to frame their stories in this manner.

A second issue is how to analyze cases of so-called honor killings, which are typically understood as punishment for transgressions of gender norms. I focused on DV intimate partner cases in order to explore the alleged distinction between DV as familiar and FGC as strange. But the lessons learned in this chapter are applicable for any form of family violence, whether "honor killings," child abuse, forced marriage, or other crimes. Does the asylum seeker participate (willingly or not) in a narrative where she is an autonomous agent fleeing and rejecting a persecutory family that propagates oppressive cultural norms in weak states? For example, consider the following proposed social group in a recent "honor killings" asylum case: "all Jordanian women who, in accordance with social and religious norms in Jordan, are accused of being immoral criminals and, as a consequence, face the prospect of being killed [at the hands of family members] without any protection from the Jordanian government."[115] In table 2.5 in chapter 2, we see 84 grants and 13 denials in honor killings cases and 271 grants and 40 denials in repressive social norms cases, also often perpetrated by family members. As mentioned in chapter 1, repressive social norm cases are often paired with other types of violence, or they may involve prototypical "exotic victim" frames that invoke particular constructions of the countries of origin (Afghanistan and Iran) that have negative relationships with the United States. Honor killings cases are most often paired with DV cases, with the highest number of asylum seekers, including for cases with singular honor killings claims, from Pakistan. In chapter 6, I thus question why and how forms of family

violence are differentially categorized, particularly when the violence is committed in particular countries.

In chapter 6, I also suggest ways to reframe autonomy not as a proclamation of independence with the accompanying rejection of family/community but as the right to form a variety of interpersonal relationships, inclusive of people who may harm but also people who are supportive and caring. In that chapter, I argue that a discursive intervention in the construction of family can institute legal reforms to expand the definition of family. It can also create more nuance in the asylum process about the characterization of the asylum seeker's family.

Rethinking autonomy in the context of family can contribute to the inclusion of undocumented immigrants into the conversation about the experiences of non-citizens. As I discuss in chapter 6, "family reunification" is allegedly a cornerstone of US immigration policy, and undocumented immigrants that are a part of a particular kind of heteronormative, nuclear family are perceived as "less dangerous" and more worthy of acceptance in the United States. I use the lens of the "family" to look at the distinction between the asylum seeker fleeing a bad family, and an undocumented person becoming "good" through evidence of being part of a normal, caring "American"-like family. It is important to reject the perceived distinction between asylum seekers and undocumented immigrants in order to better understand non-citizens' encounters with the state. How does one try to find safety in the context of violence, such as through asylum or the VAWA self-petition and the U visa discussed in chapter 2, while also resisting how state methods of immigration relief criminalize and demonize their family members and communities? As I contend in chapter 6, a deeper analysis of the family can have reverberating effects on how we understand and classify gender violence and its impact on a variety of non-citizens.

CHAPTER 4

The Innocent Worthy Victim Frame

Comparing Trafficking and Coercive Sterilization/Abortion

Trafficking and coercive sterilization/abortion seem remarkably different since trafficking has to do with consent to sex and work, while coercive sterilization/abortion concerns reproductive choices. However, after studying asylum cases, law, and analysis related to both types of violence, I discovered a common "worthy victim" frame of "innocence" at work. I see innocence as encompassing two distinct features. First, innocent victims make good choices; they do not engage in criminal activity. Second, innocence implies that a truly vulnerable victim must be juxtaposed with an evil, identifiable perpetrator.

According to the 2000 United Nations Protocol to Prevent, Suppress, and Punish Trafficking in Persons, Especially Women and Children, Supplementing the United Nations Convention Against Transnational Organized Crime, Article 3, trafficking comprises

> the recruitment, transportation, transfer, harbouring or receipt of persons, by means of the threat or use of force or other forms of coercion, of abduction, of fraud, of deception, of the abuse of power or of a position of vulnerability or of the giving or receiving of payments or benefits to achieve the consent of a person having control over another person, for the purpose of exploitation. Exploitation shall include, at a minimum, the exploitation of the prostitution of others or other forms of sexual exploitation, forced labour or services, slavery or practices similar to slavery, servitude or the removal of organs.[1]

Trafficking includes the forced movement of people across borders, or within a country's borders, with the ultimate intention to transport victims to destination countries or specific locations within a country.[2] Trafficked victims experience rape, restricted or monitored mobility, isolation and confinement, physical and psychological abuse, torture, and sometimes forced marriage. Labor trafficking is a stated concern of the United States and the United Nations. Further, men are also victims of sex trafficking.[3] But in practice, gender-based asylum and other forms of immigration relief disproportionately focus on female victims of sex trafficking.

Coercive sterilization/abortion (CS/A) occurs when countries mandate that women, and often men, get sterilized or have abortions as a part of population control policies. Thus, these women face forcible medical procedures or tactics such as intimidation, incarceration, and fines, meant to push people to "voluntarily" sterilize or have abortions. In these cases, too, while many asylum cases are of men (for sterilization), the majority of analysis is directed to women's experiences. And the male asylum seekers petition based on their relationships to their wives and girlfriends.

How do expectations of innocence operate in both types of violence? In trafficking cases, sex workers and smuggled migrants, even if they suffered persecutory harms, are not seen as truly helpless, innocent victims because they have participated in criminal activity. They are thus "left out" of considerations for immigration relief.

While asylum advocates are involved in putting forward trafficking asylum cases, the US government has put its weight behind the Victims of Trafficking and Violence Protection Act, also known as the Trafficking Victims Protection Act (TVPA), which provides special visas called T visas to trafficking victims. Because the TVPA is a more prevalent route than asylum for those fleeing trafficking-related persecution, the perception of the worthy victim emerges from the same *discursive climate* that shapes the TVPA. First, the TVPA entrenches moral panic about sex workers and prostitution. Thus, the TVPA contains provisions that allow the United States to shape the anti-trafficking policies of countries *and* nongovernmental organizations (NGOs), as well as to punish and sanction countries that do not comply with US standards that require the inclusion of anti-prostitution as a part of anti-trafficking measures. US anti-prostitution policies are encapsulated in US codification of "inadmissible aliens," which state:

> Any alien who (i) is coming to the U.S. solely, principally, or incidentally to engage in prostitution, or has engaged in prostitution within 10 years of the date of application for a visa, admission, or adjustment of status . . . is inadmissible.[4]

Second, the US government understands traffickers and smugglers as potentially part of terrorist networks. Thus, the TVPA ensures that smuggled migrants cannot in practice make claims about trafficking. Despite the efforts of asylum advocates, the United States has resisted issuing guidelines to make it easier for asylum/immigration officials to interpret trafficking asylum claims. Survivors often have to go the route of the T visa, but only if the *trafficking* brought the victims *into* the United States, effectively narrowing the number of victims who can use this option. Victims of trafficking into or within the United States have a higher chance of receiving immigration relief than victims of trafficking outside of the country who then escaped or fled to the United States, due to differing perceptions of innocence.

In coercive sterilization/abortion cases, expectations of innocence occur when immigration judges tend to focus primarily on victims who are married, rather than single or partnered but unmarried victims, indicating more legitimization of the reproductive choices of married women than those of unmarried women. Adjudicators also focus more on the loss of "potential" children due to coercive sterilization or abortion than on the harms that coercive reproductive practices inflict on women, such as through forced gynecological exams and procedures. Why is there a focus on unborn children? The 1996 Illegal Immigration Reform and Immigrant Responsibility Act (IIRIRA) discussed in chapter 2 contains a section noting that victims of China's coercive population control policies could be eligible for asylum. This type of gender violence is the only one to merit inclusion in congressional legislation about asylum eligibility. But this 1996 legislation emerged from a *discursive climate* of desires to protect "unborn children," promoted and circulated by pro-life interest groups and politicians. In turn, the endurance of the innocent worthy victim frame opens the way for pro-life groups to pressure the United States to pursue anti-abortion policies globally, and enables the United States to draw distinctions between itself as a protector of freedom and life and China as oppressive.

Thus there is a similar "innocent worthy victim" frame operating in trafficking and CS/A cases. Whereas in FGC and DV cases asylum seekers are expected to showcase autonomy and independence, in the cases I study in this chapter, there is a focus on helplessness. The persecutors are not family members but powerful entities like the government of China or terrorist/trafficking networks. Further, the US government has been deeply involved in attempts to provide immigration relief for both trafficking and CS/A. Indeed, the anti-prostitution stance in the US anti-trafficking efforts, and the anti-abortion stance in the US efforts to

address CS/A derive from a similar discursive climate that focuses on the "protection" of "truly" innocent persons.

Due to finding this shared innocence frame, I started to look for more connections between violence regarding sexual choices and violence regarding reproductive choices. I found the answer when I looked at rape cases. I first investigated rape cases, a significant percentage of gender-based asylum cases, concurrently with trafficking cases as both involve denial of consent to sex. As I will explain later in the chapter, I found it more useful to discuss rape at an interesting and unexpected intersection between sexual choices and reproductive choices, since rape can result in pregnancy. The statistics on rape resulting in pregnancy are hard to assess, as they depend on whether and how these pregnancies are reported, but estimates are that 5% to 18% of rapes result in pregnancy.[5] We do not generally have good data on how many rape-related pregnancies end in abortion or how many pregnant rape victims may have access to abortions. But US asylum and immigration law and guidelines, despite acknowledging rape as persecutory, fail to mention *forced pregnancy and forced maternity*, which occur when there is denial of abortion, as a *persecutory, coercive reproductive practice*. The discursive climate that contributes to ideas of innocence also precludes attention to forced pregnancy/maternity because of the perception that abortion is wrong, immoral, and the *end* of innocent lives. Thus, this chapter also investigates this "missing" category of gender violence. Table 4.1 provides a summary of the effects of the innocence frame.

TRAFFICKING

Two options for immigration relief for survivors of trafficking are gender-based asylum and the T visa. Although the T visa is not considered to be a form of asylum, I am including it in my discussion because it affords protection (access to legal and social services, opportunity to adjust status to legal permanent residency, etc.) similar to what asylees receive. Further, because trafficking asylum cases are notoriously difficult to win, the T visa offers an alternative possibility to some survivors.

While T visa applicants must prove to Citizenship and Immigration (USCIS) officials that they were trafficked into the United States, asylum seekers can apply if they experienced trafficking (or attempts at trafficking) elsewhere and managed to enter the United States. Trafficking asylum cases require proving persecution due to membership in a social group. The Center for Gender and Refugee Studies' gender-based asylum

Table 4.1 THE INNOCENT WORTHY VICTIM FRAME			
Type of violence	Worthy victim frame	Effects of frame on asylum seekers	Effects of frame on power relationships between united states and others
Trafficking	Innocent	Sex workers and smuggled migrants not included because of alleged "criminal activity." Sex-trafficking victims prioritized over labor trafficking victims. Trafficking victims who were rescued are prioritized over those who escaped.	United States ranks and sanctions countries according to not only how well they control trafficking but also whether they take an anti-prostitution pledge. United States links smuggling and trafficking with terrorism, focusing more on criminal activity than on harm done to survivors.
Coercive sterilization/ abortion	Innocent	Unmarried victims not included; less severe forms of population control such as forced gynecological exams and birth control insertion not included; victims of forced pregnancy and maternity (particularly due to lack of access to abortion) not included; focus on loss of "innocent unborn children" rather than on harm to women or on their reproductive choices	United States draws distinction between itself as a protector of women's rights and China (and its coercive population control practices) as an oppressor of women's rights. United States strengthens commitment to deny use of funding to global organizations that provide access to abortion services/ counseling.

cases and litigation focus primarily on "sex trafficking," inclusive of "being targeted for prostitution, threatened with kidnap, being successfully kidnapped, suffering rapes and beatings, sale into brothels, and forcible prostitution."[6]

I analyzed and consulted the Center for Gender and Refugee Studies (CGRS) attorney Stephen Knight's review of close to 100 trafficking asylum cases in the CGRS database; I discovered that trafficked asylum seekers face two main obstacles.[7] First, a social group cannot be defined by the persecution itself. So, one cannot propose membership in a social group consisting of victims of trafficking. Asylum seekers must prove that they were targeted for trafficking due to some particular characteristic.[8] But even when petitioners try to prove that they were purposely targeted, judges dismiss their claims, depoliticizing their experiences by arguing that the perpetrators were motivated by "personal" or "random" reasons. Second, asylum seekers need to illustrate their helplessness, but if they mention that they escaped their traffickers, judges are likely to argue that they are not so vulnerable after all.

As to the first point, judges have denied asylum claims based on membership of a social group including "young women." For example, in *Kuci v. Attorney General* (2008), the Third Circuit found that a group entitled "young women who have been approached or threatened with kidnapping, forced [prostitution] or killing by human traffickers" was too broad.[9] Similarly, in *Rreshpja v. Gonzales* (2005), the Sixth Circuit held that a group defined as "young, attractive Albanian women" may not constitute a social group because it was too broad, as then "any" young attractive Albanian woman could apply for asylum. However, the judges failed to realize that not every young, attractive woman would experience a fear of trafficking, or attempts at trafficking, nor would all trafficking victims apply for asylum.[10]

There are two promising developments that might bode well for social group trafficking claims. First, in the case of *Gjura v. Holder* (2nd Cir. 2012), the BIA overturned the immigration judge's asylum grant.[11] In 2012, the Second Circuit upheld the denial, rejecting the social group of "young, unmarried Albanian women." However, due to the influence of a CGRS amicus curiae brief, the court *withdrew* the published decision that "young, unmarried Albanian women do not constitute a social group." Accordingly, since the decision is no longer published, the CGRS hopes that there is room for the proposed social group to eventually be used in the future.[12]

In *Cece v. Holder* (2013) the Seventh Circuit remanded the denied trafficking case for reconsideration, issuing a legal standard that a social group may be defined by gender. This legal standard is binding only in Wisconsin, Illinois, and Indiana, under the Seventh Circuit's jurisdiction.[13] The court affirmed the accuracy of Cece's social group, "a young Orthodox woman living alone in Albania," in describing her vulnerability

to trafficking, given the sociopolitical and economic conditions in that country. The court's reasoning is instructive: "Members of a social group need not be swimming against the stream of an embedded cultural norm. Sometimes the characteristic is immutable because a shared past experience or status has imparted some knowledge or labeling that cannot be undone."[14] The court ultimately concluded that gender plus a "narrowing characteristic" (such as living alone) is sufficient, reaffirming that "gender" matters as a cognizable group.

Per the reasoning in the Kassindja case discussed in chapter 3, that gender and tribal membership are enough to constitute a social group, Gott argues that gender and nationality should be sufficient to constitute a social group, particularly for women living in countries with high rates of trafficking, such as Albania.[15] It is too early to say what the impact of this ruling might be. Perhaps it will be possible to draw upon existing feminist literature and anti-trafficking organizations' research to indicate patterns of state responsibility for trafficking, making trafficking asylum cases a bit easier to assess. But it will not be until the emergence of more cases and potentially useful guidelines and briefs from the US government that trafficked asylum seekers can feel more confident about their chances of receiving asylum.

Relatedly, asylum seekers find it difficult to prove that they were targeted when judges impute that perpetrators were motivated due to "random" or "personal" reasons. Despite evidence that traffickers stalked and singled out the asylum seekers making claims in the United States, judges have argued that the traffickers were motivated by "personal problems," because of "their own criminal enrichment," or due to general criminal harassment.[16] In cases where asylum seekers were trafficked after accepting or trying to find out more about offers of marriage, a common ploy used by trafficking rings, judges erroneously painted the traffickers as "spurned suitors."[17] So even when asylum seekers tried to explain that they were indeed targeted, the judges stripped their stories of the political context and instead pathologized the perpetrator's actions.

The second obstacle deals with how asylum seekers prove their vulnerability. Asylum seekers who describe how they were able to get away from their traffickers find that by virtue of being able to escape, they undermine their cases. So people who fled their countries in order to avoid persecution that they feared, often based on *past* experiences and harms, find that *being able to flee* the traffickers sets the asylum seeker up to fail!

Adjudicators also fail to recognize that a "past harm" of being trafficked and raped can have future persecutory effects particularly for women who escaped, such as being targeted again, particularly to punish the escape, as well as ostracism due to being raped.[18]

One asylum applicant expressed a fear of being kidnapped in the future, because she had already received threats. The immigration judge argued upon examining country reports of Albania that "'most cases' involve women who are 'lured by false promises . . . [or] sold unwillingly by their family,'" and that the applicant "has shown herself to be resistant to being lured."[19] The judge denied her asylum petition. Further, the judge acknowledged that Albania had a problem with trafficking but not with kidnapping for the purposes of forced prostitution. This decision indicates that the judge might narrowly understand kidnapping as some kind of sinister plot from which there can be no *resistance or escape*. This judge, like others, was looking for the truly helpless woman, someone duped by everyone around her, with no choices or opportunities to leave. Recall from chapter 3 that the autonomous victim is rewarded for "fighting back" and proving escape, because of the rejection of her family/culture/country. However, in trafficking cases, escaping/resisting is seen to belie the image of the enslaved, trafficked woman.

In 2004, the Seventh Circuit Court of Appeals rejected the claim in *Lleshanaku v. Ashcroft* because the petitioner escaped her traffickers and failed to report her case to the police. Because the petitioner was able to escape, the judges noted that she had managed to "resist lures to work for the gang."[20] The court also attributed its decision to the claimant's failure to report the violence to the police. But, as the claimant argued, the police were also afraid of the trafficking gangs. And, indeed, the police's fear of gangs could constitute state unwillingness to protect targeted people.

The asylum advocacy group Human Rights First suggests ways for asylum seekers to win trafficking cases. An asylum seeker can illustrate that one was targeted for trafficking due to family political ties; suggest fear of future retaliation by creating a social group based on shared past experience with other victims of trafficking; show that the trafficking occurred in connection with forced marriage; or argue that one is an independent or single women living alone in a country and transgressing norms and thus will be targeted by traffickers.[21] But with the obstacles named above, some anti-trafficking advocates point out that the T visa might be an easier route because it focuses on the *criminal activity of trafficking*.

The T Visa

The second option for immigration relief is through the T visa. [22] In 1998, the Clinton administration issued a directive to address trafficking through "prevention, protection, and support of victims" as well as prosecution of traffickers. President Clinton signed the Trafficking Victims Protection Act into law on October 28, 2000. [23] Around the same time, after US-led negotiations, on November 15, 2000, the United Nations adopted a new document, the aforementioned Protocol to Prevent, Suppress and Punish Trafficking in Persons, Especially Women and Children, supplementing the United Nations Convention against Transnational Organized Crime (Palermo Protocol), with the United Nations Office on Drugs and Crime serving as the monitoring body. The United States became a signatory to the Protocol in December 2000 and ratified it in 2005. The United States framed its commitment to ending trafficking as a part of its own legacy in ending slavery. It saw both the TVPA and Palermo Protocol as the commencement of "unprecedented momentum" in a global fight to end this type of violence.[24] Congress has reauthorized TVPA every few years since 2000, with the exception of 2011. The TVPA also requires that the US State Department issue Trafficking in Persons Reports about other countries' policies and successes in eradicating trafficking.

The T visa has a cap of 5,000 a year, with less than 1,000 actually being issued per year. Given that anywhere from 14,000 to 50,000 people are trafficked into the United States every year,[25] this cap allows the United States to express concern for victims while trying to limit the entrance of non-citizens. T visas are issued for four years (previously three years), after which the recipient is eligible to adjust his or her status to legal permanent residency.[26]

To be eligible for a T visa or T "status," survivors must be in the United States (or American Samoa, the Commonwealth of the Northern Marian Islands, or at a port of entry) *due* to trafficking. TVPA only applies to those who are "physically present" in the United States due to trafficking, which means that the victims entered the United States by being forcibly brought by traffickers, are present in the United States after a recent rescue from trafficking, or were trafficked in the past and continue to live in the United States due to some reason directly related to the trafficking.[27] People are not eligible for T status if they escaped the traffickers before law enforcement became involved, or if they escaped but cannot show that they did not have a "clear chance" to leave the United States due to trauma, injury, lack of resources, or other factors.[28] The trafficking survivor must be "admissible" to the United States, meaning she was not deported in the

past; if she is unlawfully in the country she must demonstrate that the trafficking was a central reason for that unlawful presence.

Applicants also have to prove "extreme hardship involving unusual and severe harm" if removed/deported. This standard, however, is open to interpretation. Also, Congress chose the standard of proof to be "extreme hardship" rather than other options that are easier to demonstrate, such as "well-founded fear of retribution."[29] The extreme hardship requirement sets an even higher standard than what needs to be proven in asylum cases.[30] Petitioners must prove "severe" trafficking, meaning they were kidnapped, forcibly sold and transported, or tricked into the sex work industry; *there is no room for any perceived "consent" or "choice" in the situation.*

The TVPA requires a "commercial sex act" to constitute sex trafficking, which would technically exclude those who were forced to marry against their will and then trafficked across a border.[31] The legislation does discuss labor trafficking, and two highly publicized US incidents of trafficking that preceded the creation of TVPA were forced labor cases.[32] For example, the US government acknowledges that

> traffickers often prey on individuals who are poor, frequently unemployed or underemployed, and who may lack access to social safety nets, predominantly women and children in certain countries. Victims are often lured with false promises of good jobs and better lives, and then forced to work under brutal and inhuman conditions. . . . Trafficking can also take place in labor situations such as domestic servitude, labor in a prison-like factory, or migrant agricultural work.[33]

However, in the passage and reauthorizations of the TVPA lawmakers have primarily referenced passive victims of *sex* trafficking who are under the total "slavery-like" control of the traffickers.[34]

Eligibility for the T visa also requires compliance with "reasonable requests" from law enforcement for the purposes of investigating the trafficking. Even if someone does not apply for a T visa, a federal law officer might request from an immigration official that a trafficking victim be given "continued presence" in the country if she cooperates with and aids law enforcement. Continued presence means that the victim can stay in the country, work, and receive social services for one year with the potential to renew.[35]

The TVPA of 2005 allows some exemption from the requirement to assist law enforcement, particularly if the survivor is a minor or too traumatized to cooperate. Some victims are allowed earlier access to

permanent residency, and the government is becoming more aware of the need to protect the victim's family members living abroad and to promote family reunification.[36] But both Congress and the Department of Homeland Security have failed thus far to provide guidance on who gets exempted, or to guarantee the protection of victims' interests over "prosecutorial interests."[37] Further, law enforcement officials may be unwilling to endorse and support a T visa application since that would require a formal statement from the victim, which some prosecutors contend is inappropriate or a form of interference if there is going to be a criminal trial.[38]

The CGRS data show that 52 trafficking claims were granted and 19 claims were denied between 1996 and 2013.[39] According to data from the US Citizenship and Immigration Services, between 2002 and 2012, there were 3,309 approvals and 1,671 denials of T visas.[40] While the ratio of acceptance to denials is higher with asylum than with T visas, the sheer volume of T visa cases, in a shorter period of time, as compared to asylum cases, is worth thinking about. Because of the problems with the T visa, some scholars and human rights advocates have moved away from promoting the T visa in order to push for a stronger emphasis on appropriate asylum guidelines.[41] But as it stands, the innocent victim frame operating in both asylum cases and T visa legislation has negative effects on trafficking survivors.

THE EFFECTS OF THE INNOCENT WORTHY VICTIM FRAME ON ASYLUM SEEKERS / TRAFFICKING SURVIVORS

As mentioned in the beginning of the chapter, the cases I discuss deal with sex trafficking. The United Nations Office of Drugs and Crime estimates that 79% of human trafficking cases involve sexual exploitation but notes that forced labor cases are underreported.[42] The International Labour Organisation estimates that out of the 2.4 million people trafficked worldwide, 32% are labor-trafficking victims, 43% are sex-trafficking victims, and 25% experience both forms of violence.[43] Within the United States, labor-trafficking victims constitute 54% of reported human trafficking incidents, whereas sex-trafficking victims comprise 46%; in the United States labor cases are also underreported.[44] The US Department of Justice's Office for Victims of Crimes also provides more services to labor-trafficking victims than sex-trafficking victims (after the victims escaped or were rescued from their perpetrators).

But the vast majority of governmental *investigations*, which are crucial for designating a T visa applicant's willingness to cooperate, are of

suspected human trafficking involved sex-trafficking cases.[45] The predominant focus of investigations on sex-trafficking cases ultimately limits the availability of T visas for labor-trafficking victims.[46] Governmental agencies often do not frame labor trafficking *alone* as a "gendered" form of persecution unless it is combined with sexual exploitation. Asylum advocates and adjudicators also focus more on sex than labor trafficking, perhaps following the lead of the governmental focus. The CGRS database has one case, number 3579, about labor trafficking for a Ukrainian male claimant, decided by an asylum officer, whose decision is not accessible. So even though asylum seekers do apply based on labor trafficking, these cases are hard to track down because they are not published, accessible, or analyzed.

How and why do US governmental agencies prioritize the focus of sex trafficking of women and girls? I contend that the focus on sex trafficking in the United States derives from a discursive climate of moral panic about female sex workers. Governmental responses to trafficking, in other words, are a site to reinforce anti-prostitution policies.

"Abolitionists" contribute to and shape this panic. Abolitionists have historically been involved in eliminating all forms of sex trafficking and prostitution, not allowing for the recognition of the human rights and labor rights of sex workers. Abolitionists often consist of radical feminists dedicated to ending the objectification of women. But those engaged in "moral crusades" to end both trafficking and prostitution include conservative religious groups, many of which are less committed to promoting women's rights and more interested in ending "evil".[47]

During the negotiations leading up to the passage of the TVPA, liberal feminist advocates noted that the abolitionists won "ideologically" in using the human trafficking issue as a way to demonize and abolish prostitution.[48] President George W. Bush cemented the abolitionist view of trafficking, as he routinely referenced sex trafficking as the "worst" kind of violence. He imbued his discourse with language about the lurking and spreading evil, commenting that "civilized nations" were concerned about this "challenge to our conscience."[49] Obama shifted from this particular language and framed trafficking as a "criminal civil rights violation."[50] However, the language Bush used has persisted in many ways in congressional discussions about trafficking.

Feminist critiques of abolitionist perspectives focus on how these moralistic views of trafficking construct ideas of innocence.[51] For abolitionists, the concern is that trafficking and prostitution both destroy the inherent goodness and purity of women. The innocent woman is targeted, stalked, abducted in the dead of night, and then robbed of her virginity. Also, abolitionists imagine victims to be female and trafficked for the purposes of

sex in a way that indicates she was forced and then *rescued* from rather than escaped (which would indicate some measure of "volition") from the traffickers.[52]

Further, the United States equates trafficking with slavery, specifically a "modern slave trade." Equating trafficking with slavery creates a clear perpetrator: the trafficker, the modern slave master. The Bush administration's secretary of state, Condoleezza Rice, connected the new abolitionism to the 19th-century movement to abolish slavery, framing trafficking as a "new type of global slave trade [that] prey[s] on the weak among us."[53] But it is impossible to understand the connections between slavery and different forms of trafficking without understanding the economic contexts of exploitation. The all-too-easy reference to "slavery" distracts attention from a more complex view of how neoliberal economic policies, immigration restrictionism, and exploitation of workers contribute to trafficking and indentured servitude.[54] But the evil-versus-innocent trope is powerful and pervasive even though "evil" does not explain why trafficking occurs, how it endures, where it emerges, or the different kinds of experiences of trafficked victims.

The TVPA technically includes "anyone who has received assistance with migration for the purposes of prostitution."[55] While the TVPA uses this language when describing the general problem of trafficking, eligibility for immigration relief is limited to victims of "severe forms of trafficking." This raises the bar from just the form of labor (sex work) to an element of violent or deceptive *recruitment*; the element of coercion and trickery must be present from the get-go. Chapkis points out that the reference to other types of victims, such as those who voluntarily migrated for prostitution, are useful to "swell the numbers" of victims to draw urgent attention to trafficking.[56] For pro-life political players, the rise and prevalence of abolitionist discourse will ultimately support the larger cause to protect "innocent" lives. It is no accident that US Republican Congressman Christopher Smith, a prominent player in the writing and passage of pro-life, antichoice legislation and well versed in abolitionist jargon, was a key sponsor of the TVPA. He sees both "unborn children" and "trafficked women and children" as "innocents" in need of protection.[57]

Left out of the "innocent" victim frame are those who have been smuggled into the country, those who are labeled "illegal aliens." Chapkis argues that the TVPA was passed and reauthorized in a way that entrenched a divide between "violated innocents" and "illegal immigrants."[58] The latter are imagined to be primarily men who cross illegally into the United States for their own opportunities. Indeed, the TVPA legislation makes a distinction between labor *trafficking* and labor *exploitation*. Trafficking

must include "force, fraud, or coercion," whereas exploitation includes "extremely low wages . . . , long hours, poor working conditions, lack of avenues of redress, and may be linked to various forms of mistreatment of immigrants."[59] Labor exploitation is significantly more difficult to prove and is more likely to be perceived as impacting undocumented migrants, particularly those who were smuggled.

Because victims of labor exploitation are not likely to be eligible for the T visa, some legal commentators suggest that eligible migrants apply for the second type of visa made possible by the TVPA, the U visa mentioned in chapter 2. The U visa covers a very wide range of violent crimes, inclusive of trafficking, domestic violence, other forms of gender violence, and other crimes such as extortion, torture, and kidnapping. Thus, Saucedo suggests that the Department of Labor and the Equal Employment Opportunity Commission could support U visa protection for undocumented workers in exploitative working conditions.[60] But as with the T visa, the U visa also requires the cooperation with law enforcement. This requirement is a drawback, given the criminalization, threats, and workplace raids many immigrant communities experience at the hands of police and other enforcement bodies. So, labor trafficking T visa recipients exist, but the precarious distinctions between labor trafficking and labor exploitation make it difficult to more inclusively address the wide variety of violent experiences migrants have.

I thus contend the focus on sex trafficking is also because labor issues are "too close" to the politics of smuggling. The United States and the United Nations both draw a strict distinction between trafficking and smuggling. Recall the United Nations definition of trafficking, from the beginning of the chapter, which focuses on deception, coercion, and control. Now compare that definition to the United Nations understanding of smuggling. Article 3 of the Protocol Against the Smuggling of Migrants by Land, Sea and Air, supplementing the United Nations Convention Against Transnational Organized Crime, notes:

(a) "Smuggling of migrants" shall mean the procurement, in order to obtain, directly or indirectly, a financial or other material benefit, of the illegal entry of a person into a State Party of which the person is not a national or a permanent resident;
(b) "Illegal entry" shall mean crossing borders without complying with the necessary requirements for legal entry into the receiving State.[61]

The definition does *not* hinge on an explanation of the exploitative and violent effects on those who are smuggled.

Indeed, the United Nations Office on Drugs and Crime points out that there are distinctions between trafficking and smuggling in terms of purpose, consent, and outcomes to show that trafficking is *so much worse.*[62] The distinctions, according to US Citizenship and Immigration Services, are listed as follows.[63] The smuggling of migrants, while often undertaken in degrading and/or dangerous conditions, involves consent to smuggling. On the other hand, trafficking victims have "either never consented or, if they initially consented, that consent has been rendered meaningless by the coercive, deceptive or abusive actions of the traffickers." Further, "Smuggling ends with the arrival of the migrants at their destination," whereas trafficking involves the ongoing exploitation of the victims in some manner to generate illicit profits for the traffickers. Finally, in smuggling, profits are gained from transporting the migrant or facilitating a person staying in the destination country, whereas profits in trafficking are "derived from exploitation." The trafficked victim is allegedly tricked by a fraudulent trafficker into entering the country; the smuggled migrant *is* the *fraudulent actor* through his or her *free will.* Migrants are judged based on whether they seem to "consent" to activity deemed to be "immoral," such as prostitution or willfully entering a country without proper documentation.[64]

The term "smuggled alien" arose concomitantly with the term "illegal alien" in US political discourse so as to describe those whose "first act" upon reaching the United States was to "break laws" in a "clandestine manner."[65] The TVPA, the USCIS, the Department of Homeland Security, and the Department of Justice cling to the difference between smuggling and trafficking to deter fraudulent attempts by undocumented economic migrants to take advantage of immigration relief options.[66] The prototypical victim eligible for the T visa must be under full "control" of the trafficker so as to prove that she did not willingly choose to enter the United States without proper documentation. This approach makes sense given that the Palermo Protocol and the TVPA both rely upon a criminal justice perspective emphasizing prosecution of traffickers. But this criminal justice perspective allows states to use the Protocol as an excuse to strengthen anti-immigrantism.[67]

Bhabha points out that some asylum seekers, already having fled other forms of violence, may *become* victims of trafficking because of the desperate choices they make, such as the use of "smugglers, counterfeit documents, subterfuge and clandestine behavior to circumvent mandatory visa requirements."[68] Haynes is thus concerned about the impact of anti-smuggling stances on trafficking victims.[69] However, she too makes a distinction between trafficking and smuggling victims in terms of "choice."

She notes:

> Smuggling involves delivering persons to the country they wish to enter, *initiated* by the potential migrant. Smuggling often takes place under horrible and possibly life threatening conditions, but smuggled persons are left to their own devices upon delivery. Smuggling is not as lucrative for the perpetrators, as smugglers usually make only a short-term profit on the act of moving a person, while traffickers regard people as highly profitable, reusable, re-sellable, and expendable commodities.[70]

The experiences of smuggled undocumented migrants, as Haynes notes above, are inherently exploitative and violent.[71] Thus, the alleged "choice" of smuggled migrants should be put in context. Systematic constraints, such as border patrols, vigilante groups, lack of resources to legally migrate, and immigration restrictionist measures and laws, contribute to the necessity of smuggling as well as patterns of exposure to and risk of violence.

The perceived distinction between the prototypical female trafficking victim and the conniving male smuggled alien reveals a gendered politics to who gets protected. In addition, both scenarios deny the multiple forms of agency simultaneously at play during migration; there are varying degrees of coercion, exploitation, and choice occurring in both trafficking and smuggling.[72] Interestingly, the first recipient of the T visa was a four-year-old Thai boy who was "rented" by a smuggler. That smuggler was trying to bring a Thai sex worker into the United States and needed a child to complete the picture of a "family." Despite significant attempts by the INS to deport the boy, a federal judge blocked the deportation. Then-attorney general John Ashcroft noted that the child was the perfect "first" recipient of the T-1 visa because he was typical of trafficking victims, "too young, too frightened, too trapped in their circumstances to speak for themselves."[73] And this boy, although smuggled, is framed just like a trafficking victim, because of the "simple morality tale " his story engendered.[74]

Why the US Government Promotes the T Visa over Asylum

As we start to understand that the TVPA process leaves out a vast swath of potential T visa recipients, we have to ask why the United States has poured so much more energy into the TVPA than into creating guidelines or submitting reviews of trafficking asylum cases, particularly for

guidance in the creation of a viable social group. Why not try to eliminate the problems with the asylum claims? Researchers and nonprofit organizations have demonstrated state responsibility in trafficking cases, particularly in cases with high numbers of asylum seekers, such as Albania, so it would be feasible to even use the TVPA-mandated State Department country reports in asylum cases. The difference between the two forms of immigration relief is that the T visa is linked to prosecution of traffickers. So while trying to obtain the T visa can seem like a promising route, as it focuses on criminal activity and not on creating a social group, as is required in asylum cases, there are consequences to this focus.

Granting a trafficking survivor asylum will do nothing about his or her persecutors. This explains why the United States might continue to ignore trafficking asylum claims. The reason why traffickers are so important to the United States is that the government sees them as illegal aliens intent on entering the country to do harm not only to trafficking victims but also *to the country.*

In 2002, President George W. Bush signed National Security Directive 22, which linked human trafficking to terrorism. And in 2004, Congress passed the Intelligence Reform and Terrorism Prevention Act, which established the Human Smuggling and Trafficking Center for the purposes of understanding how smuggling and trafficking networks constitute threats to US security. And the TVPA reauthorization of 2005 created an interagency task force to study the relationship between trafficking and terrorism. When President Barack Obama entered office, his administration also framed trafficking as a national security concern.[75]

Analysts also started to see a connection between immigration, trafficking, and terrorism. As two trial attorneys with the Department of Justice asked: "If gangs [such as MS-13 made up of 'foreign nationals'] are willing to traffic children into the United States for sexual exploitation, is there any reason they would not help a terrorist enter the United States with a dirty bomb?"[76] There are also concerns that money made from trafficking operations could fund terrorist organizations.

The passage of the TVPA has increased convictions against traffickers.[77] But True notes that

> the privileging of criminal justice satisfies the state because it is highly visual and seems as though the state is "doing something" while leaving immigration policy [and the causes of trafficking] unchallenged. . . . There is no feeling of catharsis for victims of trafficking. This is because their experiences of violence are not simply physical but also social and economic.[78]

As Rieger points out, trafficking survivors are "decriminalized" when they are deemed eligible for T visas. There is a presumption of criminality for all migrants *unless and until* they can prove their innocence as a "true" survivor of the "worst" forms of trafficking.[79] Indeed, as feminists have pointed out, trafficking is typically seen as a security threat that must be addressed through stringent border control. Thus, responses such as the TVPA to trafficking should be understood as ways to protect state interests, and to show how better, stronger states keep out unwanted migrants and *potential terrorists* arriving from other states.[80]

THE EFFECTS OF THE INNOCENT WORTHY VICTIM FRAME ON US POWER RELATIONSHIPS

The innocent victim frame, primarily via the TVPA, allows the United States to ramp up counterterrorism efforts in the name of protecting the vulnerable. But there are other ways that the innocent victim frame serves as an entry point for the United States to shape its relationships with other countries. Since the US governmental efforts are more focused on the TVPA than on asylum guidelines, we can explore how TVPA provisions enable increased US influence.

The TVPA legislation allocates a significant amount of the funding for annual reports about other countries' efforts to combat trafficking.[81] Hendrix claims that since the Palermo Protocol has faced enforcement problems, the TVPA is the "most effective and comprehensive system for monitoring anti-human trafficking efforts internationally"; she joins others who support the United States taking on the global leadership role of enforcing anti-trafficking norms and standards.[82] Specifically, she notes that the TVPA turns into "obligation" the human rights goals in the Palermo Protocol by requiring the secretary of state to submit annual reports to Congress about anti-trafficking attempts and measures by foreign governments. This "Trafficking in Persons Report" (TIP) evaluates both the extent of the trafficking problem and successes of anti-trafficking measures in each country that may be the origin, transit point, or destination of trafficking.

Based on these reports, the State Department then ranks these countries into Tier 1 (fully complied with minimum standards established by the TVPA), Tier 2 (did not comply but made significant efforts), Tier 2 Watch List, and Tier 3 (noncompliant and no efforts). The Tier 2 Watch List is comprised of countries that have a high number of trafficking victims, have not made improvements from the previous year, or were in Tier

3 but committed to make improvements. After two consecutive years on the watch list, countries will be moved to Tier 3. Tier 3 countries have three months to take steps, in coordination with the US Trafficking in Persons Office, to be in compliance with the minimum standards.

In addition to attempting to shape countries' policies through this ranking system, the United States has a series of enforcement measures at its disposal to penalize Tier 3 countries. The United States can enact sanctions related to nonhumanitarian, non-trade-related foreign assistance. The United States can use its influence to deny foreign assistance by international financial institutions and multilateral development banks to these countries. The US president may waive moving a country from the watch list to Tier 3 or instituting economic sanctions if doing so is in the United States' "national interests"[83] or would protect "vulnerable populations."[84] Chuang notes that the Clinton administration realized that the United States was a major destination of trafficking, but it believed that unilateral sanctions would compromise the US role in international outreach on the Palermo Protocol. However, Congress was able to push the tier system and unilateral punishment through, and it later found the support of the Bush administration.

The United States strategically decides which countries to sanction, and is rarely consistent. Under the Bush administration, although there were 14 Tier 3 countries, the government only fully sanctioned Burma, North Korea, Syria, Cuba, and Iran, those unfriendly with the United States. China and India were on the watch list rather than in Tier 3 because of concerns about the effects on the relationships between those countries and the United States.[85] In the Obama administration, there is currently a debate as to how or whether to "punish" China and Russia, which have reached their limit on how many times they can be on the watch list; the discussions on this topic clearly and explicitly invoke foreign policy concerns.[86]

More to the point of the innocent victim frame, ideas about prostitution are embedded in the TVPA. During the drafting of the Palermo Protocol, countries debated whether the definition of trafficking should include voluntary sex work, and eventually left that distinction to country discretion.[87] The United States through the TVPA committed to exclude voluntary sex work. The 2003 reauthorization of the TVPA added the language that the US government would not provide funding to any nongovernmental organizations that "promote, support, or advocate the legalization or practice of prostitution." Representative Smith authored this anti-prostitution pledge language. Not only does this language leave out sex workers, but it also allows the United States to tie aid and its

relationships with organizations and countries to this particular punitive view of sex work.

By 2005, organizations had to *explicitly* note in their policy statements that they would not support prostitution or aid prostitutes unless these workers had ended commercial sexual activity; the US Agency for International Development (USAID) would not work with the organizations otherwise.[88] The TVPA has ushered in global efforts to punish sex workers so as to rise in rank in the TIP reports.[89] For example, in order to move from Tier 3 to Tier 1, South Korea instituted widespread anti-prostitution laws, including prison time and fines for traffickers *and* sex workers, despite significant protests from organizations working with sex workers.[90] Enfolding anti-prostitution into anti-trafficking dramatically restricts who can benefit from T visa protection and ensures that the United States can influence how countries and organizations alike develop their positions on prostitution and sex workers' rights. Despite President Obama's repeals of several of the Bush administration's moralistic measures, the requirement of the anti-prostitution pledge for organizations receiving United States funding still stands.

International hierarchy gets reproduced when only certain ideas and norms, those flowing from the "hegemon," receive legitimacy. In effect, the United States is participating in protection politics that on the face of it look to cohere with international norms protecting victims of gender violence. However, the United States is reaffirming the power of the state to decide what kinds of victims are "innocent" enough to protect.

COERCIVE STERILIZATION/ABORTION (CS/A)

China's one-child policy was instituted in the late 1970s and in 2002 was standardized in the Population and Family Planning Law. As part of the policy and law, Chinese heterosexual couples must be married in order to have a child, and they must apply for a birth permit before doing so. After having one child, women must submit to sterilization or visit a gynecologist to insert an intrauterine device to prevent further pregnancies; both procedures are monitored by the state. If after having one child a woman becomes pregnant, she must terminate the pregnancy, and one spouse must get sterilized after an "unauthorized" birth. Both parents of multiple children are often forced to get sterilized, depending on the situation and decisions of local officials.

Economic benefits are conditional on complying with state policies and local official decisions about pregnancy. Richer Chinese citizens can

have additional children by paying fines. The policy/law is also enforced by governmental intimidation, such as using ultrasounds to find "abortion candidates," and detention of family members of women who have unauthorized children. The Chinese central government formally forbids forcible sterilization, infanticide, coercive abortion, imprisonment, economic sanctions, and other severe measures to enforce family planning policies, but it allows local officials to carry out such penalties.[91] The government also relies on massive advertising campaigns to ensure that all citizens are aware of the laws and policies. China has claimed repeatedly that the one-child policy is a misnomer, arguing that if both parents are only children, they can apply to have a second child and that restrictions do not apply for certain rural areas and some ethnic minorities. In 2013, China slightly eased the restrictions of its policies by noting that a couple could have more than one child if one of the parents was an only child.

In 1996, Congress enacted legislation, the aforementioned Illegal Immigration Reform and Immigrant Responsibility Act,[92] as part of a wider effort to address undocumented immigration and terrorism. Section 601 of the IIRIRA amended the Immigration and Naturalization Act, which addresses immigration and citizenship processes and requirements, Section 101(a)(42)(B), to allow for *asylum eligibility* for victims of CS/A as follows: [93]

> For purposes of determinations under this chapter, a person who has been forced to abort a pregnancy or to undergo involuntary sterilization, or who has been persecuted for failure or refusal to undergo such a procedure or for other resistance to a coercive population control program, shall be deemed to have been persecuted on account of political opinion, and a person who has a well founded fear that he or she will be forced to undergo such a procedure or subject to persecution for such failure, refusal, or resistance shall be deemed to have a well founded fear of persecution on account of political opinion.[94]

While this statute can apply to any country with such policies, Congress wrote it aimed at China.[95] The IIRIRA limits 1,000 grants of asylum per year for this type of violence. In addition, the IIRIRA did not add another ground for persecution, nor did it actually change the *definition* of refugee.[96] Rather, Congress provided criteria for adjudicating asylum claims for a particular group of foreign nationals fleeing a particular kind of persecution.

Even though China instituted the one-child policy in 1979, the United States did not acknowledge China's policy as persecutory until 1996.

Indeed, in the 1989 case of *Matter of Chang*, the BIA held that the policy was not "on its face persecutory."[97] What happened between 1979 and 1996?

Part of the answer is that Section 601 was a politically safe way to address China's human rights violations in the midst of strengthening economic relations.[98] In many gender-based asylum cases, the social group ground is often combined with political opinion, such as membership in a social group that resists a political practice or that expresses a political belief that is different from the one held by the government. However, in this case, Congress was able to point to Chinese policies through explicit reference to the *political opinion* ground. Some suggest that as compared to other types of gender violence, the US government was able to see this persecution as "state-sponsored" because of its understanding of China as a totalitarian, communist state, thus fitting nicely with older understandings about what political asylum comprises.[99] In comparison, the United States sees domestic violence and female genital cutting as a problem of state negligence or weakness, and the case of persecution due to sexual orientation and gender identity as state persecution but not necessarily by an authoritarian state.

Another key development was that pro-life organizations invested in restricting women's reproductive rights gained significant influence in US domestic politics during the 1980s and early 1990s.[100] As the pro-life movement then faced backlash and resistance in the United States, it realized its ability to sway foreign policies. As such, the movement influenced the US delegation to the second United Nations International Conference on Population in Mexico City in 1984 and a related review of US foreign policy stances on population issues.[101]

In 1984, President Reagan instituted the global gag rule that denied funding to any organizations that provided abortion services and information. Representative Christopher Smith, the congressman making several appearances throughout this chapter, penned the 1985 Kemp-Kasten amendment, which allows the United States to deny funding if an organization "supports or participates in the management of a program of coerced abortion or involuntary sterilization." Smith would later play a role in adding the amendment regarding CS/A to the IIRIRA.

Then in 1988, Attorney General Edwin Meese provided guidelines for the then-Immigration and Naturalization Service (INS) to give "careful consideration" to Chinese asylum seekers.[102] However, the Board of Immigration Appeals (BIA) refused to budge regarding its position in *Matter of Chang*, noting that these guidelines were for the INS and not binding on BIA/immigration judges. But then the Tiananmen Square

massacre occurred very shortly after the *Chang* ruling, resulting in the Emergency Chinese Adjustment of Status Facilitation Act of 1989, with an amendment that would overrule *Chang*. President George H. Bush vetoed the bill, concerned about the impact on US-China relations. But he did concede the need for protection for those fleeing China's family-planning policies.[103]

The Clinton administration also did not overturn *Matter of Chang*. But in 1993, a ship full of people escaping coercive population policies and other repressive practices in China was intercepted off of Long Island, New York, in what is known as the *Golden Venture* incident.[104] This event occurred just a few months after the first attack on the World Trade Center in New York City and during an economic recession. At the time, legislators discussed "testing out" restrictive immigration policies such as blanket detention and quicker hearings to expedite deportation of the survivors of this boat incident. However, with word of these impending changes to the immigration system, a coalition of feminists concerned about China's one-child policy and pro-life conservatives galvanized around the *Golden Venture* case. They worked with congressional members to add Section 601. Pro-life groups saw a perfect opportunity to have global influence through the immigration legislation.

As per the data discussed in chapter 2, a significant proportion of refugees, those applying from outside of the United States, are from China. Chinese applicants are also consistently among the highest affirmative and defensive asylum recipients. When it comes to gender-based asylum cases, since 1996, according to the CGRS database, there have only been 25 population control grants; 12 successful grants have been from China. These low numbers might be because attorneys have perhaps not notified or required the assistance of CGRS in claims about CS/A. This might also be because asylum seekers or asylum lawyers do not see it as a case of gender-based asylum or as a matter of needing CGRS assistance in being able to convincingly put forward a case. Rather, precisely because of the IIRIRA, attorneys might see Chinese applications as "straightforward."

Congress ensured that there would be a cap of 1,000 grants. But there is a tremendous backlog, so US Citizenship and Immigration Services and the Executive Office for Immigration Review issue "conditional asylum status" to additional CS/A cases, a status available for no other type of persecution. Chinese applicants are most likely to claim religious persecution and persecution due to coercive abortions and sterilizations. There is such an expectation that Chinese applicants will claim persecutory coercive reproductive practices that the *New York Times* recently reported on an "industry" of asylum fraud in New York City's Chinese-dominated

neighborhoods.[105] Lawyers and asylees allegedly coach Chinese asylum seekers to either lie about coercive population control measures or to falsify documents to support actual cases of abortion and sterilization. Among many Chinese immigrant communities, it is well known that asylum petitioners can recycle stories, documents, and even names in CS/A cases.

Expectations of Innocence

As I reviewed cases in both the CGRS database and through commentary in law reviews, I found three essential examples of expected "innocence." First, I found a focus on marriage. Second, there is a focus on unborn children. Third, I discovered a privileging of forced abortion / coercive sterilization over other forced gynecological procedures, such as exams or insertion of an intrauterine device, that do not necessarily end a pregnancy or irreversibly prevent all future pregnancies.

First, a review of asylum cases reveals a focus on married asylum seekers. One year after the passage of the amendment, the Board of Immigration Appeals granted asylum to the male spouse of a woman who had experienced coercive sterilization, in *In re C-Y-Z-* (1997).[106] The man's wife remained in China, and thus this was not a case of "derivative" spousal asylum. The BIA argued that spouses should be allowed to apply for asylum based on the experiences of their partners with CS/A.[107] The BIA did not provide a rationale for this ruling, and courts had to decide whether to accept the BIA's ruling.[108]

In the case *In re S-L-L-* (2006) the BIA revisited *In re-C-Y-Z* and ruled that courts could extend legal refugee protection to the *legally married spouses* of victims of the one-child policy.[109] It clarified that it interpreted IIRIRA Section 601 as an indictment of China's "intrusion in marriage"; in other words, rules about population control are a way for China to interfere in decisions spouses should be able to make without state interference. The married couple was persecuted as an "entity." Further, the experiences of CS/A caused "sympathetic suffering" for the partner of the victim.[110] However, courts have had conflicting interpretations regarding the rights of unmarried partners. This is because the BIA argues that only married spouses face the significant pressures of the one-child policy. The BIA also notes that unmarried partners would have to show "personal resistance" to the policy *and* that they are for all intents and purposes married even if they are not legally so.[111] This "personal resistance" requirement constitutes an additional burden for unmarried people.

Asylum advocates looking at CS/A have tried to ensure continued asylum protection not only for "legally and traditionally married spouses of direct victims of China's coercive family planning programs"[112] but also for unmarried partners. Nortick, for example, argues that courts should focus on the "closeness" of the relationship rather than on the legal status in order to determine if a partner has suffered persecution.[113] While not all courts have accepted the BIA's marital status restriction,[114] the Board's stance reflects the notion that attacks on reproductive freedoms matter more in the context of certain relationships.

A focus on heterosexual married relationships contributes to the construction of innocence because it perpetuates the idea that family planning and reproductive choice *should* be made in the context of a heterosexual, "legal" relationship. However, reproductive rights and justice advocates emphasize that women should be able to decide what happens with their bodies regardless of their relationship status. Sexually active single and unmarried women, and women in partnerships that are not recognized, have and continue to be painted as promiscuous, *never innocent*, if they try to exercise rights over their reproductive choices.[115]

Second, I found an emphasis on the right to preserve the life of unborn children. For example, judges often refer to aborting an unborn child or to depriving the petitioner of his or her unborn child, rather than framing the violence entirely as a forced or coercive reproductive practice that is harmful to the *women* as a denial of their basic rights and choices. When men are granted gender-based asylum, it is also because of the idea of the loss of an unborn life. In *Zhang* (2006), the Seventh Circuit court noted that "the act of forced sterilization is not a discrete act, but rather a permanent and continuous form of persecution that deprives the couple of a child or children who might have eventually been born to them."[116] The court also argued that "the forcible abortion has deprived him of his unborn child, of the ability to realize the family that his wife and he had desired, and forever deprived him of the ability to become a parent to that unborn son or daughter with his wife." One should not discount the pain these asylum seekers feel when they are not able to conceive additional children, or whether *they* see a forced abortion as primarily about the loss of an unborn child. Rather, I am interested in how asylum judges recognize suffering *more* as a loss of "innocent" fetal personhood than as the suppression of choices about one's body.

Third, and relatedly, a victim of forced sterilization/abortion is seen as more "innocent" than a victim of other "less severe" forms of coercive reproductive practices. For example, consider a woman who was forced

to have a gynecological exam or forced to insert an intrauterine device as a form of birth control. Judges waver more with these forms of coercive practices because they are not entirely convinced about the vulnerability of the victim in these cases. The distinction between more and less severe forms of coercive reproductive practices stems from the wording in the congressional legislation, which explicitly names forced sterilization and abortion but generally notes "other resistance to a coercive population control program." Does resistance to a forced gynecological exam count as "other resistance"?

In 2004, a federal court offered an opinion about "other resistance" for the first time in *Li v. Ashcroft*.[117] The petitioner resisted the one-child policy by getting married before the allowable age. She also verbally proclaimed that she disagreed with the policy. But she was forced to undergo a prolonged gynecological exam to assess whether she was pregnant. The judges upheld Li's appeal to review and remanded the case for further consideration. They noted that "[a] forced gynecological examination lasting thirty minutes and attended by threats does not meet any civilized understanding of a routine medical procedure"; the court thus believed Li's description of the forced exam as "rape-like," further noting that "rape may constitute persecution."[118] The promise of this decision is the focus on the harm done to the woman, not just the harm done because of the inability to control having future children.

But I also want to draw attention to the dissent in this case to illustrate the controversy and ambivalence over who is "worthy" of protection. The dissenting judge argued that Li was resisting just the minimum age for marriage and *not* involuntary abortions and sterilization, noting her experiences were not persecutory. This dissent moved away from the focus on the "rape-like" forced gynecological examination, that is, the actual persecutory violence, which occurred *in order* to see if she were pregnant. So these gynecological exams are certainly related to the practice of forced abortions. But the dissent argued that the exam probably was evidence of "the crudeness of Chinese village medicine and was not, as the majority implies, sadistic punishment to deter resistance."[119] The dissent reduced the severity of the asylum seeker's experience to a "disgraceful" and "degrading" exam, noting that

> our court is not in a position to change the ideology of the Communist Party of China. . . . By broadening the grant to . . . young lovers thwarted in their desire to marry, we may well be withdrawing American protection from those at the heart of it, persons subjected to forced abortions and sterilizations.[120]

Years later, in *Matter of M-F-W- and L-G-* (2008), the petitioner was forced to insert an intrauterine device (IUD) after her first child was born but hired a private doctor to remove it after it caused her medical suffering and Chinese officials refused to remove it. After a forced gynecological exam revealed that she no longer had an IUD, she was detained and eventually forced to insert a second IUD. After her arrival in the United States, she had a doctor remove the IUD and gave birth to a second child. The BIA ruled that while removal of an IUD or failure to attend mandatory gynecological appointments could constitute "resistance" to China's policies, insertion/reinsertion of IUDs as part of "routine medical procedure" does not mean that the procedure was necessarily persecutory.[121]

The BIA also argued that Congress intended to protect only victims of CS/A and not *less permanent forms of birth control*. And because she did not suffer the specific harms named in Section 601, she had to prove "resistance" to China's policy and that the persecution resulted due to the resistance, per a Department of Homeland Security ruling.[122] While the BIA acknowledged that removing an IUD or skipping doctors' appointments, both of which the petitioner did, would "thwart" China's policies, it did not find her fears legitimate or that persecution due to removal of the IUD occurred. The BIA ruled that the discomfort caused by the IUD was not because of the Chinese government's desire to persecute her. However, the BIA failed to consider that the petitioner would not have been subjected to insertion of IUD were it not for Chinese family-planning policies that the United States has codified as persecutory.

The BIA's written discussion of this case and interpretation of Congress's intent are crucial to interrogate. Why and how are forcible exams and medical procedures not elevated to the same seriousness as CS/A, particularly if Section 601 is about coercive reproductive practices? Preventing the ability to have children in a "long term" manner, such as through sterilization, and the loss of a "potential child" through coercive or forced abortion, *matter more* because Congress's concern was not for women's experiences of harm and loss of decision-making but for the loss of *potential children*. Governmental agencies involved in asylum adjudication perpetuate this concern for the loss of potential life.

THE EFFECTS OF THE INNOCENT WORTHY FRAME ON ASYLUM SEEKERS

In CS/A cases, being free from "guilt and sin" means the innocent woman marries and tries to fulfill her duty and desire to procreate, only to be

stymied by the Chinese government. In these cases, descriptions of those forced to abort or sterilize identify a clear "bad" persecutor. As a legal commentator notes:

> Women seeking asylum in the United States have reported instances where local enforcers come to their homes in the middle of the night seeking to force them to abort their babies. One woman who recently spoke before Congress related a heart-rending tale of being physically escorted to a hospital where nurses prevented her from leaving.[123]

But the coercive pressure to abort a pregnancy or to sterilize is not always at the hands of government officials but rather due to family, friends, neighbors, and associates reporting each other as a result of intimidation tactics and a system of surveillance. In other words, structural violence matters as much as the particular perpetrators.

Asylum seekers also confront expectations about how to demonstrate innocence. In one case regarding an asylum seeker who experienced multiple abortions, the court found it "incredible," refusing to believe that "any woman would suffer through four abortions."[124] Does this mean that the truly innocent woman would not have allowed additional abortions to occur?

Furthermore, the rights of unborn children are privileged over the rights of asylum seekers. The pro-life activists construct the fetus not as a "passive" entity in the womb but as a person with rights, with the ability to sense, react, and emote.[125] Pro-life, antichoice discourse assumes that the woman having an abortion is performing a criminal act of destroying "innocent" life, such that a woman who is pro-choice loses all innocence. It thus stands to reason that someone who wants the right to procreate, who would allegedly and presumably *never* have an abortion, is all the more innocent. I return to this point later in the chapter to further flesh out the effects of the innocent victim frame on asylum seekers, particularly those who might be persecuted by forced pregnancy/maternity due to lack of access to abortion.

THE EFFECTS OF THE INNOCENT WORTHY VICTIM FRAME ON US POWER RELATIONSHIPS

As with the case of trafficking, I look at the politics behind this attempt to protect victims of CS/A. Crucially, the wording inserted into the IIRIRA originally included a provision denying funding to organizations that

provided voluntary abortions, indicating the pro-life politics behind the legislation.[126] While the provision ultimately did not make it into the legislation, the politics remain.

McKinnon notes that through the extension of asylum to Chinese applicants, the United States is able to position itself as a country that celebrates choice, as opposed to Communist China, which does not.[127] Hua describes the orientalist framing of oppressive China in US discussions about the one-child policy, because China is constructed as a timelessly backward country that has not progressed past outdated and "defeated" communist ideology and "Asian traditions."[128] Thus, there is little understanding or analysis of the reasons behind the relatively recent Chinese policies but rather presumptions about deviant Chinese patriarchy.

Further, what China represents is not only oppression but also lack of regard for unborn children. For the pro-life lobby, China represents "federally endorsed abortions that they fear may lie in store for the United States."[129] Representative Smith, mentioned above, remains a persistent critic of the United States giving aid to the United Nations Population Fund (UNFPA), which is tasked with addressing reproductive health and planning. Smith asserts that UNFPA supports China's one-child policy. The Department of Health and Human Services has pushed back against the false claims about UNFPA, and UNFPA also asserts that no US funds go toward any of its China programs.[130] Further, UNFPA is one of the few organizations aiming to end coercive reproductive practices in China. But since the mid-1980s, Smith and his allies have been pivotal in the decisions of the Ronald Reagan, George H. W. Bush, and George W. Bush administrations to cut off funding to UNFPA. The United States is the only country in the world that has ever denied funding to UNFPA because of its alleged support of forced reproductive practices, despite all evidence to the contrary.[131]

President Obama restored funding in 2009 after Secretary of State Hillary Clinton assessed that UNFPA did not violate laws regarding CS/A. However, in 2011, Representative Smith held a hearing on China's one-child policy that focused largely on UNFPA. Just one week later, the House Foreign Affairs Subcommittee on Human Rights and International Programs approved H.R. 2059, which would deny US funding to UNFPA. The bill died, and the Obama administration continues to provide financial support to UNFPA. But Representative Smith and other members of Congress remain committed to removing funding at some point in the future.

Thus the denial of funding to UNFPA and a concern for asylum seekers fleeing coercive reproductive practices are both rooted in a pro-life

discursive climate. So we must link the innocent victim frame to the justification of a particular vision of what women's rights should comprise: the right to procreate, to mother, to become pregnant, and to carry a pregnancy to full term. Asylum seekers may or may not benefit, in other words, but the *act* of focusing on their traumas is less about the pain they experienced and their right to be free from suffering. Section 601 is more about ensuring certain gendered ideals about what women should and should not do with their bodies.

Asylum cases strengthen the discursive climate regarding the protection of innocent unborn life, which in turn amplifies the global reach of pro-life policy stances. Denying US funding to UNFPA affected and would affect vital programs around the world, including attempts to ensure that women can voluntarily plan the number of children they want, safe pregnancies and deliveries, and have access to tools to enjoy reproductive health, including prevention of sexually transmitted diseases.[132] To be sure, there are US sovereign agents who are fully supportive of UNFPA activities; however, the very politicians and movements involved in expressing "concern" over women's choices in China are the same ones shaping US actions toward UNFPA that aim to limit women's choices in many countries around the world where UNFPA operates. As long as Section 601 exists, naming only one kind of reproductive violence, *the politics behind this amendment lurk behind every related asylum case*. I turn now to a particular effect of the innocence frame on both asylum seekers and US power politics: how US restriction of access to abortion in other countries contributes to the persecutory violence of forced pregnancy/maternity, a category of violence left out of the US understandings of coercive reproductive practices.

A NEW CATEGORY OF VIOLENCE: FORCED PREGNANCY AND FORCED MATERNITY

When we look at the effects of innocent victim frames on asylum seekers and power politics, we have to ask about the type of violence that is missing to the point that there has, very oddly, been very little discussion in asylum advocacy circles and literature. This section departs from the empirical analysis in the rest of the chapter to point to an *empirical silence*. Since there is evidence of forced pregnancy and maternity as a gendered harm, victims of this violence should be included in asylum discussions about coercive reproductive practices (anti-abortion governmental policies), or sexual assault (when rape results in a pregnancy that a woman is not allowed to abort).

A significant number of gender-based asylum claims recorded by the CGRS involve claims of rape. Per CGRS data, there were a total of 374 grants and 78 denials involving rape claims. Conceivably, at least some proportion of these rape cases involved pregnancies; we do not know if these women were forced to carry these pregnancies to term, but it is possible. Would women who endure forced maternity/pregnancy, due to rape or government-sanctioned inability to access abortion, be able to apply for asylum?

One reason the United States does not discuss this idea of persecution is because of the prevalence of "pronatalist" reproductive policies. Pronatalism means that procreation is normalized and expected, particularly in terms of the construction of "womanhood."[133] Coercive reproductive practices are typically understood and limited to only involuntary/forced sterilization and abortion. McKinnon argues that the element of *voluntary* (rather than forced) abortion is ignored so that pro-life advocates are able to use coercive population policy cases "to discursively constitute abortion as violent to all women and families."[134] But it is also persecutory if a woman is punished for resisting her government's anti-abortion stance, because it prevents her from enjoying the basic human right to freedom of reproductive choice, particularly the right to "determine freely and responsibly the number and spacing of children."[135]

Women are affected by the anti-abortion stances not only of their own governments but also of other governments. The United States uses the innocence frame to push pro-life policies globally, which impacts women around the world. This section argues that *prevention of access to abortion is itself persecutory, which is why it is crucial to view forced pregnancy and maternity as persecutory.* The New York–based Global Justice Center (GJC) recently initiated a worldwide campaign to publicize and reverse a US policy that prohibits international organizations that receive federal funding from providing or discussing abortion services. The GJC notes that because of this policy, women and girls impregnated by rape in conflict zones and countries in "crisis" are denied their rights, encapsulated in the Geneva Conventions, to have access to nondiscriminatory comprehensive medical treatment, which would include access to safe abortions.

The GJC argues that in preventing victims of rape in conflict zones from accessing abortion services and counseling, the United States is currently in violation of Article 3 of the Geneva Convention, Articles 10 and 16 of Additional Protocol I, Articles 7 and 10 of Additional Protocol II, Article 14 of the Convention Against Torture, and international customary law.[136] *In other words, the United States is violating international humanitarian law.* Exploring how the United States contributes to gender oppression in the

very countries from which asylum seekers might flee exposes the hypocrisies of protection.

The 1973 Helms Amendment states that no federal funds can be used "to pay for the performance of abortions as a method of family planning or to motivate or coerce any person to practice abortions." This amendment has since been the cornerstone of the US position on the use of federal funds by organizations' work abroad. In 1984, President Ronald Reagan enacted the Mexico City Policy, also known as the Global Gag Rule, which prevented all NGOs receiving federal funding from performing or promoting abortion services as a "method of family planning" even if they used their own non-US funds. Before the Global Gag Rule, US and foreign recipients of US money could still use their own funds and non-US sources to provide abortion services. But with this policy, foreign NGOs had to submit in writing that they would not perform or promote abortion "as a method of family planning." President Clinton rescinded the policy in January 1993, President Bush reinstituted it in January 2001, and President Obama revoked it once again on January 23, 2009.

Two main points must be made about the Global Gag Rule. First, while reproductive rights activists applauded Obama's repeal, because it was an executive order, a Republican White House can reverse the repeal in the future. Accordingly, a permanent legislative repeal of the Global Gag Rule is still needed.[137]

Second, even President Obama's repeal left in place the US *administrative policy* of a "no-abortion clause," including services and speech, which applies to all recipients of US foreign aid and funds, even if they use their own money to perform such services.[138] So even though the Global Gag Rule is currently not in place, the Helms Amendment allows such restrictions to continue. These restrictions apply also to any United Nations agencies that use US funds.[139]

The Helms Amendment technically allows US foreign funds for abortions for victims of rape. After all, rape is clearly not "family planning" and thus pregnancies in cases of rape would be exempt from the reach of the Helms Amendment. But, in 1974, USAID *interpreted* the Helms language about "motivating" and "coercing" people to practice abortions to mean not just services but also *discussions* about abortion law, information about abortion services, or even Red Cross medical care training.[140] Then, the 1976 Hyde Amendment, a response to the 1973 *Roe v. Wade* decision, outlined restrictions of federal funding for abortions *within* the United States and *included* an exception for rape. US officials thereafter argued that *domestic* cases include exceptions for rape but that *foreign* funding does *not* provide exceptions for rape.[141] By 1978, the United States had

codified the USAID 1974 interpretation of the Helms Amendment, effectively institutionalizing the no-abortion "speech" aspect of US policy. It is now known as the "Helms gag." With the exception of the Clinton administration, which did allow the use of federal funds to perform abortions abroad in the cases of pregnancies resulting from rape, Congress has persistently inserted the Helms gag into the State-Foreign Appropriations Act. And, in 2008, USAID confirmed that the Helms gag was mandatory in *all* of its contracts with NGOs, not just with those involved in "family planning."[142]

In effect, the Helms gag is much more restrictive than the Global Gag Rule, as it forbids speech, information, and training as well as humanitarian aid projects in conflict zones that would provide comprehensive care specifically to rape victims.[143] Because so many NGOs rely predominantly on US foreign aid to remain afloat and to do their work, they make the choice not to participate in abortion counseling, services, and speech in order to keep their funds.[144] Countries do often criminalize abortion. However, whether a country criminalizes abortion is irrelevant to "providers' absolute duty to provide services in accord with the Geneva Conventions."[145] The Committee Against Torture and the Human Rights Committee have also claimed that denying abortion services, regardless of country laws, for victims of rape constitutes cruel and inhuman treatment and torture.[146] Even in cases where rape victims are not in conflict zones, this denial of access violates women's rights to comprehensive reproductive rights and justice.

The Obama administration has tried to distinguish itself in terms of its support of women's rights, particularly regarding violence against women. Its December 19, 2011, executive order "Instituting a National Action Plan on Women, Peace and Security," the USAID 2012 policy on Gender Equality and Female Empowerment, and the USAID's 2012 "United States Strategy to Prevent and Respond to Gender-Based Violence Globally," all address sexual violence. But all are silent on the issue of access to abortion for survivors of sexual violence.

To be sure, abortion rights are not limited to rape survivors. Not all rape survivors who become pregnant will choose or desire abortions. But if the United States is going to claim to address the rights of sexual violence survivors around the world, the omission of abortion is glaring. Denial of access to abortion results in a *coerced* pregnancy. *The omission of this issue is also glaring given that congressional legislation ensures that other coercive reproductive practices, particularly CS/A, are deemed to be persecutory.* The persistence of the innocent worthy victim frame strengthens pro-life policy stances, particularly because both derive from a discursive climate

that privileges antichoice ideas. The role of the United States in creating policies that contribute to persecution elsewhere would not necessarily merit mention in an asylum case. However, it is worth exploring how the United States itself distinguishes between worthy and unworthy victims of coercive reproductive policies. We cannot discuss CS/A or rape unless we include the victims of forced pregnancy/maternity.

CONCLUSIONS

Trafficking and CS/A are different types of violence. Trafficking has more in common with rape cases in terms of denial of agency to consent to sex. And CS/A is similar to forced FGC in terms of forced, irreversible alterations to bodies. But the *way* trafficking and CS/A are discussed and constructed in asylum cases is similar; they derive from similar discursive climates shaped by moralistic ideas about innocent femininity. It is "bad" to engage in sex work, to pay a smuggler, to desire a child while unmarried, to choose to terminate a pregnancy. The autonomy frame, on the other hand, is about "strong" women who are more like enlightened "Western" women in escaping violence at the hands of nonstate perpetrators.

The autonomy frame serves as a way for the United States to shape other countries' policies on women's rights and to create a distinction between civilized and barbaric societies. The innocence frame enables political actors in the United States to strengthen pro-life policies and anti-sex worker policies. It also enables US commitment to combat perceived national security threats such as terrorism and communism. The "evil-doer" in both types of violence, trafficking and coercive reproductive practices, is not simply a monster. He is the Orientalized, racialized *Other*. He is a terrorist, a communist, an international criminal. The innocent worthy victim frame allows identification of this evil perpetrator. To be sure, it is important to name perpetrators when addressing gender violence, but I draw attention to how the perpetrators in these two types of violence are understood through the lens of commitments the United States already has to fight terrorism and to confront communism. Whether one approves of US foreign policy positions or not, I am interested in how asylum/immigration cases are used as a *part* of foreign policymaking. Thus, the analysis of gender-based asylum cases reveals new dimensions of how different types of violence are understood.

In chapter 6, I challenge the innocent worthy victim frame in coercive reproductive practices cases by positing a specific path for including forced pregnancy/maternity in future gender-based asylum discourses.

Feminists can intervene in the discursive climate dominated by pro-life and abolitionist activists since the denial of reproductive autonomy is *already* labeled as persecutory in congressional legislation but is *limited* to CS/A. I specifically suggest that feminists challenge how forced pregnancy is usually framed in terms of ethnic conflict rather than as a women's rights issue in international law. I also suggest that asylum advocates think about describing forced pregnancy as a potentially harmful consequence of rape. Finally, I build on the idea that the denial of access to abortion is persecutory, looking at comparisons of asylum guidelines on how denial of medical treatment can indicate persecution. Rethinking coercive reproductive practices to consider other types of reproductive injustice would also include in the conversation the experiences of undocumented women. Undocumented women are routinely denied access to reproductive justice and experience forced pregnancy/maternity when they are detained.

In order to more deeply challenge the innocence frame in trafficking cases, in chapter 6 I also look more carefully at the moral panic around sex workers, tracing and linking it to the US legal concept of "moral turpitude," which criminalizes sex workers. Thus, in terms of the rights of sex workers to apply for asylum, there is some overlap with the experiences of sexual minorities (described in chapter 5) in terms of being framed as deviant. I explore strategies that challenge moral turpitude norms.

It is important to intervene in the framing of some asylum seekers as worthy innocent victims not only to better adjudicate asylum claims but also to challenge the classification of undocumented immigrants. Undocumented immigrants are not innocent because they are criminalized "upon entry" into the country's borders. Thus innocence discourses further entrench the notion that undocumented immigrants, as a "class" of non-citizens, cannot and should not be considered as anything but threats to the United States.

CHAPTER 5

The *Always* Deviant LGBTQ Asylum Seekers

In this chapter, I look at persecutory acts that target people due to having a non-conforming sexual orientation or gender identity. My investigation of these cases reveals the persistence of an assumption that lesbian, gay, bisexual, transgender, and queer (LGBTQ) communities are inherently deviant. As such, ironically, people targeted because their countries labeled them as deviant find that the US serves as a potential "safe haven" but also requires them to prove that they *are* normal. The result is that sexual minorities are faced with deeply contradictory and mixed messages about how to frame their asylum cases. The "non-deviant" frame emerged from a *discursive climate* of US governmental and dominant public discourses that are slowly acknowledging the rights of sexual minorities but do not fully challenge homophobia and transphobia. Feminist and queer rights advocates frame persecution due to sexual orientation and gender identity as legitimate claims, but the US immigration and asylum system maintains a stranglehold on prejudicial, harmful constructions of sexual minorities.

This chapter proceeds differently from the previous chapters. While the other two empirical chapters compare two different types of violence, this chapter examines only one type of violence, the persecution of sexual minorities. While sexual orientation and gender identity are separate issues that are often conflated, they are both non-conforming identities. Laws and practices that target people who are lesbian, bisexual, or gay often also target people with a trans gender identity. My analysis of

asylum cases in the context of this book's framework revealed a unique dimension of violence targeting sexual minorities. Sexual minorities face an impossible task of simultaneously demonstrating how they are targeted for their perceived "deviance" in their home countries while defending themselves from being constructed as deviant in the asylum process. While some asylum seekers discussed in previous chapters could be constructed as autonomous or innocent, even sexual minorities who receive asylum are constructed as not quite normal. Per my comprehensive review of cases of sexual minorities, the issue is not simply about offering the appropriate and expected narrative. It is also about the possibility that asylum seekers are opting out of applying for asylum altogether.

Before I proceed, a few words about the terminology of LGBTQ, sexual minorities, and/or queer migrants. Each of these terms is politically loaded. "LGBTQ" is a comprehensive umbrella term that indicates the history of political movements associated with rights for various marginalized communities. However, others protest the inclusion of the "T," for transgender, which is a gender identity, within "LGB," which references sexual orientation. They argue that transgender people experience discrimination and hostility from some gay, lesbian, and bisexual communities and thus that the LGBT label erases the power relationships within those communities. Another debate revolves around the inclusion of "I" on behalf of intersex individuals, or those whose reproductive or sexual anatomies reveal biological variations but have been constructed as problematic, nonstandard medical conditions; intersex individuals claim that they have been left out of LGBTQ advocacy.

Others think the term "sexual minorities" more accurately describes certain communities since terminology used in the United States may not be appropriate or make sense in other countries. Indeed, even the categories of gay, lesbian, bisexual, and transgender are actually that: categories with historical, sociocultural, and political meanings.[1] Yet others believe that "queer" better politicizes expectations of "gender conformity" and "non-deviance" by reclaiming this historically and often still pejorative term to challenge the very idea of what is "normal" and what is abnormal. [2] However, "queer" can be exclusionary or discriminatory to some. I use all of these terms to include those with varying perspectives in this conversation. Table 5.1 summarizes the effects of the non-deviance frame.

Table 5.1 THE NON-DEVIANT WORTHY VICTIM FRAME

Type of violence	Worthy victim frame	Effects of frame on asylum seekers	Effects of frame on US policies and power relationships
Persecution based on sexual orientation and gender identity	Non-deviant	Gender conformity in contradictory, paradoxical ways expected of sexual minorities; sexual minorities more likely to be detained/ penalized due to perception they commit "moral turpitude" crimes; sexual minorities discouraged from applying for asylum	United States proclaims distinction between itself as protector of sexual minorities and other countries as oppressors of sexual minorities, while distracting attention from homophobia/ transphobia that is part of the US immigration/ asylum system

THEORIZING "NON-DEVIANCE"

Feminist studies along with gay, lesbian, and queer studies/theories generally attempt to understand how the categories of "normal" and "deviant" operate and can be challenged and upended. Queer theory in particular is engaged in a critique of the normal (or normative)/deviant binary, leading to an inquiry into how "straightness" is also constructed.[3] Once we set up the label "normal," and decide who gets to be in that category, then the "opposite" would be deviant. And those who get put into that oppositional "non-normal" category find themselves subject to various practices of social control, whether that is criminalizing certain sexual activities, arbitrary arrests, punishment, violence and intimidation, loss of jobs and health insurance, loss of friends and family, or getting kicked out of schools and neighborhoods. To challenge the construct of deviance is to challenge that gender and sex are easily understood. Queer theorists thus reject essentialist understandings of gender and sex. They challenge the notion that gender and sex are determined by biology and should be monitored by arbitrary yet enduring standards of "morality."

Another way to understand deviance is through the concept of *gender conformity*. By the term gender conformity I mean the expectation

of performing, acting, and expressing gender and sexuality in ways that accept, legitimize, and normalize a variety of *privileges* around gender and sexuality. Gender conformity aligns with *masculine privilege*, which goes beyond male privilege and is rather about constructs of masculinity that afford benefits to people who embody or pass as certain types of men. Second, gender conformity promotes *heterosexual* privilege,[4] or benefiting from identifying/passing for straight and desiring/living heteronormativity. Heteronormativity is an expectation that heterosexual people and relationships are the default, desired, normal way to live; it presumes that all straight people and their sexual, identity, political, and relationship choices are "status quo," supportive of creating nuclear families that participate in and contribute to the neoliberal state. Third, gender conformity aligns with *cisprivilege*, or "the privilege enjoyed by people who identify wholly with, feel comfortable in, are seen to belong to or 'are' the gender/sex they are assigned at birth and/or raised to believe that they 'are.'"[5]

To conform means to desire and act in ways that uphold masculine, heterosexual, and cisprivileges rather than to be a gender "outlaw,"[6] where one would actively challenge or redefine binaries between male/female, straight/gay, normal/deviant. Shepherd and Sjoberg note:

> According to conventional Western discourse, if you are not female you are male; if you are not transgender, transsexual or genderqueer, you are . . . normal? By following this logic, "queer" and "trans"- are framed as (sexed) "Others" in need of explanation; as people assumed just to have or to be a "gender," we only need prefixes to describe genderqueer people who appear not to be contained within one of the two gender/sex categories we rely on to make sense of bodies.[7]

Expectations of gender conformity are evident in the previous chapters. Women are expected to prove autonomy in a way that men might not have to, as it is a "given" that a man is independent and has agency. Women are expected to be exceptionally innocent; they should be virtuous and only be involved in prostitution if they were forced or frauded into it. Women are also expected to fulfill their duties as a good mother and to want to have children. We do not expect to see straight men apply for gender-based asylum or for T visas, and rarely do discussions about gender-based asylum even address the possibility of gender violence against a straight, cisgender man. The exception is men who try to get asylum based on coercive population control measures; they are

presumed to be straight, because of the expectation that only straight men participate in childrearing.

But gender conformity, particularly in terms of expectations of non-deviance, is especially heightened and salient in the cases discussed in this chapter. Cases about persecution based on sexual orientation and gender identity *require* an interrogation of what people are doing with their bodies, or with whom they are having sex. While all asylum cases scrutinize elements about the asylum seekers' most intimate experiences, LGBTQ asylum seekers undergo much more intensive investigations into their sex lives and gender expression. Even if a case for a LGBTQ asylum seeker includes other important types of persecution, adjudicators might assess how *lesbians* are supposed to react to domestic violence, or the alleged distinctions between how a *gay man* and a *straight man* would react to torture.

In the types of cases discussed thus far, women do not have to prove that they are actually women or that they are attracted to men. They may have to show *what kind* of women they are (autonomous or innocent). But they do not have to address whether their anatomy matches their identity, or to obtain corroboration to prove that they are straight.

I searched for the existence of the "non-deviant" worthy victim frame in other types of violence, but it was the strongest and most pervasive in cases dealing with sexual orientation and gender identity. There is some overlap with the construction of innocence, particularly in terms of expectations of heteronormative sexual morality. As I discuss in chapter 6, there is a connection between sex workers, left out of the worthy victim frame in trafficking cases, and sexual minorities, as both groups have been constructed as "immoral" in US legal and sociopolitical history. However, because sex workers are simply excluded from asylum and immigration relief altogether, the non-deviant frame is more apt for analyzing queer asylum seekers, many of whom *do* receive asylum if they demonstrate worthiness. Further, innocence is proven in opposition to a perpetrator (China, traffickers, terrorists), whereas non-deviance is not. Even though asylum cases discuss homophobic or transphobic state persecution, sexual minorities ultimately must prove their normalcy in opposition to perceptions about *deviant* non-conforming behavior.

Gender conformity operates at two levels when it comes to the asylum cases I discuss in this chapter. The first is the presumption that, by default, everyone is straight and cisgender. As I will show, the entire asylum/immigration system works against sexual minorities.

The second level is that those who are not straight or cisgender are expected to act and behave in particular gender-conforming ways. If one is not straight or cisgender, one still needs to "conform" to gendered expectations. For example, consider the argument that gay couples deserve same-sex marriage rights to receive the same benefits as straight couples. On the one hand, such an argument makes sense in normalizing and legitimizing same-sex marriage; on the other, inclusion is based on conformity rather than on principle. In other words, people who are "like us" or "want what we want" will be tolerated. Another way of stating this idea is expecting that sexual minorities act in ways that are not threatening to straight privilege: they want to marry and adopt, are US citizens, have access to employment and health insurance, and do not confront, experience, or challenge racism, xenophobia, deportation, poverty, and various forms of structural inequalities and violence. Sexual minorities should benefit from rather than call into question structures of power. Duggan calls these expectations *homonormativity*, which is a "politics that does not contest dominant heteronormative assumptions and institutions, but upholds and sustains them, while promising the possibility of a demobilized gay constituency and a privatized, depoliticized gay culture anchored in domesticity and consumption."[8]

This depoliticization requires a refusal to critique the racial hierarchies between citizens and non-citizens, between queers who belong, and those who do not. Thus, gender conformity intersects with white privilege and citizenship privilege.[9] In other words, *good* queer non-citizens are constructed as worthy of belonging by distinguishing themselves from racialized, sexually perverse, dangerous outsiders.[10]

As a result of trying to fit gays and lesbians into models of straightness, asylum adjudicators expect that gay men act like women, and lesbians act like men. If asylum seekers do not have long-lasting partnerships, then they might be presumed to be immoral and promiscuous, a common stereotype of gays and lesbians. Judges might think bisexual asylum seekers are simply confused about being straight or gay. There is also an expectation that transgender people want cisprivileges. This is why there is an expectation that transgender people are *either* anatomically male with a stereotypically female identity and manner of expression, appearance, and dress, *or* anatomically female with a stereotypically male identity and manner of expression, appearance, or dress.

The non-deviance frame has a built-in contradiction: sexual minorities must demonstrate that they lived "secret lives" due to experiences or fears of persecution but also that they had engaged in sufficiently and

visibly "gay" or "queer" conduct to have been persecuted. They must show evidence not just of gay/queer behavior but also of the "essence" of their queer identity. They are at once reduced to "behavior" but the case law also indicates that some adjudicators believe that "behavior" is not enough to reveal the "authenticity" of queerness.

These contradictions occur because, to a mainstream asylum system, people who are not straight or cisgender are somehow unsettling. They apparently cannot quite be figured out, or put in a simple box. Of course, no one can be easily categorized. But because the idea of "deviance" persists so insidiously due to entrenched homophobia and transphobia, queer migrants are singled out and subjected to difficult lines of questioning.

This is crucial to point out given that asylum seekers in general, and particularly in cases of FGC and DV, are often *rewarded* for transgressing social norms and mores in their countries of origin. Indeed, political persecution is often punishment for speaking out about the way things are done and for putting forward alternative ways of being and living. *Yet, when it comes to challenging norms about gender conformity and sexuality, judges usually do not see these LGBTQ asylum seekers as trailblazers but as odd, confused, and confusing people.*

Thus, to be non-deviant, this is the message that the US asylum system sends to queer migrants: One must have a stable identity, so asylum officials can figure out who and what one is. Second, one must have control over one's behavior. One should know to control and conceal behavior when appropriate, out of modesty and safety, but one should also be very visibly queer to prove targeting because of being a sexual minority. Third, sexual minorities should want to be like (normative) straight and cisgender people. One should want a stable family, to contribute as a productive member of society, and to refrain from engaging in criminal acts.

THE DEVELOPMENT OF THE NON-DEVIANCE FRAME IN ASYLUM CASES FOR SEXUAL ORIENTATION AND GENDER IDENTITY

This section names and assesses US policies that impact sexual minorities, both residents of the United States and foreign nationals. I discuss the former ban of the entry of foreign nationals who were sexual minorities, the former HIV/AIDS travel ban, the Defense of Marriage Act of 1996, the Illegal Immigration Reform and Immigrant Responsibility Act of

1996, the REAL ID Act of 2005, the first transgender asylum cases, and the social visibility requirement for membership in a particular group consisting of sexual minorities. I demonstrate how the laws and cases presume the deviance of sexual minorities, which contribute to both discouraging sexual minorities from applying for asylum and expectations of "non-deviant" narratives during the asylum process.

Inadmissibility of Foreign Nationals Who Are Sexual Minorities

The Immigration Act of 1917 first excluded sexual minorities from migrating to the United States through references to "aliens afflicted with psychopathic personalities, sexual deviation, or mental defect," and with "loathsome or contagious diseases."[11] The Immigration Act of 1952 repealed the 1917 act but allowed the exclusion of sexual minorities as "afflicted with psychopathic personality . . . or mental defect." Further, sexual minorities who were migrants were referred to the Immigration and Naturalization Service for a public health examination, which certified the exclusion. When the Ninth Circuit court ruled that "psychopathic personality" did not "convey sufficiently definite warning that homosexuality and sex perversion are embraced therein," Congress amended the act in 1965 to explicitly exclude "aliens . . . with sexual deviation."[12] After the American Psychiatric Association removed homosexuality from its categorizations of disorders in 1973, the Department of Justice declared in 1980 that it would still exclude "homosexuals" because the congressional ban on "sexual deviants" still held. The Immigration Act of 1990 finally removed the ban, but some US governmental officials continue to use sexual orientation as a basis for banning, deporting, and denying gay and lesbian non-citizens immigration relief and citizenship.

During the 1980s, with the ban still in place, Armando Toboso-Alfonso applied for asylum based on persecution due to sexual orientation. Toboso-Alfonso reached the United States during the 1980 Mariel boatlift, an arrangement between the Cuban government and Cuban Americans for voluntary migration to the United States. When applying for asylum, he argued that gay men in Cuba were targeted because of a registry of gay men, which made him and other gay men vulnerable to frequent detention and interrogation as well as forced labor.[13] In this case, the immigration judge sided with Toboso-Alfonso, citing "the exclusion of gays and lesbians from regular immigration channels as evidence that the US government

already considered homosexuals to be a 'particularly identifiable group.'"[14] In Toboso-Alfonso's case, the ban ironically worked in his favor.

Some minor crimes committed by Toboso-Alfonso prevented him from receiving asylum, but he did receive withholding of deportation. The Immigration and Naturalization Service (INS) appealed the decision to the Board of Immigration Appeals (BIA), arguing that immigration relief "would be tantamount to awarding discretionary relief to those involved in behavior that is not only *socially deviant* in nature, but in violation of the laws or regulations of the country as well."[15] In 1990, the BIA upheld the grant of withholding of deportation as well as the decision to deny asylum due to the unrelated criminal conviction. [16]

The BIA distinguished between *behavior*, which was the main concern of the INS, and *status or identity*, by arguing for the need to protect "homosexuals as a social group." But this decision was unpublished, which meant that gays and lesbians had to "reinvent the wheel" as they applied for asylum since other courts could not cite that decision as a matter of law. The BIA also left open the idea that status *or* conduct could be considered in sexual orientation cases by clarifying that only in this *particular* case, Toboso-Alfonso was targeted due to his status of being gay. In other words, the BIA did not definitively say that sexual orientation cases should be judged based on status rather than on behavior/conduct. Finally, and crucially, the BIA did not challenge or reframe the INS's classification of this petitioner as behaving in a manner that was "socially deviant in nature."[17]

In 1990, Congress removed the prohibition of "sexual deviant" from the list of excludable "aliens."[18] The rationale for doing so, according to the Judiciary Committee at the time, was to address the lack of fairness and because "personal decisions about sexuality [are not] dangerous to other people."[19] Soon after, Marcelo Tenorio, a gay man fleeing Brazil, was awarded asylum in 1993. Although the INS appealed the decision, arguing that "sexual orientation" does not constitute a particular social group, the BIA eventually dismissed the appeal in 1999 because it disagreed with the INS reasoning.[20]

At the same time the INS was appealing Tenorio's case, it granted asylum to petitioner Ariel Da Silva, known also as Jose Garcia. Da Silva presented a case describing how Mexican police raped and harassed him due to his sexual identity. However, the INS argued that Da Silva was an individual, not a "class of people" persecuted because of their beliefs or characteristics. Thus, the fact that the police, an agent of the state, perpetrated the crimes swayed the case more than the homophobic nature of the harm.

As the INS struggled to deal with sexual orientation cases, by 1994, 40 asylum cases regarding sexual orientation were pending in the United States in the aftermath of the Toboso-Alfonso decision.[21] And Australia, Austria, Canada, Denmark, Finland, Germany, the Netherlands, New Zealand, and Sweden had recognized sexual orientation as a basis of persecution. So Attorney General Janet Reno decided to provide direction to asylum adjudicators. She released Order 1895-94, declaring the Toboso-Alfonso case as precedent, noting that "an individual who has been identified as homosexual and persecuted by his or her government for that reason alone may be eligible for relief under the refugee laws on the basis of persecution because of membership in a social group." In other words, Reno effectively declared that an asylum seeker could claim fear of persecution based solely on his or her sexual orientation. Thus it stood to reason that those targeted because of their sexual orientation were not just "individuals" but part of a "class of people" targeted for the shared characteristic of being gay or lesbian.

After Reno's order, the International Gay and Lesbian Human Rights Commission (IGLHRC) was involved in several successful asylum applications for sexual minorities, and by the end of 1996, at least 60 people working with IGLHRC received asylum on the basis of sexual orientation.[22] Per the Center for Gender and Refugee Studies (CGRS) data in chapter 2, over 100 LGBT-related claims received grants of asylum; CGRS records in its database only six denials, based on the self-reporting of attorneys. But these victories have to be tempered by concurrent or subsequent developments. For example, prior to its dissolution, INS officials had much more visibility for and interaction with asylum seekers than did immigration courts; thus its decisions carried a long-lasting impact on queer migrant communities' fear of the government. What we see in the following pages is the ongoing presumption that sexual minorities are deviant.

The HIV/AIDS Travel Ban

In 1993 the US National Institute of Health Revitalization Act codified a Human Immunodeficiency Virus (HIV) travel and immigration ban first put into place in 1987. This ban stemmed from the construction of HIV as a "foreign" virus brought by Haitians and Africans[23] and its alleged status as a "gay disease."[24] The ban was eventually lifted in 2010 (even though the 1980s ban on the donation of blood by men who have sex with men still stands in the United States). During the years of the ban, asylum seekers

received complicated messages about whether that ban applied to them or only to other immigrants to the United States.

In practice, the ban did not apply to asylum seekers and refugees. For example, a 1996 INS advisement noted that asylum seekers who were eligible for asylum and were HIV-positive could receive immigration relief. In 1999, the INS decided to make it easier for HIV-positive refugees to get an "HIV waiver." The 2000 Immigration and Nationality Act further increased the opportunity for waivers.[25] Also, being HIV-positive was never a basis for beginning deportation proceedings. Indeed, through the Ryan White Program and the AIDS Drug Assistance Program, refugees and asylees could seek treatment, counseling, and medical services.

During this time, not all HIV-positive asylum seekers were sexual minorities, but most of those HIV-positive asylum seekers were also admitted due to persecution based on sexual orientation.[26] This is possibly because, as the Ninth Circuit reasoned in *Karouni v. Gonzales* (2005), being HIV-positive would be a "confirmation" to some of being gay, and thus such a status would further elevate the persecution a gay person experienced.[27] However, it would be reasonable that an HIV ban would deter anyone arriving or living in the United States from applying for asylum if the person were HIV-positive or had AIDS, especially if the person were gay or lesbian. Additionally, if someone who was HIV-positive *did* receive asylum, because of the ban, he or she could face difficulties in adjusting his or her status to legal permanent residency, which could ultimately affect access to better healthcare. Even after the United States lifted the ban of legal admissibility of gays in 1990 due to the concerted efforts of several organizations and the support of members of Congress,[28] many asylum seekers are unsure to this day about whether they can live in the United States if they are gay or lesbian; so too there has been significant confusion after the lifting of the ban whether HIV status will result in deportation.

It is *because of these various bans*, which were premised on the idea of deviance, that sexual minorities are fearful of applying for asylum. In turn, precisely because the asylum system requires asylum seekers to be proactive and vigilant in applying for asylum, sexual minorities are disadvantaged. The ends of these bans do not mean that the construction of deviance has ended. LGBT and HIV-positive immigrant detainees are routinely denied medical treatment and experience violence and mistreatment.[29] HIV status still can shape how the United States Citizenship and Immigration Services officials assess whether immigrants and asylees seeking lawful permanent residence might be a danger to public health.[30]

amazing

key

The Defense of Marriage Act of 1996

The 1996 Defense of Marriage Act (DOMA) declared that the federal government would not recognize "same-sex or polygamous marriages for any purpose." Because so many immigrants were not able to acquire legal status or derivative asylum through a partner, both immigrants and asylum seekers tried to "create" heterosexual relationships when they moved to the United States. As Grace Poore noted about DOMA, there was an irony to a lesbian woman who "left her home country to avoid [forced] marriage, only to end up marrying [a man] in the U.S. for the right to stay."[31]

Medeiros argues that a 1982 immigration decision in some ways paved the way for DOMA. In that year, the first same-sex marriage case was presented to the INS.[32] In *Adams v. Howerton,* the claimant, a US citizen, filed a petition for his foreign-born male partner and asked the INS to recognize not only homosexuality but also the legitimacy of same-sex relationships. The INS responded by arguing that the claimant "failed to establish that a bona fide marital relationship can exist between two faggots" and that the *federal* definition of marriage was only for heterosexual couples and not same-sex partners because of the latter's inability to produce offspring.[33] The Ninth Circuit upheld denial of spousal status, legitimizing only opposite-sex marriages for federal immigration law; Raba notes that the court's reasoning not only served as precedent to DOMA but also helped to justify DOMA's provisions.[34] Thus we see the crucial intersection of immigration and federal laws.

In 2011, the Obama administration noted that Section 3 of DOMA, which defines marriage as a legal union between a man and a woman, was unconstitutional and that the government would still enforce the law but no longer defend it in court cases. The US Supreme Court, in *U.S. v. Windsor,* also ruled in 2013 that Section 3 was unconstitutional. A subsequent directive to US Citizenship and Immigration Services by the secretary of Homeland Security led to successful green card petitions for same-sex spouses. Further, in *Matter of Zeleniak*, 26 I&N Dec. 158 (BIA 2013), the BIA held that *U.S. v. Windsor* was applicable to same-sex legally married spouses seeking immigration benefits for one partner. But these victories have little meaning to at least 267,000 undocumented LGBTQ immigrants, some of whom are single immigrants whose families refuse to sponsor them, or are in partnerships where both people are undocumented.[35] Imagine a case in which one partner receives asylum, but the other partner is detained, has no eligible asylum claim, or whose asylum claim is in danger of being denied. This couple's future together would

OMG!

be in jeopardy, preventing both parties from enjoying their right to form relationships. The idea of "deviance" attached to same-sex relationships and to non-conforming sexual orientation and gender identity persists for and continues to impact a large class of migrants.[36]

How do we know that the legacy of the two bans and DOMA could continue to deter non-citizens seeking asylum? First, Raba notes that the ruling of *Adams v. Howerton* could be reinstated by courts unless DOMA is not just repealed but also replaced by legislation that clarifies that people who marry in states where same-sex marriages are legal are also considered married under federal law; she also recommends an amendment to the Immigration and Naturalization Act to extend immigration law to couples in civil unions and domestic partnerships.[37] Second, the underlying homophobia and transphobia that underscored the bans persist in interactions non-citizens have with government officials. And these systematic biases continue through other laws that impact LGBTQ non-citizens negatively, as we see with the following two sections.

The Illegal Immigration Reform and Immigrant Responsibility Act (IIRIRA) of 1996

As discussed in chapter 2, the IIRIRA affects asylum seekers because of the one-year deadline, expedited removal, and mandatory detention. This section revisits those three provisions in terms of the impact on LGBTQ asylum seekers in particular. Because of isolation within immigrant communities, particularly for LGBTQ immigrants, many are simply not aware of the one-year deadline. Asylum officers and immigration judges do have the discretion to be empathetic to how isolation could prevent knowledge about the deadline, but they are not required to take it into consideration.[38]

The second relevant specification is "expedited removal," where individuals with no or forged/fraudulent travel documents can be deported without review. Even if asylum seekers know to request a credible fear interview, they may be too traumatized to be able to tell their story to a stranger. Many gay, lesbian, and transgender immigrants may not reveal their sexual orientation or gender identity at a port of entry if they think, per confusion about the previously mentioned bans, that their identities would be "grounds for deportation." Homophobic and transphobic immigration officials may also abuse their powers and enact expedited removal *because* someone reveals he or she has a non-conforming identity.[39]

In effect, LGBTQ asylum seekers do not apply in time or request credible fear interviews because the label of deviance they faced in their home countries shapes their fears in the United States. And because the idea of queer-as-deviant has not been fully and unequivocally challenged and addressed in US laws and processes, LGBTQ asylum seekers can easily find further "proof" that it is not safe to even apply for asylum. As Neilson and Morris note, "[Sexual minorities] often continue to live a life of secrecy once they reach the United States. The fear and danger they experienced at home is transferred to their new lives in the United States within their insular communities, especially during their first year."[40] Further, queer migrants may feel pressured to keep their sexual and gender identities secret within immigrant or other communities that might otherwise advise them on the possibility of asylum if they spoke openly about their persecutory experiences.[41]

Sometimes immigrants choose lawyers who are from the same countries or have the same language skills, but this raises the possibility that the lawyers might also hold homophobic or transphobic prejudices based on expectations or norms about how others from the same community *should* be. Lawyers in general may also not introduce the topic of persecution due to sexual and gender identity when immigrants visit them because they assume or expect gender conformity.[42] Lawyers may assume everyone is straight or cisgender, or that if someone is gay or transgender, that he or she will act in a certain way or openly state it, or will answer questions about sexual orientation and gender identity in a particular way. In effect, when we consider what it means to be a "worthy victim," it is not just about what happens to those whose stories are misunderstood or do not fit into a certain box (autonomous, innocent). *It is also about those who do not even tell their stories because they believe that their very identities would make them "unworthy" of protection.* Of course, it is difficult to evaluate the percentage of asylum seekers who opt out of applying, but anecdotal evidence by asylum lawyers and immigrant community leaders reveal that fear is a very effective deterrent.[43]

The third relevant provision of the IIRIRA is "mandatory detention," which calls for the detention of asylum seekers who are in expedited removal or deportation proceedings. Immigration detention has been contracted to local prisons, where LGBTQ asylum seekers face additional risk of abuse, harassment, and violence if their sexual orientation or gender identity is discovered.[44] Some scholars also argue that the USA PATRIOT Act's provision, allowing the attorney general authority to imprison any immigrant believed to be a security threat, disproportionately impacts gay men from Muslim, Arab, and South Asian countries.[45]

Mandatory detention also disproportionately impacts queer asylum seekers and immigrants because of the "criminalization of poverty."[46] Turney points out that marginalized communities experience higher rates of poverty, which is linked with "survival crimes," such as theft, selling drugs, and prostitution.[47] Recall that the Anti-Terrorism and Effective Death Penalty Act (AEDPA) and IIRIRA expanded "deportable crimes," thus emphasizing "moral turpitude" crimes. Sexual minorities are "disproportionately accused of crimes involving sex" as well as of so-called quality-of-life issues, such as "loitering, public drunkenness, and littering."[48] Even using the "wrong" bathroom for one's "sex" can be considered a lewd act; this targets trans immigrants who might use the bathroom that matches their gender identity but not necessarily how "male" or "female" they look.[49]

Gehi, an immigration lawyer, notes that if one of her queer clients ever engaged in prostitution, she or he would then be "deportable" even if she or he was never convicted or aware that prostitution is a crime. Gehi also mentions two cases in which queer clients were "coerced by immigration officers to admitting to engaging in sex work in their country of origin" and then subjected to removal hearings.[50] Reports by various lawyers confirm that sexual minorities are *always already presumed* to be guilty of "moral turpitude," and thus profiled and harassed by the police.[51] This increases the likelihood of being detained. Turney accurately notes that

> given that these issues increase the time it takes for a determination to be made on an application, the applicant spends more time in detention. If applications are denied and the applicants choose to appeal the decision, they remain in detention while their appeal is heard. As a result, it is common for asylum applicants—even if ultimately successful—to spend years in detention.[52]

The point is that if sexual minorities are more likely to be perceived to have committed crimes of moral turpitude, which in turn damage their asylum chances, then the assumption of deviance clearly persists.

The REAL ID Act of 2005

The 2005 REAL ID Act, described in table 2.2 in chapter 2, confirmed the IIRIRA's one-year deadline. The REAL ID Act also increased asylum application requirements for credibility and corroborating evidence.[53] Corroborating evidence is difficult for LGBTQ asylum seekers because the fears around persecution may result in secrecy, which makes it difficult to

be able to prove their claims. Or, despite evidence of state-based persecutory laws, countries often hide discriminatory practices against sexual minorities by claiming that someone was imprisoned for criminal activity unrelated to sexual orientation.[54]

Further, the REAL ID Act gave federal courts the jurisdiction to review BIA decisions about exceptions to the one-year filing deadline. These exceptions include changed circumstances in the country of origin. For example, a queer asylum seeker could point to recent criminalization of same-sex acts. In addition, applicants can prove a change in their circumstances, such as "coming out" as gay, transitioning through a sex reassignment surgery, entering a same-sex relationship, or becoming active in a LGBTQ organization. Or the applicant can prove the existence of extraordinary circumstances, such as a serious illness, like posttraumatic stress disorder. The applicant must prove that these particular "circumstances were not intentionally created by the alien through his or her own action or inaction."[55] But even if the BIA grants exception, the courts can review and overturn the BIA decisions. There are significant inconsistencies in how judges interpret these exceptions and circumstances.[56]

The REAL ID Act also issued identification requirements, which require that state driver's licenses and personal identification cards comply with federal standards of identification documentation. But this impacts transgender immigrants who struggle with getting identification documents because of fluidity or changes in their gender expression or gender identity. Because of different city, state, and federal agency requirements, trans immigrants are subject to accusations of having incorrect or fraudulent identification, which also affects them when they have to prove their identity in asylum interviews.[57]

Identity requirements are emphasized in the 2007 (revised in 2010) US Citizenship and Immigration Services Affirmative Asylum Procedures Manual's section on "transsexual asylum applicants."[58] This manual recommends that asylum officers review a memorandum that defines "transsexualism [as] a condition in which an individual feels persistently uncomfortable about his or her anatomical sex, and often seeks medical treatment, including hormonal therapy and 'sex reassignment surgery.'"[59] The manual also notes that the marriage of a transsexual asylum seeker should be recognized if the person went through sex reassignment surgery, married the "opposite sex" of the "new sex," and if the marriage was recognized as a heterosexual marriage. It advises that asylum officers attempt to ascertain identity through documentation such as "re-issued birth certificate, legal name change, or medical records of [sex reassignment surgery] or other transgender-related medical treatment" but must

also be "sensitive" to any related stress and trauma.[60] The manual makes clear that the recognition of a person's gender identity requires ample legal documentation of the "new" gender identity and incorporates expectations of sex reassignment surgery.

The First Transgender Asylum Cases

I now shift to the dynamics within court cases for transgender applicants. Some successful early asylum cases involved applicants who underwent *visible* changes due to hormonal changes and treatments or surgery.[61] The manifestation of gender expression also came into play in one of the most cited cases regarding transgender asylum seekers. In 2000, the Ninth Circuit court granted asylum to Geovanni Hernandez-Montiel, a Mexican man who identified as gay and occasionally dressed as a woman, and who applied for asylum after experiencing sexual assault and intimidation at the hands of the police.[62] The petitioner presented expert testimony by a San Diego State University professor who proclaimed that "gay men with female sexual identities in Mexico," meaning gay men who assumed "stereotypical female roles" in relationships, were more ostracized and subject to abuse and violence than gay men who acted in stereotypically "male" ways. Both the immigration judge and the BIA found that the persecution was not based on an immutable characteristic because the claimant was "choosing" to alter the outward appearance to appear female.

But the Ninth Circuit court found that "gay men with female sexual identities in Mexico" did constitute a social group because his "female sexual identity" was "inherent" to his identity. It thus found that he should not be required to change it. The Court cited Goldberg's "Give me Liberty or Give Me Death: Political Asylum and the Global Persecution of Lesbians and Gay Men," *Cornell International Law Journal* (1993), the Gay Rights Coalition of Georgetown University Law Center, and an article about sexual identity in the *Berkeley Women's Law Journal*, to conclude that gendered acts and behaviors, such as cross-dressing, are crucial to one's core identity.[63] Hernandez-Montiel eventually received asylum.

This case, at first glance, seems like a victory for transgender applicants. But it is a tentative one for two reasons. First, the INS first tried to argue that the Ninth Circuit did not have jurisdiction, as Hernandez-Montiel had been allegedly convicted as a prostitute while in the United States. But because the INS did not charge the claimant with a "crime of moral turpitude," the court did still have jurisdiction. This means that *had* the

INS charged the claimant with the crime, the court would not have been involved and been able to intervene with a different legal interpretation.

In addition, the case created a very specific, exclusionary path for recognizing transgender petitioners' rights by *interpreting gender identity in the context of sexual orientation*. In *Reyes-Reyes v. Ashcroft* (2004), the Ninth Circuit court granted a review of an asylum seeker's request for relief under the Convention Against Torture and withholding of removal.[64] The court ruled that Reyes belonged to the same social group as Hernandez-Montiel, describing this male-to-female transgender asylum seeker as a gay man with "deep female identity." The court granted withholding of deportation.

On the one hand, it is important that the Ninth Circuit dismissed the cavalier manner in which the lower courts treated cross-dressing as a "fashion choice." On the other hand, I am intrigued by the combination of the terminology of "gay man" and "deep female identity." In *Reyes-Reyes*, the Ninth Circuit noted that "although Reyes has not undergone sex reassignment surgery, he has had a characteristically female appearance, mannerisms, and gestures for the past sixteen years."[65] As in the Hernandez-Montiel case, the Ninth Circuit discusses the petitioner as a "homosexual" but also mentions the asylum seeker's claim that "he may be considered a transsexual." But the Ninth Circuit claims without explanation that it does not need to consider whether transgender people comprise a particular social group. And it notes, "Geovanni is not simply a transvestite 'who dresses in clothing of the opposite sex for psychological reasons.' Rather, Geovanni manifests his sexual orientation by adopting gendered characteristics characteristically associated with women."[66]

It is unclear whether the Ninth Circuit has a very fluid understanding of gender and sexual behaviors and identities, reflecting in turn particular understandings the petitioner shared. Or is the court confusing gay men, a sexual orientation, with transgender women, a gender identity? Is it appropriate to "legitimize" the status of a gay man by referring to his "deep female identity"? Is the court dismissing transgender people based on its decision not to consider Geovanni's own claim or transgender identity as a social group? What exactly is the difference between "transvestites" and gay men with female identities? And if these cases are about gay men who gender-bend through appearance and other performative acts, are they relevant for transgender asylum seekers who would not identify themselves as gay or lesbian? Did the claimants choose the gender pronouns, or did the lawyers and the court; for example, if *Hernandez-Montiel* is a transgender asylum case, why is the claimant referenced as "he" rather than "she" in the court proceedings? The Ninth Circuit decision offered

no reflection on these issues. However, the lawyer who represented Reyes-Reyes acknowledged after the case that the claimant did identify as transgender but chose to pursue an "uncontested membership" of sexual orientation.[67]

In an analysis of these two cases and another similar one, *Ornelas-Chavez* (2006), Berg and Millbank note that the Ninth Circuit actively declined to consider whether "transsexuals constitute a particular social group" but stuck instead with framing these cases in the context of sexual orientation.[68] This can preclude transgender asylum seekers who are heterosexual or do not comment about their sexual orientation/identity. Some scholars have pointed out that transgender people are often "misrecognized" as gay because of gender-conforming ideas, such as that gay men are really "like women."[69] Neilson points out that while *Hernandez-Montiel* served as an "important bridge to other cases involving claims by individuals who push the boundaries of sexual identity," this claimant's case was more likely to succeed because of the focus on sexual orientation.[70] She notes that while persecution based on sexual orientation and persecution based on gender identity are different issues, courts may see a link between the two if patterns of discrimination against transgender individuals are based on *imputed* sexual orientation.[71] For example, the claimant might be perceived to be gay and thus face homophobic insults, discrimination, and violence; homophobic terms may be used when there is no prevalent terminology in a particular country regarding transgender people.

However, the Ninth Circuit indicates that it sees gender and sex in rigid, binaried terms; for example, it looks at social groups of gay men with "unmistakably" female identities, and who are "characteristically" female. Judges often perceive that transgender applicants must be "unmistakably and characteristically" one "sex" or the other. Transgender applicants are already perceived as confusing to asylum adjudicators because their gender identity does not "match" perceptions of their biological sex, but they are seen as particularly bizarre if they do not seem to "pick a gender," male *or* female, to normalize the "mismatch" between gender identity and biological identity. Gender fluidity, or more open ideas about what constitutes gender, sex, and the alleged distinction between the two, is then associated with deviance, in terms of deviating from binaries.

The lower courts clearly struggled in these particular cases. But at the same time, in other cases, immigration judges and the BIA accepted "transgender individuals" as their own distinct social group. And the US Citizenship and Immigration Services Training Module for Immigration Officers regarding sexual orientation and gender identity explicitly notes that "'transgender is a gender identity, not a sexual orientation.'"[72] Thus

transgender asylum seekers also receive mixed messages from different players about whether the asylum system can offer them means of immigration relief and protection.

The Social Visibility Requirement

Recall the discussion in chapter 2 about the additional burdens created in the 2006 and 2008 BIA cases of proving social visibility in social group claims. Prior to this additional requirement, courts usually assessed whether gays and lesbians constituted a social group by looking for evidence that they were at least perceived or "suspected" of being gay.[73] But US asylum adjudicators started to interpret social perception as social visibility, requiring much more proof that the group was not just perceived as gay but *visible* as gay.[74] This meant that asylum seekers would have to show that they were visible in ways that fit judges' preconceived notions about what it meant to be "out" in the world as a gay person (hanging out in gay nightclubs, for example). They would also have to show evidence of being "out" when the very problem they faced was that being visibly gay could result in severe harm or violence. As I explain below, this expectation negatively bears out in asylum seekers' experiences.

THE EFFECTS OF THE NON-DEVIANCE WORTHY VICTIM FRAME ON ASYLUM SEEKERS

In effect, these different issues illustrate that the immigration and asylum system, inclusive of laws and practices, consistently fails to account for the variety of experiences of LGBTQ communities.[75] As a result, asylum seekers might be unsure about how to present their stories and experiences, if they apply at all. My review of LGBTQ cases demonstrates that those assisted by law clinics and lawyers well versed in asylum law and efficiently able to provide details about homophobic or transphobic country conditions were quite likely to be successful. However, I also found evidence that judges displayed a significant inability to comprehend non-conforming sexual orientation and gender identity.

To be sure, when one reads the various manuals and guidelines US governmental agencies have created, particularly the scholarly and nongovernmental articles and publications they cite, it is tempting to see government agencies as inclusive. Even issuing guidelines regarding the

rights of queer asylum seekers was unimaginable not too long ago. But asylum advocates contend that the main problems queer asylum seekers face are primarily about convincing judges that sexual orientation and gender identity are "immutable." Recall that to prove persecution based on membership in a social group, one needs to show that he or she was persecuted based on possessing a characteristic he or she cannot change or should not be expected to change. Anker and Ardalan explain that since the social group ground pivots on immutable characteristics, courts should focus on "beliefs and characteristics, not . . . activities."[76] They explore the controversy over courts asking evidence of not just gay "status" but also actions, conduct, and behavior to "corroborate" sexuality.[77]

In the Toboso-Alfonso case mentioned above, the INS argued that a "conduct-based group" could not be a cognizable social group. But the BIA argued in response that the violence and threats the applicant experienced were due not to "misconduct" but to "the government's desire that all homosexuals be forced to leave their homeland."[78] Anker and Ardalan note a series of cases including *Karouni v. Gonzales* (2005), *Maldonado v. U.S. Attorney General* (2011), and *Hernandez-Montiel v. INS* (2000), in which appellate courts found that violence in response to "activities" was so severe precisely because of persecution of the applicant's core identity as a sexual minority, inclusive of rights to intimacy and relationships.[79] Anker and Ardalan argue that adjudication should be based on "unchangeable characteristics" rather than on "social perceptions of what sexual orientation or identity means and how it should manifest itself."[80]

Other scholars, such as Hathaway and Pobjoy, protest courts' expectations around the world that since sexual orientation can allegedly be "concealed," it is up to the asylum seeker to be discrete to avoid persecution.[81] Hathaway and Pobjoy argue that asylum seekers should not have to "conceal" their "core" identity, because their orientation is not a set of behaviors or conduct but rather a part of who they "really are." The authors say that it may not be "possible" for someone to be discrete or to "turn off" whatever it is that would signal one's sexual identity; they thus focus on recognizing the "endogenous harm" of having to conceal one's identity.[82]

Anker, Ardalan, Hathaway, and Pobjoy are trying to challenge the focus on the minutiae of asylum seekers' activities. They are showing that such intrusions by judges are unnecessary and problematic. Some asylum seekers have noted that they have to be prepared to give a "performance of a lifetime," being advised by their immigration lawyers to "flaunt" their sexual orientation.[83] Imagine what an asylum seeker must confront when

preparing to appear before a judge: be visibly gay, in a way that satisfies the judges' preconceived notions about what that means. But one should not be too gay, because then a judge might scold an asylum seeker for inviting or provoking persecutory behavior. But if one cannot prove persecutory harm, then a judge might assume that sexual orientation is not central enough to one's identity to warrant fear of persecution.[84]

Another consideration in "proving" one's identity as a sexual minority is how the conduct/status distinction is mapped onto the public/private binary. Lesbian asylum seekers are disadvantaged *as women*, because they are allegedly more likely than gay men to be targeted in the "private sphere." Indeed, gay men are usually more likely than lesbians to receive asylum.[85] Lesbians allegedly have a less "public" experience, according to some observers of the asylum system, and thus adjudicators' focus falls on their conduct.

Berger finds that lesbian women are more likely to receive asylum when they are perceived to have been "rebelling" against their home state.[86] They also have to discuss the repercussions of living an "out" life in the home country, or show some overtly "public" element to the persecution, such as the persecutor being involved in public criminal activity that the government was unwilling to prosecute. If lesbian asylum seekers do not sufficiently show they were persecuted on account of being gay to the satisfaction of the courts, courts dismiss their experiences as mere "harassment" or because of some other reason not connected to their sexual orientation. If they are not "out" and instead have male partners or even children, or do not participate in organizations or attend bars and social settings for lesbians, their claims of persecution are questioned.[87] At the same time, when asylum seekers prove that they were "out," courts have sometimes reasoned that asylum seekers would not be "out" if they feared for their safety.[88]

Neilson also claims that the main obstacle lesbians face in proving the harm they suffered as persecutory is the perceived "private" nature of the violence they experience.[89] She gives the example of *Pitcherskaia v. INS* (1997), as the only precedent decision involving a lesbian asylum seeker. Pitcherskaia was under surveillance in Russia because her father was a political dissident. She was arrested after participating in various protests on behalf of gay and lesbian acquaintances beaten or imprisoned for being gay rights activists. She denied being a lesbian to authorities but was labeled as a "suspected lesbian" after visiting an ex-girlfriend who was forcibly being "treated" for being gay. Pitcherskaia was also forcibly subjected to psychiatric "treatment." Neilson notes that the surveillance and arrests were "public" but that visiting the friend in the hospital as well as other gay friends in their homes were "private" acts.[90]

The immigration judge and BIA in this case found that forcible psychiatric treatment was not persecutory because the intention was to "cure," not to harm. However the Ninth Circuit reversed the BIA's claims and remanded the case. Neilson claims the Ninth Circuit's reversal effectively meant that attention was shifted from the *intent* of the persecutors (to "help" or "cure" a sexual minority) to whether the suffering and harm would be offensive to a "reasonable person."[91] Thus, this decision was a major victory for gays and lesbians persecuted by forced medical procedures such as psychiatric treatments. She concludes that there is a broader societal commitment to "eliminate" or make "invisible" lesbians and female homosexuality, which is why they are targeted "privately."[92]

There are understandable frustrations with trying to prove that some forms of violence are as serious as so-called public, political violence. But Neilson seems to inadvertently accept the public/private binary. For example, Neilson defines public activity "outside of the home," whereas the private is "within the home or other *protected* area."[93] Neilson is referencing "right to privacy" laws regarding freedom from interference by the government. But such rhetoric ultimately sanctifies the private sphere as a place of love, security, and *privacy*. The special kind of concern about what happens behind closed doors, in "private," to *particular* populations, namely women, lesbians, and transwomen, further reifies that *some* bodies are "feminized" and to be protected.[94] The issue is not just *where* the violence happens, but also what is done to people's bodies and how violence always has a political dimension. Also, as mentioned in chapter 3, sanctifying the family/household as a separate, protected space actually reinforces the public/private binary. Further, given that the hospital is where the "treatment" for gays and lesbians occurred, the claimant's visit to this institution as well as what happened to her there, would certainly count as "public" acts. But I take Neilson's point that *gendered* expectations of behavior figure into the construction of what non-conforming asylum seekers are supposed to act like.

Elsewhere, Neilson, the legal director at Immigration Equality, describes the expectations of conduct and expression in the context of trans asylum seekers. She tells the story of "Cristina," who is fleeing persecution due to her gender identity as a transwoman.[95] During her first interview, the asylum officer told her, "You're a beautiful woman, what problems would you have if you went back to your country?" As Neilson notes, Cristina so successfully eliminated the "otherness" of her trans identity through her transition to a woman that in the eyes of the asylum system, adjudicators could not imagine that she might be persecuted due to being a transgender woman.

Neilson gives another example of "Marco," a trans man who started hormone therapy and is starting to have a deeper voice and more facial hair. But, as Neilson points out, the asylum officer was confused when Marco described being a butch woman attracted to other women, who then decided to transition to a male gender identity and was still attracted to women. The asylum officer asked, "So you were a homosexual and now you're a transsexual?"[96] This officer could not comprehend that Marco was describing persecution based on a perception of deviance, focusing instead on fitting Marco into one category, same-sex attraction, *or* the other, a non-conforming transgender identity.

Interestingly, the *Hernandez-Montiel* and *Reyes* cases discussed above articulated social groups that may have been applicable for the asylum officer to understand Marco's claim. So this asylum officer may have been unaware of the court cases, may have been confused by the cases, or may think the social group does not apply for someone with a "deep male identity." Or the officer may have understood from those cases that being a lesbian with a "deep male identity" means that she must be as "fully male" as possible, which Marco is not, as he is still in the process of transitioning.

With these various problems, many asylum advocates use as a starting point the declaration in *Hernandez-Montiel* by the Ninth Circuit that sexual orientation and identity are characteristics "so fundamental to one's identity that a person should be not be required to abandon them." The Ninth Circuit later reaffirmed in *Karouni v. Gonzales* (2005) that homosexuality is as "innate" as heterosexuality in noting that "*all* alien homosexuals are members of a 'particular social group.'" The power of the immutability requirement is in proclaiming that being forced to hide one's sexual orientation or gender identity would violate one's freedom.[97] Implied in *immutability* is that a person cannot and should not be expected to change a characteristic about themselves and thus cannot avoid being persecuted simply by changing that characteristic that is being targeted. Asylum advocates thus challenge the judges' focus on visibility/behaviors, advancing instead the premise that people do not "choose" their sexual orientation or gender identity. Thus, the focus should be on a person's self-identification, not expressions of behavior or dress. But should asylum advocates take for granted that the "immutability" of sexual orientation or gender identity is applicable in all cases?[98]

Not all sexual minorities believe in the narrative that they were "born that way" or that they "always knew." Instead, they may see degrees of choice in discovering or claiming their sexual orientation or gender identity. An emphasis on the "authenticity" of being born gay or transgender, with a requisite "coming out" story that legitimizes becoming fully

aligned with a gender or sexual identity, can seem like a necessary strategy to confront the violence of homophobia, transphobia, heteronormativity, and cisprivilege. But the asylum process sets up a requirement that if people do not fit into heteronormative ideals, then they must fit into *some* category, to turn their alleged deviance into something "understandable," something that is stable and fixed enough to make intelligible violent experiences. "Immutability" and "status," in other words, hinge upon accepting sexual orientation and gender identity as a stable core.

Because the asylum process forces "an unrealistic ideal of a definitive and revelatory self," Berg and Millbank argue that it would actually be more helpful to look at both the "felt self-identification" and the "gender identity or sexual orientation imputed to them."[99] In other words, rather than focus on the "status" versus "conduct" debate, or proof of "static and concrete identity groupings," it would be more useful to focus on the violence that is targeting people because they do not conform to gendered expectations.[100] Such violence could be assessed based on both how the claimant sees himself or herself, as well as how he or she is seen in society, allowing for flexibility and fluidity in how one's identity changes and may be targeted differently over time.[101] Thus contradictory expectations and experiences would become *part* of the narrative of persecution, rather than something that the asylum seeker has to resolve in a courtroom to a judge's satisfaction. To focus on gender non-conformity would also be helpful when transgender applicants are often treated as a subset or afterthought to sexual orientation claims or presented erroneously as sexual orientation cases rather than being addressed on their own accord.

In sum, the non-deviance expectation drags asylum seekers and their advocates into contradictory messaging that does not fully capture different kinds of experiences. It can also lead to stereotyping of the "essence" of "queerness" or of how persecution/discrimination against LGBTQ asylum seekers occurs. Finally, trying to pinpoint how one *should have* behaved, lived, loved, or engaged in sex reveals the staying power of the presumption of deviance of sexual minorities.

THE EFFECTS OF THE NON-DEVIANT WORTHY VICTIM FRAME ON US POWER RELATIONSHIPS

We could simply ask: is the United States making efforts to address the treatment of sexual minorities? Does the United States grant asylum based on persecution due to sexual orientation and gender identity? The answers of yes to both questions indicate that US policies ostensibly aim to protect human rights.

On December 6, 2011, President Obama explicitly linked asylum and foreign aid in his Memorandum of International Initiatives to Advance the Human Rights of Lesbian, Gay, Bisexual, and Transgender Persons, instructing his executive departments and federal agencies to protect vulnerable LGBTQ asylum seekers, and to respond meaningfully to human rights abuses around the world.[102] This memorandum was issued right after then-secretary of state Hillary Clinton addressed the United Nations in Geneva, proclaiming the duties of all countries to respect the rights of LGBTQ individuals. In 2011, the Department of Homeland Security created "Guidance for Adjudicating LGBTI Refugee and Asylum Claims" after an extended collaborative effort between US Citizenship and Immigration Services and the pro-LGBTQ asylum seekers organization Immigration Equality. US Citizenship and Immigration Services made this document a part of mandatory training for asylum officers. The US State Department and Department of Health and Human Services have also been engaged in various conversations about providing appropriate refugee processing and resettlement for "vulnerable" populations of sexual minorities, as well as how to address the specific kinds of trauma sexual minorities face both from their persecutory experiences and during migration.[103] Others attempting to make US foreign policy more LGBTQ-inclusive emphasize that having more information about the levels of persecution in other countries would help lead to successful asylum grants.[104] In turn, they argue, activists and the United States could leverage those asylum cases to encourage and promote LGBTQ rights around the world.

When Samantha Powers, US ambassador to the United Nations, was a special assistant to the president and senior director of Multilateral Affairs and Human Rights at the National Security Council, she detailed in a December 2012 press release how US "leadership" is crucial in advancing equality for sexual minorities abroad.[105] She mentioned several topics: US governmental representatives' meetings with LGBTQ communities in other countries; conditioning foreign aid and assistance on the treatment of sexual minorities; possible protection for LGBTQ refugees particularly during resettlement; using the United Nations system to strengthen norms about the rights of sexual minorities; attempts by the Department of Justice and Department of State to pressure countries to decriminalize sexual minorities and to take violence against these communities seriously; and the role of several other departments and agencies to "guide" other countries in their treatment of sexual minorities. These various examples arguably indicate that the United States is further entrenching advocacy for sexual minorities' rights around the world.

Indeed, undocumented queer activists and scholars/activists pushing for queer immigration rights often argue that sexual minorities will need the option of asylum as long as there is a "gulf" between the global North and global South in ensuring the rights of sexual minorities.[106] Interestingly, the United States is perceived as so LGBT-friendly that Immigration Equality had to correct a *New York Times* article that argued that straight people were pretending to be gay in order to get asylum![107] But protection is often more than it seems. The non-deviant frame allows the United States to admit some exceptional asylum seekers to be able to proclaim its superiority when it comes to LGBTQ issues while also being able to reject enough asylum seekers to uphold immigrant restrictionism. The non-deviant frame plays a role in US power relationships in two ways.

First, through the asylum process, and particularly the media attention around certain cases, "queer asylum seekers' testimonies are elicited in ways that reinforce dominant nationalism and imperialism without necessarily leading to sanctuary for the individuals concerned."[108] In other words, these asylum cases, *regardless of the outcome for the asylum seeker*, provide narratives about how awful their countries are, in ways that align with and fortify US opinions about particular countries, including those with which it is unfriendly. Thus, while expectations of deviance by and within the United States stay intact, the focus on *other* countries' treatment of perceived deviance serves a way to point to *their* inferiority.

As Birdsong notes, it is crucial to note that the first successful sexual orientation case was of an asylum seeker from Cuba.[109] To be sure, many US officials, including Janet Reno, were afraid of the consequences of the Mariel boatlift. But Janet Reno did an about-turn and declared Toboso-Alfonso's case precedent, as she had to manage the dual duties of easing the burden of additional Cuban migrants while still being able to critique Cuba's human rights record.

Cantú argues that it was important not to deport a Cuban during the Cold War.[110] He notes that the eventual declaration of Toboso-Alfonso's case as precedent may have had to do with the Clinton administration showing that it supported gay rights after failing to adequately address anti-gay discrimination in the military. Other countries had far worse human rights records regarding the treatment of sexual minorities at the time, and other cases could have been made an example. Cantú also suggests that with Mexican cases in particular, the more that Mexico can be proven dangerous to all classes of people, including its queer citizens, the better the United States can justify the need to violently secure the border.[111] In other words, he asks us to consider the desire to deter migration

while also needing to let in certain migrants to denote why Mexican culture and society are so dangerous.

In the fall of 2013, in *Doe v. Holder*, the Ninth Circuit court ordered the BIA to review its decision to deny asylum to a gay Russian man who was attacked due to his sexual orientation.[112] Both the immigration judge and the BIA argued that the applicant did not convincingly prove that Russia sponsored and condoned the persecution or that Russia was unwilling to stop persecution. But the circuit court judges were convinced that Doe proved that the police dismissed his complaints of harassment and violence. Thus they claimed that the burden was actually on the United States to show that circumstances had changed sufficiently enough (for example, that Russia overturned anti-gay laws) to warrant a denial of asylum.[113]

Some media outlets as well as newspapers with gay audiences picked up the story, using the opportunity to describe anti-gay legislation and the general political climate in Russia.[114] During the writing of this book, the BIA had not yet reviewed the case, but it is worth noting that regardless of what happens to this man's case, his story has been used to publicize Russia's policies. The ruling was argued and submitted in September 2013, soon after the highly publicized Russian ban on "gay propaganda" at the Winter Olympic Games and subsequent US analysis of anti-gay legislation there. To what extent was the Ninth Circuit ruling influenced by those events?

Russia's anti-gay policies and actions do and should matter. And certainly immigration and asylum advocates have been rather vocal in the past few years about Russian policies so as to promote the rights of LGBTQ Russian asylum seekers to receive legal protection in the United States.[115] But I find it interesting that a US asylum claim can draw upon and contribute to discourses about other countries' policies even while the fate of the asylum seeker remains unclear. To be sure, these narratives help to put pressure on the United States to ensure a favorable asylum outcome, but their *endurance* and circulation matter particularly when the asylum seeker does *not* receive a grant. Indeed, Doe could very well be deported if there is not concerted intervention and mobilization by US-based gay rights activists and asylum advocates. Further, it is now up to the US attorney general to decide how to present information about Russia's treatment of gays. How much will the current US tensions with Russia over the Ukraine conflict influence the US position? To what extent will a desire to paint Russia in a particular light outweigh concerns about immigration restriction? These questions will be crucial to answer as queer Russian asylum seekers in the United States are more actively mobilizing on their own behalf; to what extent will they be able to participate in and shape the narrative

about Russia and the US-Russia relationship?[116] What happens to asylum seekers who are not able to tap into US advocacy communities?

Sussman contends that strong patterns of state persecution should be interpreted not as indicative of the inferiority of those countries but rather in the context of global politics.[117] Thus, we can politicize *why* countries persecute sexual minorities and understand better how asylum decisions are linked to global power relationships. He uses the example of Jamaica. In 2010, 30% of people who won asylum with the assistance of Immigration Equality due to persecution based on sexual orientation were from Jamaica.[118] Neilson, legal director at Immigration Equality, notes that Jamaica "is one of the most violently homophobic countries that exist in the western hemisphere." Jamaican asylum seekers, the Jamaican Forum for Lesbians All-Sexuals and Gays, and Human Rights Watch also provide empirical and anecdotal evidence of virulent homophobia in that country.

Sussman shifts from taking homophobia in Jamaica as a natural fact. He points out that Jamaica's anti-gay laws were modeled on England's antisodomy laws; Jamaica's laws should also be understood in the context of colonial legacies and US evangelical groups' influence. Further, Jamaica has stood behind its laws as a way to resist US economic pressures to change its policies. Accordingly, Sussman suggests that rather than faulting Jamaican culture, asylum advocates could track anti-LGBT laws, patterns of popular culture anti-LGBT messages, police complicity, incidences of mob violence against sexual minorities, and backlash against those falsely accused of being gay. Sussman documents violence in that country while pointing out, rather than reproducing, international hierarchy. This approach allows the creation of an impactful narrative that is more complex and nuanced. Doing so could also make it less likely that an asylum narrative would be useful in US attempts to influence other countries' policies without reflection on its own.

My second point is that the extension of rights and protection to asylum seekers through the non-deviance frame helps the United States distract attention from the discrimination, harassment, and violence queer asylum seekers face once they are in the United States.[119] Precisely because the non-deviance frame is contradictory, the United States can highlight progress and downplay the documented problems, such as mandatory detention. At a January 2014 congressional briefing, cosponsored by the LGBT Congressional Caucus and the LGBT Faith and Asylum Network, a coalition of immigration and human rights advocacy groups along with LGBTQ asylum seekers argued that the challenges they faced can be a shock to those who once thought of the United States as a

"beacon of hope."[120] As Rochelle Fortier Nwadibia, legal director of Private Courts International, noted, "Today our arms are not open wide for the modern-day asylum seeker. Instead, we find the creeping criminalization of asylum seekers . . . not the safe harbor we'd expect."

Many queer rights immigrant groups may try to strategically leverage the United States to "live up to its standards." LGBTQ asylees proclaim in a number of interviews that they are much happier living in the United States, with the protection of asylum. But this is all the more reason to see who is *left out* of receiving that same opportunity or experiencing the same kind of quality of life. Indeed, the US history of treatment of non-citizens who are sexual minorities belies the notion that the country ever was a "beacon of hope," at least in a consistent way. For those who cling to distinctions between Western and non-Western countries, it is important to know that the United States was the lone Western country in a group including Iran, Iraq, and Syria (countries forcefully criticized by the United States for their human rights violations) with an HIV ban policy.[121] Accordingly, the narrative of the United States as an unequivocal supporter of queer rights should be questioned.

In addition, Luibhéid notes that it is problematic when "freedom" is privileged as the most important or sometimes even only relevant aspect of migration.[122] What she means is that even when asylum seekers are escaping threats to their lives and freedom, seeking reprieve and safe haven in the United States, their stories remain complex. As Luibhéid notes, the "freedom" may be fleeting because of discrimination, isolation, lack of representation, and detention.[123] As I pointed out earlier, "freedom" is not an option for non-citizens who opt out of applying for asylum due to fears of what might happen if their sexual orientation or gender identity is discovered. The "freedom to be who you really are" is precisely why queer immigrants are disproportionately targeted as criminals and subsequently detained. Queer immigrants are also targeted for sexual violence once in detention centers.

Consider the story of Christina Madrazo.[124] She is a transgender woman from Mexico who was conditionally granted asylum. She was then fingerprinted and underwent background checks. But at the follow-up asylum hearing, the INS told her that it had doubts about her credibility because she had left the United States and returned. Madrazo had indeed tried to return to Mexico because of difficult economic circumstances in the United States. Government officials also noted that Madrazo had solicited sex. This strategy of economic survival shifted Madrazo from the category of saved asylum seeker fleeing persecution, to an "undocumented criminal alien." She was temporarily detained in the Krome Detention Center in

Miami, Florida, where a guard raped her. Despite the fact that she filed a complaint, the detention center failed to assign her another guard, and the same guard raped her again. After a trial, during which the accused guard eventually pled down the charges, Madrazo sued the US government for $15 million under the Torts Claims Act.

Solomon sums up Madrazo's case as revealing

> the limits of the liberal state even in arenas (such as asylum law) where it often appears to be the most generous. . . . her transgender status no longer cast her as a victim of a "primitive" land, requiring rescue by America; quite the contrary, it became a marker of her multivalent deviance from which America itself required rescue through her deportation. Madrazo's illegibility became quite literal: Krome authorities couldn't figure out whether to house her in the men's or women's dorm. So they put her in one of the punitive segregation cells.[125]

Madrazo is now waiting for a final asylum decision as well as for a decision about the lawsuit against the man who assaulted her while incarcerated. She is also now involved with the LGBT Latino/a activist organization LLEGÓ. Madrazo's story demonstrates the twists and turns as one woman is trying to find safety and belonging while confronting treatment that is discriminatory and potentially persecutory. Indeed, an asylum adjudicator assessing conditions elsewhere would likely designate mandatory detention as a persecutory deprivation of rights.

Asylum law requires "dissidence," rewarding many asylum seekers who fail to conform in their home countries, but sexual minorities are thrust into a startling expectation to "conform to a new set of regulatory ideals—be they political, sexual, or gender-related—in order to be embraced by America."[126] Solomon quotes the words of legal scholar and gay Pakistani immigrant Saeed Rahman, who won asylum in 1997:

> I felt that in America I could live freely. Even if one is harassed or attacked for being gay, there's recourse to the law. But that narrative didn't factor in that I was non-white and going to be an immigrant.[127]

As I have pointed out throughout this book, and also per my discussion of race and gender in chapter 1, asylum seekers' experiences must be understood in the context of racialization. Rahman has expressed in public and through an interview with Solomon his sadness and despair over how he had to play into certain damaging discourses about Pakistan. Further, his claim about being a nonwhite immigrant reveals the complicated experiences of asylum seekers, in terms of finding belonging and dignity. Also,

many queer asylum seekers might be still involved in the politics of resistance in their home countries, in which case they look not only at LGBTQ rights but also at different kinds of social, political, and economic justice claims, as well as the dynamics of power relationships between the country from which they fled and the country in which they have received asylum. Thus, strong distinctions may not hold in the lives of at least some asylum seekers.

CONCLUSIONS

The non-deviant worthy victim frame indicates that sexual minorities face not only contradictory expectations in courtrooms but also obstacles from US policies. But the distinction the United States draws between itself and other countries serves as a distraction from the issues within the United States and amplifies the construction of other countries as persecutory without due attention to whether non-citizens actually receive protection in the United States. Persecution against sexual minorities is unique in that other persecuted groups are not challenged to prove their identities in the same way.

At the same time, the expectation of non-deviance overlaps with the expectation of innocence discussed in the previous chapter. In particular, discourses about trafficking leave out sex workers because they are allegedly guilty of committing crimes. However, historically the criminalization of sex workers stemmed from the same moral turpitude legal codes discussed in this chapter. In chapter 6, I discuss how intervening in discourses about moral turpitude can challenge the construction of both sexual minorities and sex workers as "unworthy."

As I show in that chapter, queer immigration rights organizations intervene in the discursive climate to decouple morality and rights discourse. In addition, sex worker advocates used the 2010 United Nations Human Rights Council Periodic Review process to introduce language about the human rights of sex workers and sexual minorities in the Council's report on the US human rights record. As a result of continued advocacy, in 2011 the US State Department eventually responded to that report by declaring publicly for the first time that the human rights of sex workers should be respected. Sex worker advocates continue to use this declaration as a basis for advocacy to challenge moral turpitude codes and to secure the enjoyment of rights for sex workers, immigrants, and sexual minorities.

CHAPTER 6

Feminist Possibilities of Scholarship and Advocacy

This chapter offers possible pragmatic ways for academics, practitioners, and advocates to confront the obstacles and problems presented in this book. I find my inspiration for the possibilities of academic-activist collaboration from Swarr and Nagar's edited volume, *Critical Transnational Feminist Praxis*. They provide examples and encouragement of learning to speak and listen across disciplinary, professional, geopolitical, and other boundaries.[1] They specifically suggest that "grounding feminisms in activist communities *everywhere* is a means to interrogate all forms of implicit and explicit relations of power (e.g. racist/classist/casteist), and to contest those power relations through ongoing processes of self-critique and collective reflection."[2]

First, I examine the politics of feminist expertise, thus exploring how/whether scholarship can be useful and impactful in legal decision-making. Second, I discuss how to change the discursive climates from which worthy victim frames emerge. I suggest ways to rethink the construction of family so as to challenge the autonomy frame. I explore how to add another type of violence, forced pregnancy/maternity, to the list of possible types of coercive reproductive practices to challenge the innocence frame. Finally, I push for an examination of outdated legal codes about moral turpitude that continue to have influence on the non-deviant frame regarding persecution of sexual minorities and on the innocence frame regarding the exclusion of sex workers. For each type of frame, I suggest how feminist IR can challenge legal and political understandings about gender violence that may have ripple effects in asylum cases. I also explore specific

reforms in immigration and asylum advocacy. Finally, because ideas of "worthiness" underscore the perceived distinction not only among asylum seekers but also between asylum seekers and undocumented immigrants, I examine how these strategies are useful for addressing the experiences of non-citizens in general.

Feminist "knowledge claims" underpin these various strategies. As noted in chapter 1, feminists help to articulate, name, and shape how we understand and talk about gender violence. In doing so, they engage in making knowledge claims, which draw upon the meanings and understandings about the causes and solutions for problems in the world.[3] These claims are contested and contestable. I offer the following thoughts in the spirit of being corrected and challenged, yet being included in ongoing conversations about what to do about the gendered and racialized classifications of non-citizens.

FEMINISTS AS "EXPERTS"

One of my most exciting discoveries while studying the politics of gender-based asylum was the potential role of academics in contributing research to the cases lawyers were building. When assessing the variables that impact judges' decisions, Ramji-Nogales, Schoenholtz, and Schrag note that asylum seekers with legal counsel received grants of asylum at a rate three times higher than those without legal representation.[4] They found in particular that asylum seekers represented by the Georgetown University law clinic had an asylum grant rate of 89%.[5] The authors found comparably high rates with other law school asylum clinics and with pro bono representation by law firms associated with Human Rights First.[6] Of course, these lawyers are possibly likely to handpick cases that are more clear-cut or seem easier to win. But the authors reasoned that lawyers and law students from these clinics and firms were able to spend a significant amount of time conducting research to corroborate clients' testimony and identifying experts to "testify in court about a country's human rights violations."[7] Lawyers thus must build relationships with experts to increase the rate of success.

"Experts" have the privilege and resources to produce knowledge about countries and people's experiences. They legitimize, give context to, and raise awareness about some stories, but not others. They turn stories about countries into "reality," predicting "what could happen if petitioners are forcibly returned home."[8]

Scholars have critiqued the professionalization of human rights advocacy as strengthening the power and privilege of some to shape

understandings and ideas about victims' experiences.[9] For example, the concept of expertise assumes that some people, such as asylum seekers or activists without professional or academic credentials, are not credible in providing specific kinds of knowledge. I thus call for greater politicization of how feminist experts, in particular, interact with the asylum/immigration system.

There are two sources of knowledge in asylum cases where feminist intervention is possible: first, expert affidavits and statements; and second, academic texts and journal articles. Expert witnesses describe or write analysis of violence in the asylum seeker's country, explaining details about the form of violence experienced, and what is likely to happen if the asylum seeker is returned to her country. I suggest that those of us writing about gender violence analyze what our roles could and should be as experts. For example, I am considering serving as an "expert" for certain asylum cases, particularly after one organization requested my input when I reached out to it during the process of researching this book. But I am torn about how to delicately balance the need for a "straightforward" report with my desire to lend nuance and complexity to the process. Will I write with attention to how power relationships operate? Or will I be focused on just ensuring that the judge will be convinced and thus figure out a way to tap into the likely discursive understandings he or she already has? How will I challenge and decenter my position as an expert?

I am not alone in contemplating these issues, as many academics participate in providing expertise in asylum cases. Jennifer Coffman, an anthropologist who has served as an expert witness in gender-based asylum cases, such as the Gachumi case described in chapter 3, notes that the African Studies Association has a database of members who have served on asylum cases, and the American Anthropological Association sends requests to its members to serve as country condition experts.[10] My analysis of expert affidavits reveals that experts are trained in a wide variety of academic disciplines. What kind of biases do experts hold or might be accused of carrying?[11] Coffman openly discusses her struggles with trying to fulfill her role while also challenging problematic assumptions and representations of other cultures. She notes that she is aware of ongoing informal conversations about what it means to serve as an expert. Indeed, the UK-based Country of Origin Research and Information Center held a conference in June 2010 to discuss the challenges in producing "objective" evidence for refugee claims.[12] The colleagues of sociologist Lionel Cantú Jr., who passed away, reflect on his position as an expert witness in five cases of Mexican men applying for asylum. They highlight how he could

simultaneously appreciate the hope that the asylum system held for these asylum seekers while critiquing the stories the men were forced to adopt.[13]

Thus, I suggest more collaborative dialogue between legal and academic scholars to work through these dilemmas. Conversations with asylum advocates and lawyers about these issues are possible because the asylum advocacy world, particularly regarding gender-based asylum, is somewhat "porous." There are many ways to get to know organizations involved in asylum representation and research and to have conversations about what kind of information/research is valued and why. For example, on its website the Center for Gender and Refugee Studies (CGRS) asks for volunteers to help with human rights / country condition research.[14] Other organizations invite nonlawyers to their trainings and panel discussions about the major obstacles in the asylum process. In some cases, potential expert witnesses have opportunities to discuss cases with asylum seekers, who might detail the choices they make in telling their stories.

As another example, Chitra, my lawyer friend, and I discussed the framing of the Democratic Republic of Congo (DRC) as the "rape capital of the world."[15] Neither of us thought that the label was helpful. She told me the story of how she tried to avoid playing into the "DRC is the worst" rhetoric. In a recent case, she inserted ideas found in an academic article "Why Soldiers Rape," a nuanced, critical feminist discursive analysis of the complexities of masculinity, sexual violence, and the political-economic context in the DRC. This article was published in 2009 in *International Studies Quarterly*, a journal widely respected among international relations scholars.[16] Chitra tried to illustrate *why* her client might face sexual violence if forced to return. The immigration judge granted asylum to this particular claimant; however, she did so by referencing another unrelated case on Colombia, arguing that if the claimant were returned forcibly to the DRC, she would be kidnapped by rebel soldiers much like what happened to the claimant in the Colombia case. But the contexts of sexual violence are very different in Colombia and the DRC. Chitra noted that she did not want to challenge the judge since asylum was granted. She was also unclear about whether the judge simply dismissed Chitra's critical analysis or was just strategically choosing an easy path for granting asylum.

Based on that conversation, Chitra and I put together a presentation that was accepted to a panel called "Reconciling Theory and Practice," for the October 2012 Social Justice Feminism Conference at the University of Cincinnati. I shared with her critical feminist articles about gender-based asylum; she showed me her decision process while representing her clients and the kinds of statements asylum seekers make when describing their experiences. She also asked me to figure out a way to more easily translate

theoretical claims into accessible observations that she could use in court and that her clients could think about. We discussed how asylum seekers might theorize violence in ways that confront feminist claims. We structured the paper as a "testing ground" for thinking through positionality, accountability, and collaboration. We also saw gender-based asylum as standing at the intersection of advocacy around gender violence, immigration rights, and global relationships, thus concluding that feminist IR has a natural "entry point" into the asylum world.

The second form of knowledge production is academic scholarship. Judges often cite academic analysis in their decisions. They draw upon academic discussions of what constitutes rape, feminist explorations of violence in law reviews, and other scholarly works. Further, the US Citizenship and Immigration Services cites scholarship in its training manuals for asylum officers. For example, in the 2011 "Guidance for Adjudicating Lesbian, Gay, Bisexual, Transgender, and Intersex (LGBTI) Refugee and Asylum Claims" Training Module, the Refugee, Asylum, and International Operations Directorate recommends two rather critical analyses of asylum claims: Victoria Neilson's "Applying Gender-Based Asylum Jurisprudence to Lesbian Asylum Claims," and Ellen A. Jenkins's "Taking the Square Peg out of the Round Hole: Addressing the Misclassification of Transgender Asylum Seekers."[17] To be sure, these are suggested readings, and asylum adjudicators often misinterpret State Department country condition reports, much less more comprehensive legal scholarship. However, it is promising that these articles found their way into this training module. I suggest that feminist IR scholars and others with critical analyses of gender, race, power, and the immigration/asylum system contribute to law journals, such as the *Canadian Journal of Women and the Law, Hastings Women's Law Journal*, and *Berkeley Journal of Gender, Law and Justice*.

Knowledge claims are central to "international relations" as a discipline and as an arena of decisions and interactions. What is "known" about countries is pivotal in decisions about who gets bombed, who gets aid, who is an enemy, an ally, the Other. And those interactions and encounters, in turn, shape, delimit, and construct knowledge claims. The task ahead is to figure out how to participate in creating "responsible knowledge," which would entail thinking about what is done with knowledge and to whom, identifying whose voices are privileged in knowledge production, and studying the gaps and silences in authoritative accounts about the world.[18] Now that we have seen more vividly the effects of what is claimed about "worthy victims," we have to more seriously address the ideational component of the global, national, and local social structures that can shape, but

also be shaped by, state and nonstate actions and decisions. I turn next to specific knowledge claims and correlated strategies.

FEMINISTS AS THE PRIMARY ADVOCATES FOR VICTIMS OF GENDER VIOLENCE

A key task for feminists of any sensibility or theoretical commitment is to name, address, and challenge gender violence. As I have demonstrated throughout the book, there is much at stake in the politics of naming who counts as a victim of gender violence. The feminist IR, postcolonial feminist IR, and critical IR scholars that influenced my framework have all called for the recasting of categories that we take for granted: state/nonstate, victim/perpetrator, inside/outside, good/bad. In the case of gender-based asylum, since gender is *not* a fixed category, asylum advocates and asylum adjudicators are *already* stretching, strategizing, and playing with gender and what gender violence means in order to help clients *or* to restrict the entry of non-citizens.

How do we get better at understanding gender violence and offering better strategies for prevention and redress? I push for more effective, collaborative, intersectional feminist activism around gender violence. Much of feminist activism focuses either on very specific cases or very broadly on gender violence. However, my disaggregation of gender violence and rethinking of comparisons between types of violence should prompt feminist activists to think more carefully about how they categorize, connect, and separate out various types of violence *and* victims.

The worthy victim frame results in victim-blaming and moralizing about the choices that survivors of violence make. This is precisely what is going on when worthy victim classifications emerge, when survivors of violence are expected to react and even *be* in certain ways, and when their experiences are used in the service of political agendas. Feminist and queer activists, many of whom are survivors of violence, and feminist and queer scholars have historically participated in challenging the appropriation of victims' stories. At the same time, they/we too are complicit with speaking *for* survivors of violence. With a framework, discussed in chapter 1, that politicizes not only gender violence but also the *responses* to gender violence, we are better able to ask ourselves about the political choices we make when we theorize about the victims and survivors of gender violence.

For example, in research or activism, how are victims/survivors of violence constructed? How do we construct ourselves in relationship with

how we talk about victims? How do representations of victims change if those participating in activism or research are also survivors of violence? But in challenging the problematic victim frames, I want to go further than offering self-reflexive critique. I also call for political work in changing and shifting legal and political concepts that underpin problematic understandings of and responses to gender violence. The legal and juridical categories can make a difference in how asylum seekers are treated but also in the accepted discourses that find traction in how a variety of political players aid or address survivors of violence. *In other words, I want to change the discursive climate from which the worthy victim frames emerge.* Challenging the discursive climate will also be crucial for rethinking how undocumented immigrants are thought of as perpetually unworthy.

CHALLENGING THE AUTONOMOUS WORTHY VICTIM FRAME: RETHINKING THE FAMILY

I first suggest that feminists make a discursive intervention in the construction of families. I then explore two specific reforms regarding the use of information about family members in asylum cases and the expansion of the legal definition of family in immigration law. Doing so can disrupt the bad family-weak state frame.

Recall from chapter 3 the construction of families as "bad" in the context of family violence cases. I also discussed in that chapter how anti-FGC legislation pivots on the perception that immigrant families might "bring over" harmful "cultural" traditions.

Now contrast that picture of the family with US immigration policy's emphasis on "family ties" and "family reunification." Immigration related to family ties, through spouses, partners, and children, is the largest percentage of legal admissions into the United States. The family reunification stance is focused on the presumption that migrants who are a part of stable, unified families are allegedly less likely to commit crimes, and more likely to be economically productive, to assimilate, and to be self-sufficient.[19] One way to reconcile this apparent difference in the construction of families of asylum seekers and of undocumented immigrants is to think about how the "bad" family from which the asylum seeker allegedly flees is in a "weak state." But the immigrant family is ostensibly now located in a "strong" state that has mechanisms for implementing "law and order."

Thus, non-citizens are constructed via their relationships with family members. Feminist IR and transnational scholars studying the pernicious

effects when gender violence "crosses" borders (per the discussion in chapter 1) should retheorize the "family" so as to rethink conceptualizations of gender violence. First, how do expectations of heteronormative families underlie gender violence? Gayatri Spivak notes:

> Reproductive heteronormativity simply means that it is normal to be heterosexual and to reproduce, and it is in terms of that norm that society is made: legal structures, religious structures, affective structures, residential structures, everything. It may be displaced into that corner, this corner, and so on, but it is a very tough perennial. It is not something that will go away. It will never go away because that is what writes (and rights) being human.[20]

The centrality of a particular kind of family underscores ideas discussed thus far in this book about how families should behave, how women should want to get married and have children, and how sexual minorities should become "normalized" by desiring nuclear families. Those gendered expectations of the construction of family play a role in experiences of *and* understandings of violence. An understanding of this thread running through different types of gender violence cases will prompt, in turn, an interrogation of how feminists think about the family.

Second, how do feminists differentially categorize families? Recall the discussion at the end of chapter 3 about different types of family violence, inclusive of "honor killings." Why do feminists participate in labeling some forms of family violence as examples of *culturally* motivated harm? For example, Abu-Lughod questions whether honor killings are really a distinct crime, clearly distinguishable from domestic violence; she is puzzled by why feminists and the United Nations insist not only on this separate category but also on stating that the rates of honor killings are dramatically increasing.[21] As she notes, even if we decide to call family violence in *some* places honor killings, it is hard to come by evidence as to whether it is prevalent or increasing because of the problems in reporting and classifying this violence.[22] Yet it is feminist and human rights advocates who participate in pitting individual women against their menacing *religious* or *traditional* families. They highlight patriarchal family violence in immigrant communities in Western countries, non-Western countries in general, or communities coded as backward (such as rural ones) within non-Western countries, and diminish the prevalence of such violence in Western countries.[23]

As Gill notes, is not any type of family violence perhaps a reaction to feeling "dishonored"?[24] Abu-Lughod comments that people everywhere "fail to live up to moral ideals; betrayal, anger, and hurt prevail.

Everywhere, it seems some fathers are violent, some brothers commit incest, there are men who kill their wives and lovers on suspicion, and families and marriages can be dysfunctional and abusive."[25] A focus on the *construction* of the "autonomous individual" fleeing "bad families" can reveal how doing so "devalues not just women's but men's human experiences of dependency and relationship."[26] While us-them tropes often hold on for dear life, renewing how we think about families can shake up the old controversial debates. In other words, to challenge the racialization of gender violence requires examining the taken-for-granted centrality of the family as the primary vehicle of propagating barbaric cultures.

With this call for theoretical attention to the construction of the family, what are some pragmatic strategies forward? First, recalling my concerns in chapter 3, I offer a rethinking of autonomy, such that it is understood not only as atomistic individual actions separate from others but as one's choices about connection with others. I thus privilege knowledge claims about family structures as multifaceted and complex. Asylum seekers need to prove when the perpetrator is not the government that the violence is "supported by the legal system or social norms in the country in question" and "reflects a prevalent belief within society, or within relevant segments of society."[27] It is possible, for example, to show that some members of the family reinforce certain dominant interpretations of how women are to be treated. At the same time, an asylum seeker's story could include examples of how other members of the family and other relevant people in the person's life challenge or disagree with the dominant gender norms and thus support the asylum seeker's decision to leave. This attention to complexity in describing families already happens in practice, but I contend that there should be a more deliberate, explicit attempt to redefine and reframe autonomy. The asylum seeker's autonomy should be illustrated by *both* the decision to leave and reject abusive and violent treatment and *also the decision to form and maintain other relationships with supportive family, kin, friends, and community members.*

Approaching autonomy in this way allows nuance. Thus family members who are supportive are not "extraordinary" or anomalies but rather offer challenges to dominant norms. Also, there would be less pressure to reject families because it is the family members who would be crucial in testifying to other family members' violence. In their analysis of proving asylum credibility, Bohmer and Shuman note that relatives and other "associates" of asylum seekers can provide important and essential information about persecutory experiences.[28] Such a tactic would make more sense in the context of expanding the understanding of family and networks of support and care.

Second, in considering the experiences of non-citizens in general, it is important to reimagine what counts as a family in the law. Some political actors are slowly recognizing the "family" beyond blood and marital ties, noting "alternative relationships of care" that are equally socially meaningful.[29] For example, in 2001, the Law Commission of Canada published "Beyond Conjugality: Recognizing and Supporting Close Personal Adult Relationships," with Canadians participating in online forums with their thoughts on the state's treatment of various types of relationships.[30] The commission took a stand that "autonomy" meant the ability to develop personal relationships.[31]

It also argued that as family reunification is a primary goal of immigration, then "family" has to be reinterpreted as "deeply rooted relationships of interdependence," allowing for non-citizens to say "who is the most important to them, and who is part of what they consider family in the broadest sense."[32] The Canadian government has not integrated the commission's findings, but I find the 2001 report an intriguing model of inquiry and examination. Tasmania, Australia, Alberta, Canada, and the state of Hawaii have also experimented with different models of family and relationships in the law.

Some legal scholars have also suggested that the US immigration system's overhaul should include a different definition of family, beyond just biology but also inclusive of "function."[33] In other words, we should examine the roles various people play in a person's life. Legal scholars, for example, explain that the Immigration and Naturalization Act does not explicitly define family but that in practice immigration officials assume an exclusionary heteronormative definition. Thus, through amendment, a common congressional method for adding or changing certain words in sections of the act, there could be an expansion of the definition of family to include a variety of interpersonal relationships.[34]

Many immigrant rights activists see the right to family life as an integral part of immigration rights advocacy for same-sex couples. But other activists express concerns about the requirements of assimilating to certain expectations of gender conformity, particularly "U.S. ideals of family and domesticity,"[35] if they wish to become citizens or legal residents. Queer immigrant rights groups and scholars writing about queer migrants challenge how family reunification/family unity, particularly the heteronormative family unit, is prioritized in US immigration policy. Those who do not fit or desire that model will lose out in terms of both avoiding deportation or detention and receiving support from advocacy networks and lawyers.[36] What about people who do not have the resources to support a non-citizen partner? Those who choose to be single or are not

in relationships? Those in relationships who do not want to subscribe to particular family configurations? Those rejected by some of their family members because they are queer? Queer immigrant rights advocates also highlight that HIV-positive undocumented immigrants without families often fall through the cracks.[37]

Rethinking the definition of family, particularly in the context of the right to family life, can be useful in mobilizing support for non-citizens in fear of deportation and policing. For example, Das Gupta describes how the "family" is a powerful "political subject" used by immigration advocates.[38] She shows how the New York based Families for Freedom supports immigrant men with criminal convictions particularly by framing them as caregivers, thus challenging the idea that only female migrants are caregivers, or that only those without criminal convictions have or are deserving of socially meaningful lives. This organization thinks about family as including anyone who is "impacted [by] or wants to help a loved one" and resists distinctions drawn between "good" law-abiding immigrants and "the criminals."[39]

This strategy of recasting "criminal" immigrants as caring family members challenges the criminalization, detention, and deportation of men of color. For example, consider the Violence Against Women Act (VAWA) self-petition and U visa options discussed in chapter 2. The VAWA self-petition allows undocumented immigrants to independently request legal status without depending on an abusive partner who is a US citizen or legal permanent resident. Petitioners must be currently or previously married to their abusers. The U visa allows petitioners to seek immigration relief if they can prove being significantly affected by violence, are willing to cooperate with law enforcement to address the crime, and may have any kind of relationship with the perpetrator. As Gehi and Munshi point out, the VAWA option can strengthen state-based racial discrimination against and punishment of immigrant communities.[40] And Reuters reports that the requirement to cooperate with law enforcement agencies to receive the U visa only works when there is already a level of trust between the police and immigrant communities.[41] Thus, it makes sense that immigrant rights organizations are considering community-based alternatives to criminalization as a variety of family formations negotiate their responses to interpersonal and state violence.[42]

Feminist theorists have historically challenged and politicized the social construction of families.[43] I thus push for doing so in the context of comparative constructions of gender violence as well as of immigration and asylum politics. Accordingly, we should reconceptualize not just what counts as a family but also rethink autonomy in terms of connection.

CHALLENGING THE INNOCENT WORTHY VICTIM FRAME: ADDING A NEW CATEGORY OF VIOLENCE

I ended chapter 4 with a reflection on stretching the category of coercive reproductive practices to include forced pregnancy/maternity that would result from lack of access to abortion, among other factors. Doing so will not necessarily upend the innocent victim frame, but it could point out its cracks and contradictions. Think of the entire range of what reproductive justice comprises: the right to procreate; the right to have an abortion; access to prenatal, maternal, and postnatal comprehensive healthcare; the right to make choices about how to prevent pregnancy; the right to safe sex education and prophylactics; access to support for those who have suffered infertility, forced pregnancy or forced/coercive abortion, and miscarriages.[44] Yet Congress only saw fit to protect asylum seekers fleeing coercive sterilization/abortion. Despite the influence of pro-life lobbies and the usefulness of the innocence frame in US politics, I contend it is possible to create a new category of violence. In order to add this category, I suggest first feminist IR intervention in how forced pregnancy is theorized. I also suggest specific reforms for immigration and asylum advocates to link rape to pregnancy in the context of persecution, and to frame the prevention of abortion as a gendered harm.

First, feminists can challenge how the discussion of pregnancy due to rape in international law focuses more on what that pregnancy symbolically represents about "ethnic" conflict than on the persecutory effects on the woman when she is prevented from making a choice about her pregnancy. Various United Nations documents, including the 1993 Vienna Declaration and Programme of Action, the 1995 Beijing Platform for Action, and other United Nations documents mention forced pregnancy as a human rights violation. But the Rome Statute that created the International Criminal Court (ICC) and entered into force in 2002 framed forced pregnancy primarily as an issue of the targeting of ethnic groups. Article 7(2) of the ICC statute defines forced pregnancy as "unlawful confinement of a woman forcibly made pregnant with the intent of affecting ethnic composition of any population or carrying out other grave violations of international law."

The Rome Statute defines genocide, war crimes, and crimes against humanity. Genocide differs from the other two crimes because of the requirement to show intent to destroy a particular group.[45] But forced pregnancy is the "only sexual crime provision within the Rome Statute that requires specific intent."[46] Forced pregnancy is considered to be an example of a war crime or a crime against humanity, but prosecutors

must establish intent even though general war crimes and crimes against humanity do not require intent to be proven.[47] As Drake illustrates, prosecuting forced pregnancy is difficult in terms of the requirements of international criminal law.[48] She shows how it is easier, relatively speaking, to prosecute rape as a crime against humanity and as a war crime in the ICC than it is to prosecute forced pregnancy.

Why is this the case? The focus on intent understandably stems from the reactions of the international community and human rights advocates to the specific kinds of forced pregnancy crimes that occurred in Rwanda and the former Yugoslavia. In Rwanda, 250,000–500,000 women were raped; [49] while the numbers were reported to not be as high in the former Yugoslavia (20,000–50,000),[50] the women who became pregnant as a result were pressured or actually forced to carry pregnancies to term. The International Criminal Tribunal for Rwanda, in *Prosecutor v. Akayesu* (1998), claimed that "deliberate impregnation" could constitute intent to "prevent births within the group" per the United Nations Convention for the Prevention and Punishment of the Crime of Genocide.[51] Forced pregnancy was discussed in the Serb leader Radovan Karadzic's case at the International Criminal Tribunal for the Former Yugoslavia. The Trial Chamber noted, "Some camps were specially devoted to rape, with the aim of forcing birth of Serbian offspring, the women often being interned until it was too late to undergo an abortion."[52] In the United States, the Alien Tort Statute was used to sue Karadzic. In *Kadic v. Karadzic,* a description of his crimes included "murder, rape, *forced impregnation*, and other forms of torture."[53] The case's amici curiae brief specifically mentioned forced pregnancy/maternity as a strategy to "destroy the ethnicity of the Bosnian-Muslim population."[54]

Forced pregnancy was a sticking point for the participants in the 1998 diplomatic conference that created the framework for the ICC. In an attempt to assuage concerns that mentioning forced pregnancy would imply or explicitly address access to abortion, Delegate Hamdan of Lebanon phrased forced pregnancy in the context of intent to alter ethnic identity, so as to narrow the scope of women for whom abortions would be acceptable as an option.[55] Scholars have since debated how to successfully frame forced pregnancy as an act of genocide.[56]

But I call for increased attention to forced pregnancy as disentangled from the ethnic component. While pregnancy might be the intended result of rape, it might also be an *unintended* consequence of rape that *then* creates a persecutory and oppressive situation for rape victims. I am not arguing that gender and race/ethnicity should be treated separately, but that we should explore how and why gender and race/ethnicity

become intertwined in ways that downplay women's experiences of sexual violence.

Not all cases of sexual violence that could result in pregnancy have an ethnic component to them. Accordingly, rape is not *only* a method of ethnic cleansing, genocide, or destruction of an ethnic/racial group. Rape is also strategically used in the context of socioeconomic turmoil, during wartime and peacetime, as a way to punish transgressions of gender norms, or as a way to reinforce patriarchal practices that shame women who are raped or, even worse, impregnated—physical proof that she is no longer "pure." For example, while there is a lot of attention to sexual violence in the Democratic Republic of Congo, the sexual violence is not because of politicized "ethnic" or "racial" identities but rather because of the interplay of masculinity, class, and militarization.[57] Out of the 1.8 million rapes in DRC, if 5% result in pregnancy, there could potentially be 90,000 rape-related pregnancies.[58] Out of these pregnancies, a significant number could be forced if they are unwanted and women do not have access to abortions due to the US policies explained in chapter 4. But the predominant focus on rape-caused pregnancy in the context of ethnicity restricts exploration of this form of persecution. So since international legal understandings can impact asylum cases, it is important for feminists to rethink how rape-caused pregnancy is discussed.

Feminist IR scholars have a place in the discussion of a new category of violence, given their involvement in the classifications of violence and in the developments in international law on gender crimes. They/we should also continuously situate the idea of reproductive justice as a matter of asking why *this* crime but not *that* crime is addressed. For example, US legislative concern about some countries' coercive reproductive policies has effectively elided the US history of forced sterilization.[59] Estimates are that about 60,000 people, including racial minorities, poor people, and those deemed "unfit" to parent, were sterilized in the United States because of state eugenics programs between 1907 and 1980.[60] Asking about the discursive climate from which a worthy victim frame emerged allows us to crack open the categorization of violence, to uncover who counts as a victim worthy of concern.

I now turn to two specific ways for immigration and asylum advocates to think about forced pregnancy/maternity. *First*, rape and sexual assault are increasingly framed as persecution in asylum law. However, asylum advocates have not explicitly and consistently linked rape to potential pregnancy. It is possible that this is because there has not yet been an asylum case about rape resulting in pregnancy, or asylum seekers do not want to reveal this information. There is anecdotal evidence that judges

respond particularly strongly to stories about women who have experienced emotional trauma they suffered *as* mothers or because of being denied the opportunity to be a mother (due to coercive sterilization and abortion). So too judges seem to respond to descriptions of rape that involve consequences *related* to reproduction, that is, women who have been so severely injured that they can no longer get pregnant or bear children.[61] *This* is the loss to which many judges react: the loss of opportunity to be a "good mother," not the loss experienced due to sexual violence or inability to get an abortion.

But it is still worth raising the issue of abortion to at least name whose experiences are mourned and whose are ignored. Asylum advocates should consider discussing forced pregnancy as a potential consequence of rape given that asylum law *encourages* the description of the *effects* of persecutory experiences in order to make a credible case. For example, in cases of female circumcision, the Center for Gender and Refugee Studies advises lawyers to document their clients' experiences of the "lingering effects of persecution" such as "pain during sex, inability to enjoy sex, complications during childbirth, psychological problems."[62] In addition to describing the emotional, physical, and psychological trauma of rape, advocates might consider cataloging "effects," such as the trauma and medical complications associated with forced pregnancy, forced maternity, and forced delivery, and the potential, subsequent inability to bond with one's child. Even if pregnancy does not happen to every woman who is raped, the *possibility* should be considered in discussing the possible consequences of rape. *Future fear* of persecution is also a plausible approach for asylum seekers. Might there be social groups of "women from eastern Congo who are fearful of forced impregnation due to rape," or "women who come from a society that places a stigma on bearing children out of wedlock, particularly after rape"?

The *second* important strategy is to take access to abortion seriously, particularly in the context of rape. Despite the awareness of rape in conflict situations, discussions about reproductive rights are limited to the issues of contraceptive use and maternal health. The academic and practitioner literature on sexual violence focuses on the causes of sexual violence in the context of political and economic conditions in various countries,[63] maternal care for rape victims,[64] or healing centers to help women bond with their children produced from rape.[65] The US State Department reports on various countries explicitly discuss sexual and gender-based violence but mention only the following in the reproductive rights section: number, spacing and timing of children; access to contraceptives; prenatal and maternal care.[66] The few comments I found on trauma related to forced

pregnancy due to rape, and the need to have access to *comprehensive* health services, was mentioned by the Global Justice Center (GJC-discussed in Chapter Four) and affiliated organizations.[67]

I suspect, particularly based on conversations with GJC staff, that the lack of discussion about abortion might very well be due to the censoring of abortion speech in US policy.[68] "Abortion" is absent in the discussions and publications by the International Committee of the Red Cross, the International Rescue Committee, the United Nations Population Fund, the United Nations Office of Humanitarian Affairs, and the Office of the Special Representative of the Secretary General on Sexual Violence in Conflict, all of which receive US federal funds. The GJC notes that there is silence among the very organizations that might otherwise partner with feminist and women's rights organizations concerned about rape resulting in pregnancy.

However, those not censored by the Helms gag, such as US-based asylum advocates and feminist scholars, can certainly pose a key question. If coercive sterilization/abortion is grounds for asylee status, as discussed in the previous chapter, why is forced pregnancy/maternity not? Framing the question in this way is crucial for asylum advocates if they are to convince governmental actors less susceptible to pro-life lobby pressure, such as the Board of Immigration Appeals, to consider forced impregnation as a ground of persecution because of denial of access to abortion.

One could also frame access to abortion in the context of medical treatment. "Coercive medical and psychological treatment" is considered a persecutory harm. As advocates for HIV-positive and transgender asylum seekers seeking access to medical procedures note, the *denial* of medical treatment could also be a *part* of a persecutory pattern.[69] Asylum judges usually do not consider denial of access to medical treatment as persecution. However, international law tribunals have found that failure to provide life-sustaining medical treatment can constitute persecution.

Whether because of a country's or the United States' policies, is denial of access to abortion contributive to fear? Is abortion potentially "life sustaining"? I contend the answer to both questions is yes.

The pregnancy resulting from rape and a child resulting from rape are physical manifestations and "proof" of rape, and can thus result in persecution of both the woman and the child.[70] Many scholars are focusing on what happens to *children* born due to wartime rape.[71] But one can argue that because women are not able to get abortions, they are forced to be pregnant and thus face danger to their lives, not only in terms of possibility of death or injury in high-risk pregnancies and traumatic deliveries, but also in terms of targeted attacks. The GJC notes that forcing women

to carry unwanted pregnancies to term can constitute a form of torture and can also be life-threatening, considering that unsafe abortion, along with hemorrhage and sepsis due to childbirth, is one of the leading three causes of maternal mortality.[72] Indeed, the United Nations Millennium Development Goal to address maternal mortality cannot be met without taking seriously the issue of access to safe abortions.[73]

In sum, these strategies are inspired by the desire to challenge the innocent victim frame when it comes to coercive reproductive practices. The creation of a new category of persecution could have reverberating effects in how feminists understand gender violence, particularly by linking crimes around consent to sex with crimes regarding reproductive rights. Access to abortion should not be limited to cases of rape. At stake in this discussion is the basic right to access an abortion; as discussed in chapter 4, preventing access to exercise choice over one's body and to appropriate medical treatment is persecutory.

I recommend coupling the strategies I suggest here with those that address reproductive rights of immigrant women in the United States. The US-based Public Education Project, a reproductive justice organization, notes that detained immigrant women, whether asylum seekers or those without asylum claims, are routinely denied access to abortion.[74] While Immigration and Customs Enforcement technically grants access to abortion in "emergency situations," in reality women are unlikely to be able to seek the services of local abortion providers. In one case, a woman who was raped during her journey into the United States was repeatedly denied her requests for an abortion; she was deported while ten weeks pregnant and had to pay for an illegal abortion in her home country of Honduras.[75] Walden argues that non-citizens, particularly those held in detention facilities, have the constitutional right to access abortion.[76] This is why Planned Parenthood and other US-based women's rights organizations mobilize around the need to include access to reproductive healthcare, including access to safe abortions, in US immigration reform.[77] The Center for Reproductive Rights, in a supplemental document for the 2013 United Nations review of US compliance with the International Covenant on Civil and Political Rights, noted US deficiencies in upholding the human rights of pregnant women in detention and immigrant women seeking affordable abortions.[78] To fundamentally challenge the innocence frame requires a comprehensive focus on reproductive justice for non-citizens.

In terms of shifting the innocence discourse around trafficking, recall that I discussed how smuggled migrants and sex workers are left out of the worthy victim frame. Various scholars have offered suggestions for

breaking down the "innocence" trope. Examples include decoupling T visa grants from the prosecutorial process; eliminating the preference for trafficked victims that are rescued over victims who escaped; and, using civil remedy tools such as civil suits and torts claims by trafficked victims against traffickers that focus on economic restitution for survivors.[79] Others call for re-examining violence committed against smuggled migrants and exploited migrant workers, so as to be more explicitly attentive to the racialized and gendered violence undocumented immigrants face.[80] I suggest an additional route, *one that addresses how both sex workers and sexual minorities are treated as immoral.*

RETHINKING THE NON-DEVIANT WORTHY VICTIM: CHALLENGING THE CONCEPT OF MORAL TURPITUDE

In this section, I consider feminist interventions in the idea of deviance and reforms in legal codes of moral turpitude. When I started to research moral turpitude, discussed in chapter 5, I discovered this legal concept's roots in early 19th-century racialized and gendered norms.[81] African Americans and indigenous Americans in general, white men who committed fraud, and female prostitutes were considered to have less "credibility" in legal settings because of their presumed, inherent "deviance." Indeed, these "morally bankrupt" people were apparently even more suspect than people who committed violence. These "honor codes" have had a remarkable hold on how the US legal and criminal justice systems operate, playing a role as well in immigration and asylum decisions. These codes explain why sex workers are not considered to be "innocent" in the genealogy of US legal thought, and why sexual minorities are considered to be deviant.[82]

Moral turpitude as a legal concept has received remarkably little scholarly attention; as the scholars who do study it point out, legislators and judges demonstrate great reluctance in challenging or addressing what exactly comprises moral turpitude.[83] Moral turpitude generally and vaguely indicates "vileness," "baseness," and "depravity."[84] But the classification of the crimes can change over the years depending on shifts in hegemonic ideas about what constitutes morality.[85]

In 1875, the United States passed legislation to exclude convicts and prostitutes as inadmissible aliens. Crimes Involving Moral Turpitudes were introduced in 1891 in a federal immigration statute. Then, the Immigration Act of 1917 outlined the following categories of inadmissible aliens:

> All idiots, imbeciles, feeble-minded persons, epileptics, insane persons; persons who have had one or more attacks of insanity at any time previously persons of constitutional psychopathic inferiority; persons with chronic alcoholism; paupers . . . persons afflicted with tuberculosis in any form or with a loathsome or dangerous contagious disease; . . . persons who have been convicted of or admit having committed a felony or other crime or misdemeanor involving moral turpitude; . . . prostitutes, or persons coming into the United States for the purpose of prostitution or any other immoral purpose.[86]

As noted in chapter 5, sexual minorities were historically included in legal references to mental illness/psychopathy. Notice the explicit inclusion of sex workers. Also recall the discussion in chapter 2 that immigration legislation in 1996 expanded the types of crimes, inclusive of turpitude, that could constitute deportable offenses. But even the lawmakers responsible for this legislation were confused about what exactly constituted a crime of moral turpitude.[87] Crimes of "economic survival," such as shoplifting and prostitution, are deportable offenses. But there is still no statutory definition as such, with Congress giving power to the judicial system to decide which crimes count.[88]

Walsh, Eckhardt, and Russell suggest that linking sexual behavior and dishonesty only further marginalizes people who participate in prostitution or who are sexual minorities.[89] In their analysis of the Supreme Court case *Lawrence v. Texas,* which concluded that sodomy did not constitute turpitude, these authors found that both the Supreme Court justices and those who filed amicus briefs relied upon historical ideas about the link between morality and sexual acts. For example, some of the briefs submitted argued that the government *does* have the right to control and police "morality."[90] The justices decided to rule based on due process grounds (meaning that consensual sex counts as one of the liberties protected under substantive due process in the Fourteenth Amendment). The arguably more pertinent equal protection grounds, also under the Fourteenth Amendment, would have been a much clearer indictment of sodomy laws as "sex discrimination based on gender role stereotypes."[91]

The authors also note that the greater criminalization of prostitutes than of clients reveals a need to control "dangerous sexuality," associated with a breaking apart of families and a "decline" in "morals [and] national pride."[92] Thus, even with feminist victories regarding the rights of women to control their own bodies, moral turpitude laws "articulate that a woman's choice in or number of sexual partners bears on her fitness as a citizen, or on her truthfulness."[93] Even with attitudinal changes and apparent victories regarding discrimination against sex workers and

sexual minorities, the policing of morality continues because of the ambiguity and holding power of the moral turpitude concept. Unfortunately, turpitude law is "virtually invisible to the general public."[94]

In sum, at the root of "innocent" and "non-deviant" worthy victim frames is the moral panic about the wrong kind of immigrant, the wrong kind of citizen *and* non-citizen, having an influence on American society. Challenging these fear-based ideas may seem like a herculean task. But I suggest that starting with moral turpitude is a feasible way to challenge how asylum seekers and immigrants are classified as "good" and "bad" migrants.

Feminist postcolonial and feminist IR scholars have documented feminist resistance to gendered legal ethical codes,[95] so they are well suited to challenge the endurance of such a concept. In particular, they trace how morality is racialized, coded in ways to designate appropriate *sexual* behavior for "others" in particular.[96] The desire to name and punish immorality, then, is rooted in deep fears about how foreign strangeness will be brought "here."[97] Recall the information in chapter 4 about past or current prostitution rendering non-citizens "inadmissible." Early immigration laws in the late 1800s targeted prostitution in part because of fears of uncontrollable women entering the country but also to prevent Chinese women, who were *all* assumed to be prostitutes, from immigrating to the United States and to curb Chinese population growth and settlement.[98] Tracking the racial undercurrent of moral turpitude will require examining asylum cases, arrests of non-citizens, and the explanations provided for deportation proceedings. How is sexuality patrolled, and whose bodies are deemed "unfit" for entry and belonging?

By persistently and consistently linking the rights of non-citizens to challenges to the legal codes of moral turpitude, the role of anachronistic honor codes can be subverted. This may seem like an abstract suggestion, but immigration rights advocates are already doing it. The Immigration Defense Project worked with other immigration advocacy organizations to successfully build a legal challenge to the decision in the *Matter of Silva-Trevino*, which expanded the ways non-citizens could be charged with moral turpitude.[99] As a result of amici curiae briefs, many of the federal circuit courts rejected the case's legal reasoning, which would have allowed unprecedented inquiry into evaluating crimes of moral turpitude, rather than relying on the legal proceedings alone. Critical Resistance, an organization dedicated to abolishing prisons, creates fact sheets about challenging immigration policies, explicitly providing tools for naming and challenging ideas about moral turpitude, even naming specific cases when moral turpitude was used against undocumented workers.[100] I also

take cues from queer immigrant rights movements, which have been calling more attention to the idea of moralistic exclusion that affects both sexual minorities and immigrants, and also more broadly anyone who does not conform to ideals of "good citizenship."[101] The Queer Migration Research Network,[102] a forum for discussing the kinds of issues raised in this section and in chapter 5, Lambda Legal,[103] a US-based organization that addresses the civil rights of sexual minorities, and Karma Chávez's work on coalition building between and within immigrant, queer, and queer immigrant communities, all serve as a point of entry for dismantling the dangerous effects of moral turpitude.

Sex worker rights groups have also challenged the concept of moral turpitude. Sex workers have been organizing to address their rights, particularly in the context of the anti-prostitution, anti-trafficking legislation discussed in chapter 4. It was not until 2011 that the United States officially stated that it has an obligation to protect sex workers' human rights. The event that catalyzed this recognition was the United Nations Human Rights Council Periodic Review of the human rights record of the United States in 2010. As US-based and transnational organizations and activists created reports to contribute to the process, sex worker advocates helped to draft the first statement about the human rights of sex workers in the United States.[104] Two US activists flew to Switzerland for the United Nations meeting to discuss the issue; they also met with representatives from Uruguay, the country that specifically recommended addressing sex worker rights. The Working Group Report recommended that the United States engage in awareness-raising campaigns to challenge stereotypes and violence against LGBT communities, ensure access to services for sex workers, and address discrimination based on sexual orientation and gender identity.[105]

As activists waited for the US response to the extensive report on various human rights issues, sex worker advocates mobilized to raise awareness among federal and government officials about the recommendations and how to think about sex worker rights outside of the paradigm of criminalization. Finally, in 2011, the US State Department accepted these recommendations and noted: "We agree that no one should face discrimination in access to public services or violence based on sexual orientation or their status as a person in prostitution."[106] The grouping together of sex workers and LGBTQ communities is particularly interesting and strategic, given that both are targeted by moral turpitude laws.

But sex workers continue to face discrimination, criminalization, and violence. Human Rights Watch interviewed over 300 sex workers in the United States as well as sex worker advocates, lawyers, and police

officers.[107] It also included in its research violence against transgender individuals participating in or presumed to participate in sex work. As a result, Human Rights Watch recommended that the United Nations

> Call upon the United States to ensure that police and prosecutors cease using condoms as evidence of prostitution and related offenses; Call upon the United States to reform or repeal overly broad loitering statutes that invite discrimination and punishment based on identity or status rather than criminal behavior; Call upon the United States to protect the human rights of sex workers, transgender persons, and LGBT youth by police, both in and out of police custody.[108]

These recommendations directly confront moral turpitude codes. Sex worker advocates believe that the State Department response is a starting point to collectively address sex worker rights, immigrant rights, workers' rights, and discrimination against LGBTQ communities who engage, or are perceived to engage, in sex work. Increasingly, it will be possible to hold the United States accountable to its statement, with a potentially reverberating effect in asylum and immigration cases with sex workers and sexual minorities.

CONCLUSIONS

The task ahead is collaborative work between asylum lawyers/advocates and feminist scholars. Lawyers are on the front lines of witnessing how distinctions about migrants play out in the daily lives of their clients. Lawyers participate in perpetuating, challenging, rethinking, and transforming the worthy victim frames discussed in this book. Many asylum lawyers are unfortunately incompetent, fraudulent, or exploitative.

But other lawyers and their translators, paralegals, and interns perform legal acrobatics to negotiate the difficult line between the need to win the asylum case, and the desire to understand the complexities of country conditions or the nuances of gender persecution. These lawyers figure out ways to honor their clients' humanity and integrity, to convey the anguish of people who still love their countries but feel they have no choice left except to seek a new home. These lawyers visit their asylum clients in immigration detention centers. These lawyers try to track down clients who have "disappeared" into the general population out of fear, understanding that sometimes some people might be better off living

under the radar than exposing themselves to the possibility of deportation if they go through the asylum process.

Academics also have a role in engaging with these practitioners, particularly as "experts" in creating and circulating knowledge claims that asylum decision-makers often rely upon in making their decisions. As long as there are inconsistent and recalcitrant understandings by judges about violence and what survivors of such violence should or should not do, advocacy networks and scholars have to persistently politicize, challenge, and address the information and "knowledge" that is used by asylum decision-makers. Such "knowledge" might come in the form of an article, an expert affidavit, or in discursively and strategically challenging the worthy victim frames as suggested above.

Those involved in the asylum process are complicit with, but also potentially transformative agents in, immigration discourses. We can engage in critical analysis of the worthy victim frames without denouncing the life-altering decisions asylum seekers make when representing their stories and communities. More importantly, asylees and undocumented immigrants involved in advocacy around these issues are taking the lead in challenging discursive climates. This chapter suggests possible paths for intervention in changing dominant understandings relevant in asylum claims and in the lives of undocumented immigrants. These steps can engender a challenge to the good migrant / bad migrant distinctions among asylum seekers and between asylum seekers and undocumented migrants by persistently confronting the gendered and racialized construction of worthiness.

CHAPTER 7
Conclusions

Rather than summarize my arguments, I offer an imagined "Question and Answer" session. First, in the spirit of continued collaboration, dialogue, and conversation, this format allows me to engage with skeptical readers. Second, it allows me to present the arguments in a way that is more accessible for audiences outside of academia.

IS GENDER-BASED ASYLUM ONLY FOR WOMEN AND/OR SEXUAL MINORITIES?

Gender-based violence is usually understood and categorized as harms that occur predominantly to women and sexual minorities. In the analyses I read about gender-based asylum, I found a tendency to see gender-based asylum as a special category reserved for those whose experiences would not be seen as a "prototypical" case of political persecution, where state actors actively target politically active male citizens. Domestic violence and female genital cutting are constructed as private/"cultural" violence, with the state *failing* to act. In the cases of trafficking and coercive sterilization/abortion, when perpetrators are identified as *political* players, such as trafficking networks supported or condoned by the state, or countries such as China with coercive reproductive policies, the victims are seen as helpless rather than as political dissidents. Even in the case of coercive sterilization/abortion, where Congress notes that asylum seekers may oppose Chinese policies and thus be persecuted because of *political opinion*, the analysis in chapter 4 reveals the importance of expectations of feminized, heteronormative innocence. Straight men do apply

for gender-based asylum when they express fear of persecution due to coercive sterilization, but they do so in the context of marriage, with the harm being interpreted as an attack on the institution of marriage and the ability of heterosexual couples to plan families. In the case of persecution based on non-conforming sexual orientation and gender identity, even when state persecutory laws are named, asylum adjudicators expect sexual minorities to prove that they are not deviant. In all these cases, the offensive laws and practices aim to control the bodies of women and sexual minorities, but victims of gender-based violence are not assumed to be politically persecuted.

Accordingly, it makes sense that asylum lawyers and advocates would presume that straight cismen would not *need* to apply for gender-based asylum because they are seen as the prototypical asylum seekers. Straight cismen are most likely to be constructed as "heroic" refugees escaping persecution due to their courageous political stances; they are not constructed as victims of *gender* violence. However, some scholars point out that the asylum process hurts men as well. Recall in chapter 2 Gerard's point that constructions of vulnerability as feminized can work in the favor of female asylum seekers. In addition, as Bohmer and Shuman's work illustrates, straight cismen also suffer from problematic expectations of how credibility should be demonstrated.[1]

The answer to this question ultimately depends on how gender-related persecution is understood. What counts as gender persecution? Who counts as its victims? Who benefits from making a gender-based claim? The answer also depends on the politics of asylum lawyers and advocates. Some may believe that gender-based asylum is only for cisgendered women, as women are more likely than men to be disproportionately impacted and targeted by gendered patterns of violence. Some may argue that stretching gender-based asylum to persecution based on sexual orientation and gender identity, while gendered, may dilute concentrated efforts to provide options for straight, female asylum seekers. Yet others might see gender-based asylum as a viable option for any person who has experienced persecution that is gendered or due to gendered expectations.

I am in favor of casting a very wide net for those eligible to apply for gender-based asylum, as the proliferation of categories of gender-based violence can more inclusively address asylum seekers who might otherwise be ignored. For example, Steinke argues that men should be eligible for asylum when they face forms of family violence due to their sexuality or choices to transgress gendered norms.[2] Do the exigencies of immigration restriction demand that gender-based asylum be limited to very specific

kinds of violence, such as men perpetrating domestic violence against their female partners, that judges already have a hard time acknowledging as "real" persecution? Or does limiting gender-based asylum to women and sexual minorities potentially reinforce the marginalization of these asylum seekers? For example, does it perpetuate the idea that women and sexual minorities *only* experience gender-related violence and no other form of harm? These are questions worth debating, but I caution that we should be vigilant about how we categorize gender violence and its survivors. Indeed, one of the goals of this book is to politicize *how* we respond to gender violence.

ARE THE WORTHY VICTIM FRAMES RELEVANT IN ASYLUM CASES (IN GENERAL) THAT DO *NOT* FOCUS ON GENDER-RELATED PERSECUTION? ARE THE WORTHY VICTIM FRAMES RELEVANT IN THE CASES OF THE UNDOCUMENTED CHILDREN DISCUSSED IN THE FIRST LINES OF THE BOOK?

I sought to challenge and deconstruct the question "Who is worthy of protection?" by starting with gender-based asylum cases. This is because the lack of gender as a ground of persecution invites and requires interrogation of how gender violence is constructed. Digging deeper into how violence is understood creates space to explore the classification of victims. Feminist engagements with the construction of victimhood, particularly regarding survivors of gender violence, serve as an apt point of departure for connecting types of violence with typologies of victims.[3] Finally, as discussed in chapter two, the protection of women and sexual minorities carries a particular kind of political currency for countries to prove their superiority. In this context, gender-based asylum cases are the most appropriate starting point for interrogating how the United States decides who to protect and who to keep out.

But an understanding of how types of violence correlate with specific *kinds* of worthiness is useful for any asylum case. Future research could explore the differences between religious and racial persecution, for example, in constructions of the kind of victim that is seen as most credible. I remind the reader of the general problems with the creation of worthy victim frames, reiterated in table 7.1, which could be relevant in a variety of asylum cases. Table 7.1 shows the issues that worthy victim frames create for non-citizens, including asylum seekers and undocumented

Table 7.1 SUMMARY OF PROBLEMATIC EFFECTS OF THE WORTHY VICTIM FRAMES

Problems with worthy victim frames regarding experiences of non-citizens	Problems with worthy victim frames regarding distinctions between countries
Ignores experiences of asylum seekers whose stories do not "fit" into worthy victim frames.	Misses how gender violence is due to intersecting, global patterns, not just to problems in "worse" countries.
Denies agency to asylum seekers who are both critical of but also supportive of/connected to their countries/communities of origin.	Distinguishing between "better" and "worse" countries can negatively impact relationships between countries.
Asylum seekers incentivized to lie or misrepresent claims to fit into worthy victim frames.	Countries that believe they are "better" at handling human rights issues may try to control or influence countries perceived as "worse" at handling human rights issues.
Frames do not capture "noncultural" reasons violence occurs.	Distinctions between "better" and "worse" countries distract attention from human rights violations/problems committed by "better" countries.
Asylum seekers' stories disconnected from the experiences of undocumented immigrants, who also experience violence and have legitimate reasons for entering the United States.	"Better" countries may contribute to violent conditions in "worse" countries.

immigrants. It also illustrates problems with how worthy victim frames contribute to and strengthen perceived distinctions between "better" and "worse" countries.

Regarding the relevance of the frames for undocumented children, the value of my research on worthy victim frames is to remind us to look for gendered notions of worthiness in cases that *do not seem* to be about gender. Children may receive derivative asylum, or they can receive "Special Immigrant Juveniles Status." For Special Immigrant Juveniles Status, the state in which the child resides must determine that the child is a minor, has no parent or guardian, and would face abuse, neglect, or abandonment if reunited with the parent. The state must also find that being returned to his or her country would be against the child's interests; at this point, a US immigration court would consider the child's case. It is important that lawyers and judges ask whether the child might have experienced gender

violence. Indeed, the Center for Gender and Refugee Studies has issued "talking points" for lawyers, advocates, and researchers about women and girls in particular fleeing forms of sexual violence occurring in Guatemala, El Salvador, and Honduras.[4]

During a recent discussion with an asylum lawyer, she contended that rates of domestic violence and rape, particularly at the intersection of state power and gang violence, are so high that *any* girl fleeing from Honduras should be eligible for asylum.[5] Just as women fleeing certain countries can claim fear of forced female genital cutting only by referencing a social group based on their gender and tribal membership/ethnicity, so too, the argument goes, that girls fleeing Honduras could claim gender-based persecution simply by referencing a social group based on gender and nationality. If asylum lawyers attempt to develop this line of thinking, then the worthy victim frames analyzed in this book would be relevant for exploring which Hondurans actually get asylum.

In addition, human rights advocates note that the congressional reauthorization of the Trafficking Victims Protection Act in 2008 added provisions requiring that all unaccompanied "alien" children undergo screening procedures to see if they are victims of trafficking.[6] Here is an opportunity to explore the extent to which the "innocence" frame plays a role when assessing children's claims. Are gendered notions of innocence relevant in *all* cases of children?

Indeed, not all children are seen as automatically innocent, particularly if they participated in violence. This point is relevant in two Board of Immigration Appeals (BIA) decisions from February 2014. Asylum advocates are currently critiquing these two decisions because the BIA argued that the social visibility requirement for social group persecution cases is mandatory; this means that a particular persecuted group needs to have characteristics that are noticeably "visible" in society.[7] I discussed in chapter 2 how this creates a higher standard to meet for social group cases. But these cases are also about young men claiming persecution because they were resisting or had left membership in gangs. As momentum builds in critiquing the BIA's decisions, I want to privilege a focus on "worthy victims," and explore why and how understandings of masculinity shape judges' expectations of how gangs forcibly recruit and punish boys and young men in particular. In which cases are those boys seen as innocent; in which cases are they seen as violent and criminal? In sum, I find that there are several reasons the worthy victim frames are applicable and relevant in a variety of cases.

THIS BOOK SEEMS TO DEMONSTRATE THAT ASYLUM SEEKERS LIE OR MISREPRESENT THEMSELVES; IS IT NOT APPROPRIATE TO PROTECT THE UNITED STATES FROM FRAUDULENT MIGRANTS SEEKING TO ABUSE THE ASYLUM SYSTEM?

Yes, asylum seekers may craft their stories in particular ways that do not fully align with their experiences. Those suspicious of asylum seekers may assume that lying or exaggerating are indications of malicious intent. However, I contend that such acts reveal more about what the asylum system/process incentivizes. Gender is not a ground for persecution, and there is a tension between immigration restriction and human rights obligations. Both factors, by engendering unpredictable and arbitrary decision-making, contribute to the emergence and endurance of "worthy victim frames" that help to qualify which asylum seekers are "worthy" of protection. Such frames elicit attempts to prove worthiness, which may not match the veracity of the asylum seeker's experiences. Recall, for example, the discussion in chapter 3 about Mary Gachumi, who tried to make her story match Kassindja's precedent female genital cutting case. The fear and trauma asylum seekers face, as they try to figure out how to prevent deportation, can lead to desperate decisions. Recall also the example in chapter 4 about how lawyers advise Chinese non-citizens to take advantage of the coercive sterilization/abortion clause of the Illegal Immigration Reform and Immigrant Responsibility Act. Asylum seekers often use language and narratives given to them by their lawyers and advocates, who, in turn, are attempting to navigate the limitations of the asylum system. Asylum seekers are thus taking advantage not of US generosity but rather of *particular narratives* that actually exist because of *US political agendas* (such as desires to influence other countries, or the influence of the pro-life lobby). In the previous chapter, I discussed how to intervene in the discursive climates so as to challenge the problematic framings of gender violence that can indeed distort asylum seekers' stories.

IS THIS BOOK ARGUING THAT THE UNITED STATES SHOULD NOT CONTROL ITS BORDERS? DOESN'T THE UNITED STATES HAVE THE RIGHT TO DETERMINE WHO ENTERS THE COUNTRY?

The question is not as simple as whether the United States should or should not control its borders. As I discuss in chapter 2, the very concept of the border is made possible by the construction of an "outsider" that, in turn,

makes necessary state actions to protect itself. My intention with the discussion in this book is to shift the conversation from whether the United States should or can control its borders to how borders are drawn *through* US actions toward non-citizens. We should ask how countries identify threats and undesirable outsiders not simply as a way to shield themselves and their citizens from harm but rather to ensure state power and justification for actions taken to reinforce that power. In practice, these attempts to secure and control do not deter the migration of non citizens, and they make the journeys to cross into the country more violent. And, as also discussed in chapter 2, border control is wrapped up with the desire to protect; thus security issues cannot be disentangled from the politics of protection. The more appropriate starting point would be *how* the United States manages its borders and with what consequences.

THE DISTINCTIONS DRAWN BETWEEN "BETTER" AND "WORSE" COUNTRIES ARE NOT NECESSARILY PROBLEMATIC; WOULDN'T THE ASYLEES LIVING SAFELY IN THE UNITED STATES AGREE THAT THE UNITED STATES IS "BETTER"?

Arguably, asylum seekers, refugees, undocumented immigrants, and authorized immigrants demonstrate that the United States is a better country in which to live than others precisely through the choice to risk so much to migrate to the United States. For example, for the many persecuted sexual minorities who reside in the United States, it does indeed seem that they found safety, at least from the formerly threatening situation. In March 2013, the Williams Institute at the University of California–Los Angeles[8] released a report estimating that 267,000 of the 11 million undocumented immigrants living in the United States identify as a sexual minority.[9] The Center for American Progress explored these immigrants' origin countries, noting that about 80 countries criminalize LGBTQ people, with Iran, Mauritania, Saudi Arabia, Sudan, and Yemen punishing certain transgressions of gender conformity with death. The report also gives the example of lack of access in those countries to medical care for HIV-positive people.[10] Some of these persecuted individuals, the report mentions, seek countries with "safer and . . . more tolerant environments."[11] The United States, to many, fits that bill. While, as the report details, there are several measures the United States would need to take to improve the treatment of LGBTQ non-citizens, is the United States not "better" for sexual minorities than, say, Saudi Arabia?

Once again, I reframe the question. *Why* is one country "better" than another country; what caused the dynamics that pushed people out of their countries into another country? And how do those dynamics get translated into the social rankings of countries? How do the frames generated in the asylum process serve to reinforce US power relationships? Thus, even those committed to seeing the United States as "better" could learn about the factors that shape US global actions.

I am interested not only in why people would migrate to the United States or any other country, versus others, but also in why the act of migration contributes to the construction of countries in particular ways. Some countries are the "safe havens." Other countries are the rape capitals of the world, the rogue states, places of unimaginable horrors. Is it possible to advocate for the rights of asylum seekers and refugees *without* such hierarchies? There are consequences to social hierarchies, as discussed before; a focus on ranking impoverishes the study of human rights violations around the world. The hierarchies also distract us from the empirical realities that the United States is not consistently "better," as I discussed in the earlier chapters. As I explained, the United States does not adequately deal with domestic violence, excludes the experiences of sex workers and smuggled migrants who experience violence, contributes to oppressive conditions that prevent women from accessing the right to abortion, perpetuates homophobia and transphobia, and violates the rights of non-citizens through detention.

The United States being "better" for an asylee is dependent not on some inherent goodness of the country but rather on the unpredictable confluence of other factors. A grant of asylum depends on the presentation of a particular story, the capriciousness of asylum adjudicators whose decisions are rarely transparent or easy to understand, or the political expedience of protecting certain non-citizens. The experiences of asylum seekers *after/if* they receive asylum depends on the particular encounters and interactions with various governmental agencies, immigrant communities, and civil society.

I am concerned about the "absented" and "disappeared" migrants, whose stories *do not result* in US immigration relief. We can actually honor many migrants' enjoyment of asylum by revealing how their host states might see the very *next* asylum seeker or immigrant as undeserving of those same rights and desires. Their host state might deny services to a refugee; arbitrarily criminalize them; contribute to the situation that drove them out of their home country through foreign policies; or make their inclusion in the United States conditional. I see the following tasks as necessary: first, to rigorously question the asylum system; second, to

explore the fragile distinction between asylum seeker and undocumented immigrant; and third, to ask *why* the United States is seeking to protect the persecuted. Approaching asylum in this manner, rather than comparing countries as better or worse, is more productive in understanding state sovereign power and responsibility and the human rights of non-citizens.

WHAT ARE SPECIFIC CONTRIBUTIONS FEMINIST IR CAN MAKE TO ADDRESS THE HUMAN RIGHTS OF NON-CITIZENS?

As mentioned in chapter 3, Fauziya Kassindja, celebrated as an example of a successful gender-based asylum case, was detained upon her arrival in the United States. She was held in a maximum security prison in New Jersey, where she was shackled, placed in isolation, tear-gassed, and beaten.[12] But the outrage over "female genital mutilation" and the accompanying mobilization to end this practice effectively elided concerted *feminist* analysis of her detention experiences. Feminist IR scholars have specific insights that can help us think through a crucial human rights violation of non-citizens: detention.

States exercise their power not only through protection and/or restriction. They also do so by attempting to *manage* non-citizens. Going forward in a feminist IR analysis of immigration detention, in addition to drawing upon and engaging in scholarly conversations happening in other disciplines such as feminist geography, sociology, or criminal justice, I suggest feminists pay attention to issues raised by immigration rights advocates. The two main topics activists discuss can be summarized as the *dispersal of state power*, and *the scrutiny of non-citizens*.

First, immigration advocates present testimonies that explain how many immigrant encounters with policing and detention do not occur *only at the border*. This is because many undocumented immigrants and asylum seekers are already *part* of US society. They accidentally or intentionally overstay a visa. They realize after entering the country for a job or to join a family member that they qualify for asylum. They are in the process of adjustment to legal status but get caught selling marijuana or commit a crime of "moral turpitude." They grow up in the United States and do not become aware of their undocumented status until they try to apply for driver's licenses or college. They are trafficked into the country or enter as a sex worker and have been working at a brothel or as part of a prostitution ring for several months or years. They are already "inside."

To be sure, we do need to maintain a focus on what happens "at the border." Feminist scholars examine the effects of the fortification, hardening,

and militarization of the borders between the United States and Mexico, and the United States and Canada, on the people who cross those lines.[13] We learn from feminist IR in particular that the securitization of the state results in insecurity for some (increased number of rapes and deaths of undocumented immigrants crossing into the border), while allegedly providing security for others (some US citizens, the US state).[14]

But recall the earlier discussion in chapter 2 about the "dispersal" of state power, meaning the spreading out in multiples spaces the enactment of sovereign decision-making. The state exercises power in and through the diffusion of a multiplicity of detention facilities. Andrijasevic points out that the experiences of migrants cannot be reduced to being excluded, trapped, or detained "at the border"; much of immigrants' experiences occurs after they have crossed "literal" borders, forcing us to rethink borders as not a stark line between inside and outside but "diffused, dispersed and networked."[15] Immigration detention is not purely a story of being trapped "in between states," even though that is a significant part of being "in limbo."[16] Indeed, if one explores the "Detention Facility Locator" on the Immigration and Customs Enforcement (ICE)'s website, the Google maps show how far *into* the country the detained immigrants are being kept.[17]

Detention centers are also dispersed *outside* of national borders.[18] The United States increasingly uses "offshore" methods for preemptively detaining and apprehending undocumented immigrants, some of whom could potentially be asylum seekers. Examples of offshore detention include military bases and detention centers in other countries, such as in Central America and the Caribbean.[19] Further, in 1997 the Immigration and Naturalization Service, in response to President Clinton's directive to crack down on migrant smuggling in wake of the *Golden Venture* incident discussed in chapter 4, created 40 offices overseas with 150 US personnel to establish a permanent presence of US immigration officials around the world.[20] Feminist IR investigations of US carceral practices in Cuba, Iraq, and other places would be useful in exploring how the US warehouses and contains *potential* immigrants and asylum seekers.[21]

We can better understand the detention of immigrants by using feminist IR conceptual tools that illustrate all the different ways state sovereignty continually gets reproduced and authorized, particularly by blurring the distinction between inside/outside.[22] As international refugee policy and IR scholar Gil Loescher argues, there exist various state practices meant to decrease and manage the numbers of undocumented migrants:

> extending border controls through stringent visa requirements, imposing sanctions against airlines and other carriers for transporting undocumented

> individuals, stationing immigration officials abroad, detaining asylum seekers before they reach national borders, negotiating agreements to send home those refused asylum, and threatening to withdraw financial and development aid if regional host countries will not take back those asylum seekers rejected in the West.[23]

These actions entail a multiplying effect of state power.

Second, immigration advocates have mobilized on behalf of detained immigrants filing lawsuits about their mistreatment in correctional facilities. Detention centers regulate mobility by rendering the scary "unknown" immigrant into an overly scrutinized "known" entity as every single aspect of his or her life is monitored and managed. But at the same time, these detainees' whereabouts are concealed and hidden from public access.[24] These non-citizens are also continuously subject to transferal and dispersal.[25] In effect, detention exercises control over every aspect of detainees' lives but with little attention to their humaneness or rights.

Examples of the mistreatment of and violence against detained immigrants abound. Recall from chapter 5 Cristina Madrazo's story of being raped twice by her prison guard. Also, in 2011, 17 lesbian, gay, bisexual, transgender, and intersex asylum seekers and other migrants who had experienced abuse and violence in US immigration detention centers lodged a complaint with the US Department of Homeland Security's Office of Civil Rights and Civil Liberties. As a result, this office and Immigration and Customs Enforcement created the first dedicated protective custody immigration detention unit for gay, lesbian, and transgender migrants in Santa Ana City Jail, California. There are also various rules at other detention centers for keeping sexual minorities "segregated" from the rest of those jailed.[26] However, many advocates argue that segregation does not prevent attacks and violence and fails to address the issue of detention in the first place.

In March 2013, Americans for Immigrant Justice announced a lawsuit on behalf of four immigrant women claiming abusive treatment.[27] Various other criminal complaints detail the sexual violence at the hands of the nonimmigrant prison population, including sex offenders, or prison guards. Couples and entire families can end up in detention centers while attempting to address situations of domestic violence.[28] Pregnant detainees are shackled, sometimes even while giving birth, even though ICE claims that it never restrains pregnant women except under "truly extraordinary circumstances."[29] President Obama signed an omnibus spending bill that included a provision to ban the practice of shackling pregnant women by ICE, and states have been passing legislation to end

the practice as well. But immigration rights activists remain dubious about the future treatment of detainees, particularly in private institutions.

Given the litany of complaints and piecemeal but often unsuccessful attempts at reform, we must ask: what does detention accomplish?

> Jailing is a necessary element of our desire to sort the good from the bad. There can be no sorting without order and no order without control. In turn, government officials charged with watching and sorting 22 million people, the number of people in the United States who are not citizens and could be subject to removal for violating immigration laws, cannot control the sorting process without tightly holding the bodies of the potentially unfit.[30]

We have seen this all before. In the name of battling terrorism, gangs, and poverty, and creating law and order, the United States has increasingly relied on incarceration.[31] And Gottschalk reminds us that the 9/11 attacks were not the catalyst for a variety of draconian immigration detention practices, such as "secret detentions; physical abuse; closed court proceedings; denial of contact with family members, attorneys, and the media; notoriously arbitrary administrative reviews; . . . state resistance to habeas corpus reviews"; rather, the post 9/11 detention of immigrants has been a continuation of policies from the past 25 years.[32]

Feminist IR is appropriately situated to think through "tightly holding" of bodies precisely because it is so focused on what is done to bodies. Jindy Pettman notes that "it should be possible to write the body into a discipline that tracks power relations and practices which impact so directly and often so devastatingly on actual bodies."[33] Bodies are made to signify security by being included or excluded in violent ways, whereby people are forced to "embody different gendered ideas and ideals."[34] Feminist IR tools for finding out how bodies are treated should help theorize and address the multiple ways that the state tries to "know everything" about the bodies it deems threatening and confusing. But feminist IR can also track resistance and mobilization, particularly in testimonies, activism, lawsuits, and other actions *by* people who are tightly held and closely monitored.[35] *Their* entry point into politics is not just through the immigration/asylum system or because of the violence they suffered but also because they point out the fragility and futility of these states and systems in defining them.

In turn, we see the unraveling of the assumption that immigration detention is necessary to "keep out/control dangerous people." Detention and other punitive measures do not work in deterring immigration. They just make the journeys and experiences more likely to result in violations of civil and human rights.

In sum, feminist IR can give us another lens for thinking through how detention affects non-citizens. More broadly, feminist IR is both enriched by and critical for analyzing gender-based asylum, which ultimately is about the rights and experiences of non-citizens who claim to have suffered or fear suffering gender-related persecution. In this book, I have prioritized a focus on what state power, whether in the form of protection or restriction, does to people's bodies and their stories. Understanding better the experiences of asylum seekers specifically and undocumented immigrants more generally thus requires feminist inquiry. I return to Cynthia Enloe's remark that feminist IR is something that one *does*. Feminist IR analysis of gender-based asylum can invigorate asylum and immigration studies by compelling us to "think and re-think, to listen and re-listen, to explore and re-explore."[36]

NOTES

CHAPTER 1

1. Jana Winter, "Illegal Immigrant Kids Exposed Federal Agents to Lice, Scabies, Tuberculosis and Chicken Pox, Report Says," Fox News.com, August 1, 2014, accessed August 2, 2014, http://www.foxnews.com/politics/2014/08/01/unaccompanied-illegal-immigrant-kids-exposed-federal-agents-to-lice-scabies/.
2. Michelle Goldberg, "Yes, Mr. President, the Border Kids are Refugees," *Nation*, July 16, 2014, accessed August 2, 2014, http://www.thenation.com/article/180682/our-refugee-crisis.
3. In the summer of 2014, President Barack Obama vowed to "fast-track" the deportation of undocumented children. Rebecca Elliott and Jon Herskovitz, "Obama Vow to Speed Deportation of Children at Odds with Public Opinion," Reuters, August 11, 2014, accessed September 2, 2014, http://www.reuters.com/article/2014/08/11/us-usa-immigration-children-idUSKBN0GB0AJ20140811.
4. At the moment, the Obama administration is increasing opportunities for children to apply for refugee status before they travel to the United States, but as I explain in chapter 2, applying for refugee status from outside of the United States is different from applying for asylum from within the United States. Michael D. Shear, "Obama Approves Plan to Let Children in Central America Apply for Refugee Status," *New York Times*, September 30, 2014, accessed October 2, 2014, http://www.nytimes.com/2014/10/01/us/obama-approves-plan-to-let-children-apply-for-refugee-status-in-central-america.html?module = Search&mabReward = relbias%3Ar%2C{%221%22%3A%22RI%3A6%22}&_r = 3.
5. "Critical" theories unmask how structures and practices operate, seeking to challenge how power hierarchies get perpetuated through the production of knowledge. See Raymond Duvall and Latha Varadarajan, "On the Practical Significance of Critical International Relations Theory," *Asian Journal of Political Science* 11, no. 2 (2003): 75–88; Meghana Nayak and Eric Selbin, *Decentering International Relations* (London: Zed Books, 2010).
6. Laura Shepherd, ed., *Gender Matters in Global Politics: A Feminist Introduction to International Relations* (New York: Routledge, 2010); J. Ann Tickner and Laura Sjoberg, eds., *Feminism and International Relations: Conversations about the Past, Present and Future* (New York: Routledge, 2011). I also draw upon feminist IR frameworks offered by the scholarship of Anna Agathangelou, Annick T. R. Wibben, Marysia Zalewski, Cynthia Enloe, and Christine Sylvester. It is not within the scope of this chapter or book to discuss the subdivisions of feminist

IR (political economy, security studies, militarization and wars, gender violence, postcolonial politics, social movements, transnational advocacy, migration studies, social movements, international law and tribunals, queer studies, etc.). When I use the term "feminist IR," I am referencing scholars in the disciplines of political science, international relations, and other related fields, such as critical geography, who focus on the issues named. I do not consider whether these scholars claim the label of feminist IR but instead focus on the theoretical approaches to gender and global politics.

7. Thomas Spijkerboer, *Gender and Refugee Status* (Burlington, VT: Ashgate, 2000); Carol Bohmer and Amy Shuman, *Rejecting Refugees: Political Asylum in the 21st Century* (New York: Routledge, 2007); Efrat Arbel, Catherine Dauvergne, and Jenni Millbank, "Introduction: Gender in Refugee Law-From the Margins to the Centre," in *Gender in Refugee Law: From the Margins to the Centre*, ed. Efrat Arbel, Catherine Dauvergne, and Jenni Millbank (New York: Routledge, 2014), 1–16; Jane Freedman, *Gendering the International Asylum and Refugee Debate* (London: Palgrave Macmillan, 1997); Alison Gerard, *The Securitization of Migration and Refugee Women* (New York: Routledge, 2014).
8. Laura Sjoberg and J. Ann Tickner, "Introduction: International Relations through Feminist Lenses," in Tickner and Sjoberg, *Feminism and International Relations*, 2.
9. Cynthia Enloe, foreword to Shepherd, *Gender Matters*, xviii.
10. Mary Hawkesworth, *Globalization and Feminist Activism* (New York: Rowman and Littlefield, 2006), 99.
11. Valerie Oosterveld, "Gender, Persecution, and the International Criminal Court: Refugee Law's Relevance to the Crime against Humanity of Gender-Based Persecution," *Duke Journal of Comparative and International Law* 17 (2006): 49–89.
12. Ibid.
13. Margaret Keck and Kathryn Sikkink, *Activists beyond Borders: Advocacy Networks in International Politics* (Ithaca, NY: Cornell University Press, 1998); Rhonda Copelon, "Gender Crimes as War Crimes: Integrating Crimes against Women into International Criminal Law," *McGill Law Journal* 46 (2000): 217–40; Sally Engle Merry, "Constructing a Global Law: Violence against Women and the Human Rights System," *Law and Social Inquiry* 28, no. 4 (2003): 941–77; S. Laurel Weldon, "Inclusion, Solidarity, and Transnational Social Movements: The Global Movement against Gender Violence," *Perspectives on Politics* 4, no. 1 (2006): 55–74.
14. Keck and Sikkink, *Activists beyond Borders*, 171, 168–169.
15. Quoted in ibid., 172.
16. Keck and Sikkink, *Activists beyond Borders*, 27.
17. Mala Htun and S. Laurel Weldon, "The Civic Origins of Progressive Policy Change: Combating Violence against Women Global Perspective, 1975–2005," *American Political Science Review* 106, no. 3 (2012): 548–69.
18. Article 1 of the United Nations Declaration on the Elimination of Violence Against Women, 48/101, 1993, defines violence against women as "any act of gender-based violence." Women's human rights and feminist activists started to more explicitly mention gender-based violence but described mainly acts targeting women. United Nations Population Fund, "Gender Equality: Ending Widespread Violence Against Women," accessed May 12, 2012, http://www.unfpa.org/gender/violence.htm. See also Janet Halley, "Rape at Rome: Feminist Interventions in the Criminalization of Sex-Related Violence in Positive

International Criminal Law," *Michigan Journal of International Law* 30 (2008–9): 82–88 for the reasons why some feminist networks created the shift in language.

19. Meghana Nayak and Jennifer Suchland, "Gender Violence and Hegemonic Projects: Introduction," *International Feminist Journal of Politics* 8, no. 4 (2006): 469.
20. Regarding the idea of treating gender violence as self-explanatory, I find it helpful to draw upon the framework offered in Maria Eriksson Baaz and Maria Stern, *Sexual Violence as a Weapon of War? Perceptions, Prescriptions, Problems in the Congo and Beyond* (London: Zed Books, 2013), which explores the "comfortable" term "wartime rape" so as to challenge its construction and examine how other types of violence receive significantly less attention and how actors use "wartime rape" as a way to entrench and challenge power relationships.
21. Nayak and Suchland, "Gender Violence," 469.
22. Sally Engle Merry, *Human Rights and Gender Violence: Translating International Law into Local Justice* (Chicago: University of Chicago University Press, 2006).
23. Sally Engle Merry, *Gender Violence: A Cultural Perspective* (Oxford: John Wiley & Sons, 2009), 27, 28.
24. Jacqui True, *The Political Economy of Violence against Women* (New York: Oxford University Press, 2012). Note True's preference for the terminology "violence against women."
25. Martin Rein and Donald Schön, "Reframing Policy Discourse," in *The Argumentative Turn in Policy Analysis and Planning*, ed. Frank Fisher and John Forester (Durham, NC: Duke University Press, 1993), 146.
26. Celeste Montoya, *From Global to Grassroots: The European Union, Transnational Advocacy, and Combating Violence against Women* (New York: Oxford University Press, 2013), 15–20. Note Montoya's preference for the terminology "violence against women."
27. Ibid., 119–20.
28. See C. Roggeband and Mieke Verloo, "Dutch Women Are Liberated, Migrant Women Are a Problem: The Evolution of Policy Frames on Gender and Migration in the Netherlands, 1995–2005," *Social Policy and Administration* 41 (2007): 271–88; Mieke Verloo and Emaneula Lombardo, "Contested Gender Equality and Policy Variety in Europe: Introducing a Critical Frame Analysis Approach," in *Multiple Meanings of Gender Equality: A Critical Frame Analysis of Gender Policies in Europe*, ed. Mieke Verloo (Budapest, Hungary: Central University Press, 2007), 21–49;
    Andrea Krizsan and Raluca Maria Popa, "Frames in Contestation: Gendering Domestic Violence Policies in Five Central and Eastern European Countries," *Violence against Women* 20, no. 7 (2014): 758–82.
29. R. Charli Carpenter, "Recognizing Gender-Based Violence against Civilian Men and Boys in Conflict Situations," *Security Dialogue* 37, no. 1 (2006): 83–103.
30. Cynthia Enloe, "Womenandchildren: Making Feminist Sense of the Persian Gulf Crisis," *Village Voice*, September 25, 2000.
31. Jonneke Koomen, "'Without These Women, the Tribunal Cannot Do Anything': The Politics of Witness Testimony on Sexual Violence at the International Criminal Tribunal for Rwanda," *Signs* 38, no. 2 (2013): 253–77.
32. Bohmer and Shuman, *Rejecting Refugees*, 171.
33. Connie Oxford notes that asylum seekers, asylum adjudicators, and asylum advocates all operate with ideas about masculinity, femininity, and women's

agency. Connie G. Oxford, "Protectors and Victims in the Gender Regime of Asylum," *NWSA Journal* 17, no. 3 (2005): 18–38.

34. Bruce J. Einhorn, "Consistency, Credibility, and Culture," in *Refugee Roulette: Disparities in Asylum Adjudication and Proposals for Reform*, ed. Jaya Ramji-Nogales, Andrew Scheonholtz, and Philip G. Schrag (New York: New York University Press, 2009), 191.
35. Ibid., 191–92.
36. John Norris and Bronwyn Bruton, "The Price of Failure," *Foreign Policy*, October 5, 2011, http://www.foreignpolicy.com/articles/2011/10/05/the_price_of_failure?page = 0,0.
37. Uma Narayan, *Dislocating Cultures: Identities, Traditions, and Third-World Feminism* (New York: Routledge, 1997).
38. Stephen Steinberg, "Immigration, African Americans, and Race Discourse," *New Politics* 10, no. 3 (2005), accessed June 15, 2014, http://newpol.org/content/immigration-african-americans-and-race-discourse. See also Aviva Shen, "Boston's 10,000 Undocumented Irish Wait for Immigration Reform," *Think Progress*, July 11, 2013, http://thinkprogress.org/immigration/2013/07/11/2284021/boston-undocumented-irish-immigrants/.
39. Lisa Marie Cacho, *Social Death: Racialized Rightlessness and the Criminalization of the Unprotected* (New York: New York University Press, 2012), 4.
40. Ivette Sanchez, "Of Anchor Babies and Welfare Queens," *Columbia Political Review*, May 4, 2011, accessed June 15, 2014, http://cpreview.org/2011/05/of-anchor-babies-and-welfare-queens/.
41. Anna M. Agathangelou and Heather M. Turcotte, "Postcolonial Theories and Challenges to 'First World-ism,'" in Shepherd, *Gender Matters*, 45.
42. Ibid., 47.
43. See ibid., 55.
44. Narayan, *Dislocating Cultures*.
45. Keck and Sikkink, *Activists beyond Borders*, 27.
46. Even the distinction between "Western" and "non-Western" countries can be hard to determine. The term "non-Western" often means the global South, including formerly colonized and nonaligned countries. "Western" indicates the global North, former colonial states and white settler states. For more on these categories see Nayak and Selbin, *Decentering International Relations*, 2–3, nn. 2, 3, 4, 5.
47. Narayan, *Dislocating Cultures*.
48. Lama Abu-Odeh, "Comparatively Speaking: The 'Honor' of the 'East' and the 'Passion' of the 'West,'" *Utah Law Review* 2 (1997): 287–307.
49. Sheila Jeffreys, *Beauty and Misogyny: Harmful Cultural Practices in the West* (London: Routledge, 2005); Simone Weil Davis, "Loose Lips Sink Ships," *Feminist Studies* 28, no. 1 (2002): 7–35.
50. Hope Lewis and Isabelle R. Gunning, "Cleaning Our Own House: 'Exotic' and Familiar Human Rights Violations," *Buffalo Human Rights Law Review* 4 (1998): 123–140; Sherene Razack, "Domestic Violence as Gender Persecution: Policing the Borders of Nation, Race and Gender," *Canadian Journal of Women and the Law* 8, no. 1 (1995): 45–88.
51. Marina Matešić, "The Politics of Gender Asylum in the U.S.: Protection of Women Asylum Seekers in the Context of Global Inequalities," *Migracijske i etnićke teme* 30, no. 1 (2014): 15.
52. Aristide Zolberg, *A Nation by Design: Immigration Policy in the Fashioning of America* (Cambridge, MA: Harvard University Press, 2006). While I do not have

room to explore the history of immigration policies in the United States, Zolberg offers a comprehensive study of how immigration policies historically racialized different groups and consequently contributed to nation-building.

53. Matešić, "Politics of Gender Asylum," 19.
54. Michelle McKinley, "Cultural Culprits," *Berkeley Journal of Gender, Law and Justice* 24 (2009): 147.
55. Razack, "Domestic Violence," 47.
56. Ibid., 48.
57. Sherene Razack, *Looking White People in the Eye: Gender, Race, and Culture in Courtrooms and Classrooms* (Toronto: University of Toronto Press, 1998), 91.
58. Susan M. Akram, "Orientalism Revisited in Asylum and Refugee Claims," *International Journal of Refugee Law* 12, no. 1 (2000): 7–40.
59. Ibid., 10.
60. Ibid., 18.
61. Meghana Nayak, "Orientalism and 'Saving' US State Identity," *International Feminist Journal of Politics* 8, no. 1 (2006): 42–61.
62. David L. Eng, *The Feeling of Kinship: Queer Liberalism and the Racialization of Intimacy* (Durham, NC: Duke University Press, 2010).
63. Alicia Arrizón, *Queering Mestizaje: Transculturation and Performance* (Ann Arbor: University of Michigan Press, 2006); Eithne Luibheid, ed., "Queer/ Migration," special issue, *GLQ: A Journal of Lesbian and Gay Studies* 14, nos. 2–3 (2008).
64. Katie E. Oliviero, "The Immigration State of Emergency: Racializing and Gendering National Vulnerability in Twenty-First-Century Citizenship and Deportation Regimes," *Feminist Formations* 25, no. 2 (2013): 2–3.
65. Seyla Benhabib and Judith Resnik, eds., *Migrations and Mobilities: Citizenship, Borders, and Gender* (New York: New York University Press, 2009); Anne Sisson Runyan, Amy Lind, Patricia McDermott, and Marianne H. Marchand, eds., *Feminist (Im)Mobilities in Fortress(ing) North America: Rights, Citizenships, and Identities* (Burlington, VT: Ashgate, 2013).
66. Marjaana Jauhola and Jennifer Pedersen, "Who Might We Become? An Interview with Cynthia Weber," *International Feminist Journal of Politics* 12, no. 1 (2010): 105–15.
67. Nayak and Suchland, "Gender Violence."
68. Judith Butler, *Undoing Gender* (London: Routledge, 2004), 35 quoted in Laura J. Shepherd, "'Victims, Perpetrators and Actors' Revisited: Exploring the Potential for a Feminist Reconceptualisation of (International) Security and (Gender) Violence," *British Journal of Politics and International Relations* 9 (2007): 240.
69. Nayak, "Orientalism."
70. Laura Shepherd, "Veiled References: Constructions of Gender in the Bush Administration Discourse on the Attacks on Afghanistan Post-9/11," *International Feminist Journal of Politics* 8, no. 1 (2006): 19–41.
71. Karen Musalo, "Protecting Victims of Gendered Persecution: Fear of Floodgates or Call to (Principled) Action?" *Virginia Journal of Social Policy and the Law* 14, no. 2 (2007): 121.
72. Karen Musalo, "When Rights and Cultures Collide," *Issues in Ethics* 8, no. 3 (1997), http://www.scu.edu/ethics/publications/iie/v8n3/rightsandcultures.html.
73. Deborah Anker, "Refugee Law, Gender, and the Human Rights Paradigm," *Harvard Human Rights Journal* 15 (2002): 153–54.

74. Connie G. Oxford, "Gender-Based Persecution in Asylum Law and Policy," PhD dissertation, University of Pittsburgh, 2006, 164.
75. Efrat Arbel, Catherine Dauvergne, and Jenni Millbank, "Introduction: Gender in Refugee Law—from the Margins to the Centre," in Abel, Dauvergne, and Millbank, *Gender in Refugee Law*, 6.
76. I examined the entire text and legal history of at least ten cases per type of violence. I also examined at least ten articles published in academic and legal journals analyzing each type of gender-based asylum. Finally, I consulted other scholars' and lawyers' comprehensive reviews of case data to which they had access.
77. I consulted University of California–Hastings Center for Gender and Refugee Studies, Immigration Equality, Columbia Law School's Sexuality and Gender Law Clinic, the Political Asylum/Immigration Representation Project, Minnesota Advocates for Human Rights Refugee and Asylum Project, Harvard and Georgetown law clinics, the Tahirih Justice Center, Human Rights First, and the United Nations High Commissioner for Refugees.
78. Bohmer and Shuman, *Rejecting Refugees*; Stephen Legomsky and Cristina Rodriguez, *Immigration and Refugee Law and Policy*, 5th ed. (New York: Foundation Press, 2009); Ramji-Nogales, Schoenholtz, and Schrag, eds., *Refugee Roulette*; Karen Musalo, Jennifer Moore, and Richard A. Boswell, *Refugee Law and Policy: A Comparative and International Approach* (Durham, NC: Carolina Academic Press, 2011).
79. As is discussed in chapter 2, affirmative asylum cases are heard by asylum officers, and defensive asylum cases are heard by immigration judges. Defensive asylum cases are easier to access. As of early 2014, due to the decision in a court case, *Martins v. USCIS*, in November 2013, lawyers should be able to access the notes and interviews conducted by asylum officers under the Freedom of Information Act. As a nonlawyer researcher, I would have to request access to the notes through a lawyer who is representing a client interviewed by an asylum officer. Due to the time frame of this project, I was not able to take advantage of this ruling. Thus, the majority of my empirical analysis was conducted by looking at immigration court cases. In some cases, I was able to consult legal scholars' analysis of their experiences with asylum officers.
80. I offer here a few words on my selection of cases. As we see in table 2.5 in chapter 2, repressive social norms cases are predominantly from Afghanistan and Iran, two countries considered to be oppositional to the United States in terms of religious and cultural norms. As I discuss in chapter 3, repressive social norms cases involving "honor killings" are most often from Pakistan. Thus, in these cases, if repressive social norms are the primary harm, they typically fit squarely into a general "exotic" frame and contribute to perceptions about the distinctions between the United States and countries in which these norms are dominant. But I was more interested in additional dimensions and nuances of the racialization of gender violence claims, so I focused on other types of violence. Also, per my analysis of the Center for Gender and Refugee Studies data I compiled (described in chapter 2), repressive social norms and forced marriage cases are often paired with female genital cutting or domestic violence cases. Persecution due to repressive social norms is also mentioned in a significant proportion of cases about persecution due to sexual orientation or gender identity. Thus, I did not examine repressive social norms or forced marriage separately. In addition, in my analysis, I grouped sex slavery cases

with trafficking cases, because conditions of slavery are included in the United Nations and US definitions of trafficking. Finally, one of the most famous cases, *Fatin v. INS* 12 F. 3d 1233 (3d Cir. 1993), regarding an asylum seeker from Iran, helped to create the language that feminism could constitute political opinion. Feminism as political opinion / women's rights activists cases in the Center for Gender and Refugee Studies database were minimal; when not paired with domestic violence or female genital cutting cases, these women's rights activists claims were present in cases regarding repressive social norms (primarily Afghanistan and Iran with one case in Sudan). Deborah Anker notes that the Harvard Immigration and Refugee Clinic has won gender asylum cases regarding feminism as a political opinion. Deborah E. Anker, "Legal Change from the Bottom Up: The Development of Gender Asylum Jurisprudence in the United States," in Abel, Dauvergne, and Millbank, *Gender in Refugee Law*, 46–72. I primarily examined feminism as political opinion / women's rights activism when paired with membership in a social group. I often found that social groups were created by looking at the group of people who resisted a particular practice, thus including at least implicitly political opinion into social group construction.

81. In chapter 5, I say more about the terminology relevant to the rights of sexual minorities.
82. Freedman, *Gendering*; Bohmer and Shuman, *Rejecting Refugees*; Arbel, Dauvergne, and Millbank, *Gender in Refugee Law*; Gerard, *Securitization of Migration.*
83. Freedman, *Gendering*; Bohmer and Shuman, *Rejecting Refugees*; Gerard, *Securitization of Migration.*

CHAPTER 2

1. The Refugee Act of 1980, Public Law 96-212.
2. Edward M. Kennedy, "Refugee Act of 1980," *International Migration Review* 15, nos. 1–2 (1981): 141–56.
3. United Nations 1951 Convention Relating to the Status of Refugees.
4. Article 1A (2).
5. Article 33.
6. "Memorandum from Phyllis Coven, US Department of Justice, Considerations for Asylum Officers Adjudicating Asylum Claims from Women" (1995), accessed June 4, 2013, http://www.state.gov/s/l/65633.htm.
7. Deborah E. Anker, "Legal Change from the Bottom Up: The Development of Gender Asylum Jurisprudence in the United States," in *Gender in Refugee Law: From the Margins to the Centre*, ed. Efrat Arbel, Catherine Dauvergne, and Jenni Millbank, 46–72 (New York: Routledge, 2014), 55.
8. "Partnership in Resettlement," UN Refugee Agency, accessed October 15, 2013, http://www.unhcr.org/pages/4a16c9246.html.
9. Jaya Ramji-Nogales, Andrew I. Schoenholtz, and Philip G. Schrag, "The Asylum Process," in *Refugee Roulette: Disparities in Asylum Adjudication and Proposals for Reform*, ed. Jaya Ramji-Nogales, Andrew I. Schoenholtz, and Philip G. Schrag (New York: New York University Press, 2009), 12.
10. Jaya Ramji-Nogales, Andrew I. Schoenholtz, and Philip G. Schrag, "The Immigration Courts," in Ramji-Nogales, Schoenholtz, and Schrag, *Refugee Roulette*, 33.
11. Ibid., 15 n. 4. Legal status (i.e. student visa) is retained even with a denial of asylum.

12. Tina Javaherian, "Seeking Asylum for Former Child Soldiers and Victims of Human Trafficking," *Pepperdine Law Review* 29, no. 2 (2012): 433.
13. *Kovac v. INS*, 407 F.2d 102 (9th Cir. 1969).
14. See Immigration Equality Asylum Manual, accessed November 5, 2014, http://www.immigrationequality.org/get-legal-help/our-legal-resources/immigration-equality-asylum-manual/3-asylum-basics-elements-of-asylum-law/.
15. Leonard Birdsong, "A Legislative Rejoinder to 'Give Me Your Gays, Your Lesbians, and Your Victims of Gender Violence, Yearning to Breathe Free of Sexual Persecution," *William Mitchell Law Review* 35, no. 1 (2008): 197–225.
16. *Matter of Mogharrabi*, 19 I&N Dec. 439 (BIA 1987)
17. Carol Bohmer and Amy Shuman, *Rejecting Refugees: Political Asylum in the 21st Century* (London: Routledge, 2008), 197–98.
18. Ibid., 205.
19. Heaven Crawley, "Gender, Persecution and the Concept of Politics in the Asylum Determination Process," *Forced Migration Review* 9, no. 6 (2000), 17–20.
20. *Matter of Acosta*, 19 I&N Dec. 211 (BIA 1985).
21. Ibid.
22. See *Sanchez-Trujillo v. INS*, 801 F. 2d 1571 (9th Cir. 1986) and *Hernandez-Montiel v. INS*, 225 F. 3d 1084 (9th Cir. 2000).
23. *Matter of C-A-*, 23 I&N Dec. 951 (BIA 2006).
24. *Matter of S-E-G-*, 24 I&N Dec. 579 (BIA 2008).
25. Leslye Orloff and Olivia Garcia, "Dynamics of Domestic Violence Experienced by Immigrant Victims," National Immigrant Women's Advocacy Project, American University Washington College of Law, accessed July 12, 2014, http://niwaplibrary.wcl.american.edu/cultural-competency/dynamics-of-violence-against-immigrant-women/1.1-Dynamics-of-Domestic-Violence-in-Immigrant-Families-MANUAL-BB.pdf.
26. Stephanie Mencimer, "Immigration Judge to Asylum Seeker: You Don't Look Gay," *Mother Jones*, October 7, 2010, accessed July 12, 2014, http://www.motherjones.com/mojo/2010/10/bush-immigration-judge-gay-asylum seeker.
27. Jessica Marsden, "Domestic Violence Asylum after *Matter of L-R-*," *Yale Law Journal* 123, no. 7 (2014), accessed August 12, 2014, http://www.yalelawjournal.org/article/domestic-violence-asylum-after-matter-of-l-r.
28. Data gathered by the Transactional Records Access Clearinghouse's Immigration Project at Syracuse University, accessed November 5, 2014, http://trac.syr.edu/immigration/reports/361/.
29. Ramji-Nogales, Schoenholtz, and Schrag, "The Immigration Courts," 47.
30. Bohmer and Shuman, *Rejecting Refugees*, 223–24.
31. Alison Gerard, *The Securitization of Migration and Refugee Women* (New York: Routledge, 2014), 66.
32. Ibid., 65.
33. Ibid., 64.
34. Those countries are the Czech Republic, Croatia, Italy, Latvia, Austria, Cyprus, Belgium, Hungary, Sweden, Moldova, the Netherlands, France, Germany, Luxembourg, Bulgaria, Ireland, Norway, Portugal, Spain, Finland, Turkey, Argentina, Colombia, Costa Rica, Chile, Mexico, Bolivia, Paraguay, Nicaragua, Uruguay, and Uganda. New Zealand does not have legislation but in practice recognizes gender-based asylum claims.
35. Alison Brysk, "Changing Hearts and Minds: Sexual Politics and Human Rights," in *The Persistent Power of Human Rights: From Commitment to Compliance*, ed.

Thomas Risse, Stephen C. Ropp, and Kathryn Sikkink (Cambridge: Cambridge University Press, 2013), 259–74; Deborah E. Anker, "Legal Change from the Bottom Up: The Development of Gender Asylum Jurisprudence in the United States," in Arbel, Dauvergne, and Millbank, *Gender in Refugee Law*, 46–72.

36. Anker, "Legal Change," 53.
37. See discussion at "End the Deadline," hosted by Human Rights First, accessed August 15, 2014, http://www.endthedeadline.org/.
38. "Refugee Admissions," US Department of State, accessed August 14, 2014, http://www.state.gov/j/prm/ra/.
39. There are multiple ways international relations theorists attempt to understand international hierarchy. I conceptualize international hierarchy by drawing upon Ann Towns, *Women and States: Norms and Hierarchies in International Society* (Cambridge: Cambridge University Press, 2010).
40. Ibid., 44–45, emphasis original. For her definition, Towns draws upon Talcott Parsons, *The Social System* (New York: Free Press, 1951).
41. Towns, *Women and States*, 11–12, emphasis original.
42. Michelle A. McKinley, "Cultural Culprits," *Berkeley Journal of Gender, Law and Justice* 24, no. 2 (2009): 103.
43. The countries in the global North/West (including eastern European countries) are United States, Canada, Australia, New Zealand, the UK, Switzerland, Czech Republic, the Netherlands, Sweden, Finland, Italy, Portugal, France, Germany, Luxembourg, Ireland, Bulgaria, Norway, Spain, Croatia, Belgium, Hungary, Austria, Cyprus, Latvia. The countries in the global South are Panama, South Africa, Paraguay, Uganda, Turkey, Mexico, Bolivia, Costa Rica, Colombia, Chile, Nicaragua, Uruguay, and Argentina.
44. Towns, *Women and States*, 7–8.
45. Ibid., 9.
46. Ibid., 55, 65–70.
47. Ibid., 79–80.
48. Ibid., 120–21.
49. See ibid., 182–83.
50. Ibid., 200–201.
51. Ibid., 186–89.
52. See Terrell Carver, "Whither Diversity?" *International Feminist Journal of Politics* 11, no. 1 (2009): 30–34.
53. Paula Bronstein, "The Worst Places in the World to Be a Woman," CBSnews.com, June 14, 2011, accessed June 20, 2014, http://www.cbsnews.com/news/the-worst-places-in-the-world-to-be-a-woman/.
54. Emine Saner, "Gay Rights around the World: The Best and Worst Countries for Equality," *Guardian*, July 30, 2013, accessed August 14, 2014, http://www.theguardian.com/world/2013/jul/30/gay-rights-world-best-worst-countries.
55. Freedom House Survey Team, "Freedom in the World 2013: Democratic Breakthroughs in the Balance," accessed February 3, 2014, http://www.freedomhouse.org/sites/default/files/FIW%202013%20Charts%20and%20Graphs%20for%20Web_0.pdf.
56. United Nations Development Programme, Human Development Reports (2014), table 4: "Gender Inequality Index," accessed September 1, 2014, http://hdr.undp.org/en/content/table-4-gender-inequality-index.
57. Meghana Nayak and Eric Selbin, *Decentering International Relation* (London: Zed Books, 2010).

58. See Sally Engle Merry's faculty website at http://anthropology.as.nyu.edu/object/sally.merry.
59. Bryan Baker and Nancy Rytina, "Estimates of the Unauthorized Immigrant Population Residing in the United States: January 2012," Office of Immigration Statistics, Department of Homeland Security, accessed January 3, 2013, http://www.dhs.gov/sites/default/files/publications/ois_ill_pe_2012_2.pdf.
60. Amnesty International, the Lawyers Committee for Human Rights, "Refugee Women at Risk: Unfair U.S. Laws Hurt Asylum Seekers," 2002, accessed June 12, 2014, https://www.humanrightsfirst.org/wp-content/uploads/pdf/refugee_women.pdf; Human Rights Watch, "Unfair Immigration Policies," accessed September 15, 2014, http://www.hrw.org/united-states/us-program/unfair-immigration-policies; US Conference of Catholic Bishops, Office of Migration Policy and Public Affairs, "Immigrant Detention," July 2014, accessed June 12, 2014, http://www.usccb.org/about/migration-policy/position-papers/upload/Immigrant-Detention-Backgrounder-july-2014.pdf; Efrat Arbel and Alletta Brenner, "Bordering on Failure: Canada-U.S. Border Policy and the Politics of Refugee Exclusion," Harvard Immigration and Refugee Law Clinical Program, Harvard Law School, November 2013, accessed June 15, 2014, http://harvardimmigrationclinic.files.wordpress.com/2013/11/bordering-on-failure-harvard-immigration-and-refugee-law-clinical-program1.pdf.
61. US Citizenship and Immigration Services asylum officer basic training, "One Year Filing Deadline," March 23, 2009, accessed August 14, 2014, http://www.uscis.gov/sites/default/files/USCIS/Humanitarian/Refugees%20%26%20Asylum/Asylum/AOBTC%20Lesson%20Plans/One-Year-Filing-Deadline-31aug10.pdf.
62. National Immigrant Justice Center, "Repeal the One-Year Asylum Deadline," accessed August 14, 2014, https://www.immigrantjustice.org/repeal-one-year-asylum-deadline.
63. Cathleen Caron, "Asylum in the United States: Expedited Removal Process Threatens to Violate International Norms," *Human Rights Brief* 6, no. 2 (1999): 27–28.
64. Pooja Gehi, "Struggles from the Margins: Anti-immigrant Legislation and the Impact on Low-Income Transgender People of Color," *Women's Rights Law Reporter* 30 (2009): 319.
65. Alisa Solomon, "Trans/migrant: Christina Madrazo's All-American Story," *Queer Migrations: Sexuality, U.S. Citizenship, and Border Crossings*, ed. Eithne Luibhéid and Lionel Cantú Jr. (Minneapolis: University of Minnesota Press, 2005), 17.
66. Jonathan Simon, "Refugees in a Carceral Age: The Rebirth of Immigration Prisons in the United States," *Public Culture* 10, no. 3 (1998): 581.
67. Deborah Anker and Michael Posner, "The Forty Year Crisis: A Legislative History of the Refugee Act of 1980," *San Diego Law Review* 19 (1981): 9–89.
68. Simon, "Refugees in a Carceral Age," 582, 583.
69. Ibid., 585.
70. Robert Suro, "US is Renewing Border Detentions," *New York Times*, February 8, 1990, accessed January 14, 2014, http://www.nytimes.com/1990/02/08/us/us-is-renewing-border-detentions.html.
71. "Analysis of Immigration Detention Policies," American Civil Liberties Union, August 18, 1999, accessed July 14, 2014, https://www.aclu.org/immigrants-rights/analysis-immigration-detention-policies.

72. Michael Welch and Liza Schuster, "Detention of Asylum Seekers in the UK and USA: Deciphering Noisy and Quiet Constructions," *Punishment and Society* 7, no. 4 (2005): 404.
73. Ibid., 405.
74. Quoted in ibid.
75. US Department of Homeland Security, Bureau of Immigration and Customs Enforcement, "ENDGAME: Office of Detention and Removal Strategic Plan, 2003–2012: Detention and Removal Strategy for a Secure Homeland," June 27, 2003, accessed July 15, 2014, http://www.cryptogon.com/docs/endgame.pdf; Jenny Manrique, "Detained Asylum Seekers Find It Harder to Win Release," *New York Times*, June 1, 2009, accessed July 14, 2014, http://www.nytimes.com/2009/06/02/nyregion/02asylum.html?_r = 0.
76. Human Rights First, "U.S. Detention of Asylum Seekers: Seeking Protection, Finding Prison," June 2009, accessed July 14, 2014, http://www.humanrightsfirst.org/wp-content/uploads/pdf/090429-RP-hrf-asylum-detention-report.pdf, 33.
77. C. T. Turney, "Give Me Your Tired, Your Poor, and Your Queer: The Need and Potential for Advocacy for LGBTQ Immigrant Detainees," *UCLA Law Review* 58 (2011): 1343–88.
78. Amnesty International, "USA: Jailed without Justice, Immigration Detention in the USA," March 25, 2009, accessed August 4, 2014, http://www.amnestyusa.org/research/reports/usa-jailed-without-justice?page = show#FN7; National Immigration Forum, "The Math of Immigration Detention: Runaway Costs for Immigration Detention Do Not Add Up to Sensible Policies," August 2013, accessed August 5, 2014, http://www.immigrationforum.org/images/uploads/mathofimmigrationdetention.pdf.
79. Bill Frelick, "U.S. Detention of Asylum Seekers and Human Rights," Migration Policy Institute, March 1, 2005, accessed June 14, 2041, www.migrationpolicy.org/article/us-detention-asylum seekers-and-human-rights.
80. Juliet Stumpf, "The Crimmigration Crisis: Immigrants, Crime, and Sovereign Power," *American University Law Review* 56, no. 2 (2006): 367–419; Anil Kalhan, "Rethinking Immigration Detention," *Columbia Law Review* 110 (2010): 42–58; Gerard, *Securitization of Migration*.
81. Frances Webber, *Crimes of Arrival: Immigrants and Asylum Seekers in the New Europe*, (London: Statewatch, 1996): 1–10; Jonathan Simon, "Refugees in a Carceral Age: The Rebirth of Immigration Prisons in the United States," *Public Culture* 10, no. 3 (1998): 577–607.
82. Lutheran Immigration and Refugee Service and the Women's Commission for Refugee Women and Children, "Locking Up Family Values: The Detention of Immigrant Families," February 2007, accessed January 12, 2014, http://lirs.org/wp-content/uploads/2012/05/RPTLOCKINGUPFAMILYVALUES2007.pdf; Julia Preston, "U.N. Official Says He's Been Denied Access to U.S. Immigrant Jails," *New York Times*, May 15, 2007, accessed June 14, 2014, http://www.nytimes.com/2007/05/15/us/15deny.html?_r = 0; Natalie J. Sokoloff and Susan C. Pearce, "Locking Up Hope: Immigration, Gender, and the Prison System," *Scholar and Feminist Online* 6, no. 3 (2008): 1–6, accessed July 24, 2014, http://sfonline.barnard.edu/immigration/sokoloff_pearce_01.htm; Robyn Sampson and Grant Mitchell, "Global Trends in Immigration Detention and Alternatives to Detention: Practical, Political and Symbolic Rationales," *Journal on Migration and Human Security* 1, no. 3 (2013): 97–121.

83. Alisa Solomon, "Detainees Equal Dollars: The Rise in Immigrant Incarcerations Drives a Prison Boom," *Village Voice*, August 14–20, 2002, accessed March 14, 2014, www.villagevoice.com/issues/0233/solomon.php; Meredith Kolodner, "Private Prisons Expect a Boom; Immigration Enforcement to Benefit Detention," *New York Times*, July 19, 2006, accessed November 15, 2014, http://query.nytimes.com/gst/fullpage.html?res = 9901E2D9163FF93AA25754C0A9609C8B63.
84. National Immigrant Justice Center, "Eliminate the Detention Bed Quota," accessed April 13, 2014, http://www.immigrantjustice.org/eliminate-detention-bed-quota#.U-ApkEhdLSA; William Selway and Margaret Newkirk, "Congress Mandates Jail Beds for 34,000 Immigrants as Private Prisons Profit," Bloomberg.com, September 24, 2013, accessed July 13, 2014, http://www.bloomberg.com/news/2013-09-24/congress-fuels-private-jails-detaining-34-000-immigrants.html.
85. "A Broken, Dangerous System," *New York Times*, December 4, 2011, accessed June 3, 2014, http://www.nytimes.com/2011/12/05/opinion/a-broken-dangerous-system.html?_r = 4; Nina Bernstein, "Report Critical of Scope of Immigration Detention," *New York Times*, October 6, 2009, accessed June 14, 2014, http://www.nytimes.com/2009/10/07/us/politics/07detain.html.
86. Samantha Powers, "U.S. Leadership to Advance Equality for LGBT People Abroad," White House Blog, December 13, 2012, accessed March 14, 2014, http://www.whitehouse.gov/blog/2012/12/13/us-leadership-advance-equality-lgbt-people-abroad.
87. Anil Kalhan, "Rethinking Immigration Detention," *Columbia Law Review* 110 (2010): 42–58.
88. Gerard, *Securitization of Migration*, 54.
89. Sylvanna M. Falcón, "Rape as a Weapon of War: Advancing Human Rights for Women at the US-Mexico Border," *Social Justice* 28, no. 2 (2001): 31–50; Gerard, *Securitization of Migration*, 190.
90. Thomas Biersteker and Cynthia Weber, eds., *State Sovereignty as Social Construct* (Cambridge: Cambridge University Press, 1995); Cheryl Shanks, *Immigration and the Politics of American Sovereignty, 1890–1990* (Ann Arbor: University of Michigan Press, 2001); Anne Demo, "Sovereignty Discourse and Contemporary Immigration Politics," *Quarterly Journal of Speech* 91, no. 3 (2005): 291–311; Joseph H. Carens, *The Ethics of Immigration* (Oxford: Oxford University Press, 2013).
91. Demo, "Sovereignty Discourse."
92. David Campbell, *Writing Security: United States Foreign Policy and the Politics of Identity* (Minneapolis: University of Minnesota Press, 1998); Jutta Weldes, Mark Laffey, Hugh Gusterson, and Raymond Duvall, eds., *Cultures of Insecurity: States, Communities, and the Production of Danger* (Minneapolis: University of Minnesota Press, 1999); Anna M. Agathangelou and L. H. M. Ling, "Power and Play through Poisies: Reconstructing Self and Other in the 9/11 Commission Report," *Millennium: Journal of International Studies* 33, no. 3 (2005): 827–54; Meghana Nayak and Christopher Malone, "American Orientalism and American Exceptionalism: A Critical Rethinking of US Hegemony," *International Studies Review* 11, no. 2 (2009): 253–79; Nayak and Selbin, *Decentering International Relations*; Wendy Brown, *Walled States, Waning Sovereignty* (Cambridge, MA: MIT Press, 2014)

93. Roxanne Doty, *Anti-immigrantism in Western Democracies: Statecraft, Desire, and the Politics of Exclusion* (New York: Routledge, 2003), 14.
94. Ibid., 2.
95. Ibid., 14.
96. Ibid., 3.
97. Nevzat Soguk, *States and Strangers: Refugees and Displacement of Statecraft* (Minneapolis: University of Minnesota Press, 1999).
98. In her comprehensive study of United Nations Security Council intervention during humanitarian crises, Carrie Booth Walling notes that when most of the Security Council members *share* understandings about the nature of the conflict/issue, this body is more likely to intervene. Through her case studies, she illustrates that the Security Council at times conceives of state sovereignty as *complementary* to human rights norms. In other words, while most scholars studying international relations posit sovereignty norms as oppositional to human rights norms, this particular study examines how sovereignty and human rights might coconstitute each other. I find this book a useful example of how sovereignty and human rights are not necessarily in opposition to each other. Carrie Booth Walling, *All Necessary Measures: The United Nations and Humanitarian Intervention* (Philadelphia: University of Pennsylvania Press, 2013).
99. Gerard, *Securitization of Migration*, 66.
100. Ibid.
101. Idean Salehyan and Marc R. Rosenblum, "International Relations, Domestic Politics, and Asylum Admissions in the United States," *Political Research Quarterly* 61, no. 1 (2008): 105.
102. Randolph B. Persaud, "Situating Race in International Relations: The Dialectics of Civilizational Security in American Immigration," in *Power, Postcolonialism and International Relations: Reading Race, Gender and Class*, ed. Geeta Chowdhry and Sheila Nair (New York: Routledge, 2002), 56–81.
103. J. Ann Tickner, *Gender in International Relations* (New York: Columbia University Press, 1992), 6. See also R. W. Connell, *Masculinities* (Berkeley: University of California Press, 1995); Charlotte Hooper, *Manly States: Masculinities, International Relations, and Gender Politics* (New York: Columbia University Press, 2001); Jane L. Parpart and Marysia Zalewski, eds., *Rethinking the Man Question: Sex, Gender and Violence in International Relations* (London: Zed Books, 2008).
104. Laura Sjoberg, "Gendered Realities of the Immunity Principle: Why Gender Analysis Needs Feminism," *International Studies Quarterly*, 50, no. 4 (2006): 889–910; Helen Kinsella, *The Image before the Weapon: A Critical History of the Distinction between Combatant and Civilian* (Ithaca, NY: Cornell University Press, 2011).
105. Carol Bohmer and Amy Shuman, "Contradictory Discourses of Protection and Control in Transnational Asylum Law," *Journal of Legal Anthropology* 1, no. 2 (2010): 212–29.
106. Jacqueline Bhabha, "Boundaries in the Field of Human Rights: International Gatekeepers? The Tension between Asylum Advocacy and Human Rights," *Harvard Human Rights Law Review* 15 (Spring 2002): 161.
107. Wendy Brown, *States of Injury: Power and Freedom in Late Modernity* (Princeton: Princeton University Press, 1995), 174–75.
108. Doty, *Anti-immigrantism in Western Democracies*, 12.

109. Shampa Biswas and Sheila Nair, eds., *International Relations and States of Exception: Margins, Peripheries, and Excluded bodies* (New York: Routledge, 2010), 12.
110. Ibid., 6.
111. Bohmer and Shuman, "Contradictory Discourses," 221–24.

CHAPTER 3

1. Bonita C. Meyersfeld, "Reconceptualizing Domestic Violence in International Law," *Albany Law Review* 67 (2003): 371–426; MariaCaterina La Barbera, *Multicentered Feminism: Revisiting the "Female Genital Mutilation" Discourse* (Palermo: Compostampa, 2009); Ronagh J. A. McQuigg, *International Human Rights Law and Domestic Violence: The Effectiveness of International Human Rights Law* (New York: Routledge, 2011); Laura L. Finley, ed., *Encyclopedia of Domestic Violence and Abuse* (Santa Barbara, CA: ABC-CLIO, 2013); Angelique Mulholland, "16 Organisations, Charities and Grassroots Groups Working to Stop Female Genital Mutilation," Pixel Project's "16 for 16" Campaign, December 1, 2012, accessed August 3, 2014, http://16days.thepixelproject.net/16-organisations-charities-and-grassroots-groups-working-to-stop-fgm/.
2. Valorie K. Vojdik, "Conceptualizing Intimate Violence and Gender Equality: A Comparative Approach," *Fordham International Law Journal* 31, no. 2 (2007): 487–527.
3. United Nations Children's Fund, "Female Genital Mutilation/Cutting: A Statistical Overview and Exploration of the Dynamics of Change," 2013, accessed September 4, 2014, http://www.unicef.org/media/files/FGCM_Lo_res.pdf.
4. Sharmon Lynnette Monagan, "Patriarchy: Perpetuating the Practice of Female Genital Mutilation," *Journal of Alternative Perspectives in the Social Sciences* 2, no. 1 (2010): 160–81.
5. John Tierney, "A New Debate on Female Circumcision," *New York Times*, November 30, 2007, accessed June 20, 2014, http://tierneylab.blogs.nytimes.com/2007/11/30/a-new-debate-on-female-circumcision/?_php = true&_type = blogs&_php = true&_type = blogs&_r = 1; Bettina Shell-Duncan, Katherine Wander, Ylva Hernlund, and Amadou Moreau, "Legislating Change? Responses to Criminalizing Female Genital Cutting in Senegal," *Law and Society Review* 47, no. 4 (2013): 803–35.
6. L. Amede Obiora, "Little Foxes That Spoil the Vine: Revisiting the Feminist Critique of Female Circumcision," *Canadian Journal of Women and Law* 9 (1996): 46–73.
7. Fauziya Kassindja's name was spelled as "Kasinga" in court proceedings; I refer to the accurate spelling of her name.
8. Julia Preston, "In First for Court, Woman Is Ruled Eligible for Asylum in U.S. on Basis of Domestic Abuse," *New York Times*, August 29, 2014, http://www.nytimes.com/2014/08/30/us/victim-of-domestic-violence-in-guatemala-is-ruled-eligible-for-asylum-in-us.html?_r = 2; 26 I&N Dec. 388 (BIA 2014), the *Matter of A-R-C-G- et al.*, Respondents.
9. Berger also discusses the role of autonomy in the DV case of Silvia, noting how the immigration judge perceived her as "worthy" of asylum "at least partially because she is rebelling against the 'backward' culture of Guatemala." But the judge neglected how racial differences between Silvia and her husband played a role in the violence she experienced. Susan Berger, "Production and

Reproduction of Gender and Sexuality in Legal Discourses of Asylum in the United States," *Signs* 34, no. 3 (2009): 671, 670.

10. Hope Lewis and Isabelle R. Gunning, "Cleaning Our Own House: 'Exotic' and Familial Human Rights Violations," *Buffalo Human Rights Law Review* 4 (1998): 123–40; Lisa Wade, "Learning from 'Female Genital Mutilation': Lessons from 30 Years of Academic Discourse," *Ethnicities* 12, no. 1 (2012): 26–49.
11. All information on the Kassindja case are accessible from the Center for Gender and Refugee Studies, accessed September 4, 2014, http://cgrs.uchastings.edu/our-work/matter-kasinga-1996.
12. See *Matter of Kasinga*, 21 I&N Dec. 357 (BIA 1996). By "gender identity," the BIA means a cisgender woman. Gender identity may also be used to designate one's identity as a man or a woman, usually invoked to address cases of transimmigrants. This will be discussed further in chapter 5.
13. *Matter of Kasinga*, 21 I&N, Dec. 377 (BIA 1996); Natalie Rodriguez, "Give Us Your Weary but Not Your Battered: The Department of Homeland Security, Politics and Asylum for Victims of Domestic Violence," *Southwestern Journal of International Law* 18 (2011): 324–25.
14. Center for Gender and Refugee Studies, "Staff and Board," accessed November 14, 2013, http://cgrs.uchastings.edu/about/staff.
15. Isabelle R. Gunning, "Global Feminism at the Local Level: Criminal and Asylum Laws Regarding Female Genital Surgeries," *Journal of Gender, Race and Justice* 3 (1999–2000): 48.
16. Connie G. Oxford, "Protectors and Victims in the Gender Regime of Asylum," *NWSA Journal* 17, no. 3 (2005): 29.
17. Chitra Aiyar, in discussion with the author, September 12, 2011.
18. Quoted in Carol Bohmer and Amy Shuman, "Gender and Political Asylum," Foreign Policy Association Blog, April 13, 2011, accessed February 12, 2014, http://foreignpolicyblogs.com/2011/04/13/gender-political-asylum/.
19. All information on the Alvarado case is accessible from Center for Gender and Refugee Studies, "Matter of R-A-," accessed July 24, 2014, http://cgrs.uchastings.edu/our-work/matter-r.
20. Helen P. Grant, "The Floodgates Are Not Going to Open, but Will the U.S. Border?" *Houston Journal of International Law* 29, no. 1 (2006–7): 1–53.
21. Carol Bohmer and Amy Shuman, "Gender and Political Asylum," Foreign Policy Association Blog, April 13, 2011, accessed January 24, 2014, http://foreignpolicyblogs.com/2011/04/13/gender-political-asylum/.
22. Susan Sachs, "The Nation: Fears of Rape and Violence; Women Newly Seeking Asylum," *New York Times*, August 1, 1999, accessed January 21, 2014, http://www.nytimes.com/1999/08/01/weekinreview/the-nation-fears-of-rape-and-violence-women-newly-seeking-asylum.html.
23. Anita Sinha, "Note: Domestic Violence and U.S. Asylum Law: Eliminating the 'Cultural Hook' for Claims Involving Gender-Related Persecution," *New York University Law Review* 76 (2001): 1584.
24. Aubra Fletcher, "The REAL ID Act: Furthering Gender Bias in U.S. Asylum Law," *Berkeley Journal of Gender, Law and Justice* 21, no. 1 (2006): 111–31; Katherine E. Melloy, "Telling Truths: How the REAL ID Act's Credibility Provisions Affect Women Asylum Seekers," *Iowa Law Review* 92 (2007): 637–76.
25. Information on the *L-R-* case, including the DHS brief, is available at the Center for Gender and Refugee Studies, "Matter of L-R-," accessed August 12, 2014, http://cgrs.uchastings.edu/our-work/matter-l-r.

26. Julia Preston, "New Policy Permits Asylum for Battered Women," *New York Times*, July 15, 2009, accessed January 21, 2014, http://www.nytimes.com/2009/07/16/us/16asylum.html.
27. *Matter of Kasinga*, 21 I&N, Dec. 377 (BIA 1996).
28. "Breaking News: Tahirih Wins Key Immigration Case," Tahirih Justice Center, April 26, 2011, accessed November 12, 2012, http://www.tahirih.org/2011/04/matter-of-a-t/.
29. Ibid.; see also Lisa Frydman and Kim Thuy Seelinger, "Kasinga's Protection Undermined? Recent Developments in Female Genital Cutting Jurisprudence," *Benders's Immigration Bulletin* 13 (2008): 1073, 1080.
30. "Breaking News."
31. *Matter of ARCG- et al.*, 26 I&N Dec. 388 (BIA 2014), accessed September 13, 2014, http://www.justice.gov/eoir/vll/intdec/vol26/3811.pdf.
32. Blaine Bookey, "Domestic Violence as a Basis for Asylum: An Analysis of 206 Case Outcomes in the United States from 1994 to 2012," *Hastings Women's Law Journal* 24, no. 1 (2013): 107–48.
33. Ibid., 110.
34. Sara L. McKinnon, "Positioned in/by the State: Incorporation, Exclusion, and Appropriation of Women's Gender-Based Claims to Political Asylum in the United States," *Quarterly Journal of Speech* 92, no. 2 (2011): 178–200.
35. Ibid., 179.
36. Anthony Fontes, "Refuge from Femicide: Facing Gendered Violence in Guatemala," *Berkeley Review of Latin American Studies* (2010), accessed July 12, 2014, http://vcro-vm-i004-dev07.berkeley.edu/research/human-rights-refuge-femicide-facing-gendered-violence-guatemala.
37. McKinnon, "Positioned in/by the State," 193–94.
38. Jessica Marsden, "Domestic Violence Asylum after *Matter of L-R-*," *Yale Law Journal* 123, no. 7 (2014), accessed November 3, 2014, http://www.yalelawjournal.org/note/domestic-violence-asylum-after-matter-of-l-r.
39. See Berger, "Production and Reproduction."
40. Adele M. Morrison, "Changing the Domestic Violence (Dis)Course: Moving from White Victim to Multi-cultural Survivor," *University of California–Davis Law Review* 39 (2006): 1061–120.
41. McKinnon, "Positioned in/by the State," briefly mentions the importance of looking at the "construction of family" (98 n. 43).
42. Preston, "New Policy Permits."
43. *Matter of Acosta*, 19 I&N Dec. 211(BIA 1985).
44. *Sanchez-Trujillo v. INS*, 801 F.2d 1571 (9th Cir. 1986), 1576.
45. US Committee for Refugees and Immigrants, "Domestic Violence Based Asylum Immigration Judge Decisions/Briefs and Affidavits," accessed March 15, 2012, http://www.refugees.org/resources/for-lawyers/asylum-research/domestic-violence-based-asylum/immigration-judge.html.
46. Florence Immigrant and Refugee Rights Project, "How to Apply for Asylum, Withholding of Removal and/or Protection under Article 3 of the Convention Against Torture," (2011), accessed July 10, 2014, http://www.justice.gov/eoir/probono/Asylum%20-%20English%20%283%29.pdf, 7.
47. *Matter of Kasinga*, 21 I&N, Dec. 377 (BIA 1996).
48. *Matter of Kasinga*, 21 I&N, Dec. 377 (BIA 1996).
49. *Matter of Kasinga*, 21 I&N, Dec. 377 (BIA 1996).
50. For example, see the postcolonial feminists referenced in chapter 1.

51. Celia W. Dugger, "A Refugee Body's Is Intact but Her Family is Torn," *New York Times,* September 11, 1996, accessed September 2011, http://www.nytimes.com/1996/09/11/nyregion/a-refugee-s-body-is-intact-but-her-family-is-torn.html?pagewanted = all&src = pm.
52. US Citizenship and Immigration Services Refugees and Asylum International Operations Asylum Division, "Female Asylum Applicants and Gender-Related Claims Asylum Officer Basic Training," March 12, 2009, accessed June 12, 2014, http://www.uscis.gov/sites/default/files/USCIS/Humanitarian/Refugees%20%26%20Asylum/Asylum/AOBTC%20Lesson%20Plans/Female-Asylum-Applicants-Gender-Related-Claims-31aug10.pdf.
53. Kerry Kennedy Cuomo, "Interview with Fauziya Kassindja," PBS, *Human Rights Defenders*, accessed January 24, 2014, http://www.pbs.org/speaktruthtopower/fauziya.html.
54. Information on the *A-T-* case is accessible from the Center for Gender and Refugee Studies, accessed July 3, 2014, http://cgrs.uchastings.edu/our-work/matter-t.
55. *Niang v. Gonzales*, 422 F. 3d 1187 (10th Cir. 2005). See also Amy McCarthy, "Niang v. Gonzales," *Washington and Lee Journal of Civil Rights and Social Justice* 12, no. 2 (2006): 331–38.
56. Zsaleh E. Harivandi, "Invisible and Involuntary: Female Genital Mutilation as a Basis for Asylum," *Cornell Law Review* 95 (2010): 608.
57. *Mohammed v. Gonzales*, 400 F. 3d 785 (9th Cir. 2005); *Niang v. Gonzales*, 422 F. 3d 1187 (10th Cir. 2005).
58. *Niang v. Gonzales*, 422 F. 3d 1187 (10th Cir. 2005).
59. *Niang v. Gonzales*, 422 F. 3d 1187 (10th Cir. 2005).
60. Michelle A. McKinley, "Cultural Culprits," *Berkeley Journal of Gender, Law and Justice* 24, no. 2 (2013): 110.
61. See Deborah Anker, "Refugee Status and the Violence against Women in the Domestic Sphere: the Non-state Actor Question," *Georgetown Immigration Law Journal* 15 (2001): 391–403.
62. Department of Homeland Security's Position on Respondent's Eligibility for Relief, *In re* Rody Alvarado-Pena, File No. A 73 753 922, 27.
63. *Matter of RA-*, 22 I&N Dec. 906 (A.G. 2001; BIA 1999), 911.
64. Bookey, "Domestic Violence," 114, 116.
65. Center for Gender and Refugee Studies Database Case #42 (1994), quoted in ibid., 123 n 53.
66. Center for Gender and Refugee Studies Database Case #373 (1996), quoted in ibid., 124 n. 53.
67. Center for Gender and Refugee Studies Database Case #222, (2002), quoted in ibid., 130 n. 92.
68. Center for Gender and Refugee Studies Database Case #614 (2001), quoted in ibid.
69. Center for Gender and Refugee Studies Database Case #813 (2003), quoted in ibid.
70. Center for Gender and Refugee Studies Database Case #1204 (2003), quoted in ibid.
71. Center for Gender and Refugee Studies Database Case #641 (2004), quoted in ibid., 135 n. 114.
72. Center for Gender and Refugee Studies Database Case #5146 (2009), quoted in ibid., 140 n. 138.

73. Quoted in Berger, "Production and Reproduction," 671.
74. Center for Gender and Refugee Studies Database Case #3346 (2003), quoted in Bookey, "Domestic Violence," 127 n. 75.
75. Laura S. Adams, "Fleeing the Family: A Domestic Violence Victim's Particular Social Group," *Loyola Law Review* 49, no. 2 (2003): 287–99.
76. Ibid., 298.
77. Ibid.
78. Elsa Bullard, "Insufficient Government Protection: The Inescapable Element in Domestic Violence Asylum Cases," *Minnesota Law Review* 95 (2011): 1884–85.
79. Ibid., 1887–88.
80. Connie Oxford, "Protectors and Victims in the Gender Regime of Asylum," *NWSA Journal* 17, no. 3 (2005): 31.
81. Ibid.
82. Ibid., 27–30.
83. *Matter of A-R-C-G et al.*, 26 I&N Dec. 388 (BIA 2014).
84. Conversation with author, skype, November 12, 2014.
85. Jennifer E. Coffman, "Producing FGM in U.S. Courts: Political Asylum in the Post-Kasinga Era," *Africa Today* 53, no. 4 (2007): 74.
86. Ibid., 76.
87. Gregor Noll, "Asylum Claims and the Translation of Culture into Politics," *Texas International Law Journal* 41 (2006): 495.
88. Ibid., 493.
89. Ibid.
90. Ibid., 495.
91. Wendy Brown, "Is Equality Secular?" Forum: Postcolonial and Liberal Discourses of the Family in Secular Politics. Center for Race and Gender, University of California, Berkeley, November 17, 2010, accessed April 28, 2012, http://crg.berkeley.edu/content/equality-secular.
92. Meghana Nayak, "The False Choice between Universalism and Religion/Culture," in "Critical Perspectives: Responses to Valerie Hudson, Donna Lee Bowen, Perpetua Lynne Nielsen, 'What Is the Relationship between Inequity in Family Law and Violence Against Women? Approaching the Issue of Legal Enclaves,'" *Politics and Gender* 9, no. 1 (2013): 120–25.
93. Bullard, 1885–1886.
94. Bullard, "Insufficient Government Protection," 1885–86.
95. Uma Narayan, *Dislocating Cultures: Identities, Traditions, and Third-World Feminism* (New York: Routledge, 1997).
96. US State Department, "United States Written Responses to Questions from the United Nations Human Rights Committee Concerning the Fourth Periodic Report," July 3, 2013, accessed September 3, 2014, http://www.state.gov/j/drl/rls/212393.htm.
97. Caroline Bettinger-Lopez, "Introduction: Jessica Lenahan (Gonzales) v. United States of America: Implementation, Litigation, and Mobilization Strategies," *Journal of Gender, Social Policy and the Law* 21, no. 2 (2012): 207–29.
98. Stacy Missari and Christine Zozula, "'Women as . . .': Personhood, Rights and the Case of Domestic Violence," *Societies Without Borders* 7, no. 1 (2012): 52–73. See also Indian Law Resource Center, "IACHR Decision Brings Hope to Native Women," August 18, 2011, accessed November 5, 2014, http://www.indianlaw.org/content/iachr-decision-brings-hope-native-women.

99. See for instance, Office of the Vice President, "1 is 2 Many: Twenty Years Fighting Violence against Women and Girls," 2014, accessed January 2, 2015, http://www.whitehouse.gov/sites/default/files/2014_vawa_report.pdf.
100. Jennifer Podkul, "Domestic Violence in the United States and Its Effect on U.S. Asylum Law," *Human Rights Brief* 12, no. 2 (2005): 18.
101. Rodriguez, "Give Us Your Weary," 344–45.
102. Center for Gender and Refugee Studies, "Getting Away with Murder: Guatemala's Failure to Protect Women and Rodi Alvarado's Quest for Safety" (2005), 19, quoted in Berger, "Production and Reproduction," 668.
103. U.S. Congress 2006, quoted in Berger, "Production and Reproduction," 672.
104. Berger, "Production and Reproduction," 669.
105. Kristin Bumiller, *In an Abusive State: How Neoliberalism Appropriates the Feminist Movement against Sexual Violence* (Durham: Duke University Press, 2008).
106. Khadijah F. Sharif, "Female Genital Mutilation: What Does the New Federal Law Really Mean?" *Fordham Urban Law Journal* 24, no. 2 (1996): 411 n. 9; "Gender-Based Asylum: Protecting and Promoting Access to Asylum for Women and Girls Fleeing Gender-based Persecution," Tahirih Justice Center, accessed June 12, 2014, http://www.tahirih.org/advocacy/policy-areas/gender-based-persecution/.
107. Illegal Immigration Reform and Immigrant Responsibility Act of 1996, Division C of Pub. L. 104-208, 110 Stat. 3009-546.
108. See Sections 644 and 655 of the Illegal Immigration Reform and Immigrant Responsibility Act of 1996, Pub. L. 104-208, 110 Stat. 3009 (September 30, 1996).
109. Sharif, "Female Genital Mutilation," abstract.
110. Leti Volpp, "Migrating Identities: On Labor, Culture, and Law," *North Carolina Journal of International Law of International Law and Commercial Regulation* 27 (2001–2): 513; Lila Abu-Lughod, "Seductions of the 'Honor Crime,'" *differences* 22, no. 1 (2011): 17–63.
111. Elizabeth H. Boyle, Fortunata Songora, and Gail Foss, "International Discourse and Local Politics: Anti-Female-Genital-Cutting Laws in Egypt, Tanzania, and the United States," *Social Problems* 48, no. 4 (2001): 536.
112. Elizabeth Heger Boyle, *Female Genital Cutting: Cultural Conflict in the Global Community* (Baltimore, MD: Johns Hopkins University Press, 2002), 41.
113. Isabelle R. Gunning, "Female Genital Surgeries and Multicultural Feminism: The Ties That Bind; The Differences That Distance," *Third World Legal Studies* 13 (1995): 17–47; McKinley, "Cultural Culprits." Further, as a thought experiment, given the reaction to FGC, where is the accompanying "outrage" regarding (often forced) genital alteration surgeries performed on intersex individuals in the United States and around the world to "normalize" their genitals. Nancy Ehrenreich with Mark Barr, "Intersex Surgery, Female Genital Cutting, and the Selective Condemnation of 'Cultural Practices,'" *Harvard Civil Rights–Civil Liberties Law Review* 40 (2005): 71–140.
114. Clare C. Robertson, "Getting beyond the Ew! Factor: Rethinking U.S. Approaches to African Female Genital Cutting," in *Genital Cutting and Transnational Sisterhood: Disputing U.S. Polemics*, ed. Stanlie M. James and Claire C. Robertson (Champaign: University of Illinois Press, 2002), 75.
115. The first quote is in the words of the judges of the Seventh Circuit; the second quote represents the asylum seekers' proposed social group. *Sarhan v. Holder*,

658 F. 3d 649 (7th Cir. 2011). In this case the Seventh Circuit recognized "honor killings" as a form of gender-based persecution.

CHAPTER 4

1. United Nations Protocol to Prevent, Suppress, and Punish Trafficking in Persons, Especially Women and Children, Supplementing the United Nations Convention Against Transnational Organized Crime, Article 3, A/55/383.
2. See Jennifer K. Lobasz, "Beyond Border Security: Feminist Approaches to Human Trafficking," *Security Studies* 18 (2009):321 n. 4 for a discussion on the difference between "domestic" and "international" trafficking. See also Andrea L. Johnson, "A Perfect Storm: The U.S. Anti-trafficking Regime's Failure to Stop the Sex Trafficking of American Indian Women and Girls," *Columbia Human Rights Law Review* 43, no. 2 (2012): 617–710, for a discussion of the trafficking of Native Americans between cities and often within reservations.
3. See, for example, "Male Trafficking Victims" Fact Sheet, US Department of State, June 1, 2013, accessed June 20, 2013, http://www.state.gov/j/tip/rls/fs/2013/211624.htm.
4. U.S.C. § 1182.
5. M. M. Holmes, H. S. Resnick, D. G. Kilpatrick, and C. L. Best, "Rape-Related Pregnancy: Estimates and Descriptive Characteristics from a National Sample of Women," *American Journal of Obstetrics and Gynecology* 175, no. 2 (1996): 320–25; E. Mulugeta, M. Kassaye, and Y. Berhane, "Prevalence and Outcomes of Sexual Violence among High School Students," *Ethiopian Medical Journal* 36, no. 3 (1998): 167–74; Felicia H. Stewart and James Trussell, "Prevention of Pregnancy Resulting from Rape: A Neglected Preventive Health Measure," *American Journal of Preventive Medicine* 19, no. 4 (2000): 228–29; Maria de Bruyn, *Violence, Pregnancy and Abortion: Issues of Women's Rights and Public Health*, 2nd ed. (Chapel Hill: Ipas, 2003); Robert R. Hazelwood and Ann Wolbert Burgess, *Practical Aspects of Rape Investigation: A Multidisciplinary Approach* (Boca Raton, FL: CRC Press, 2009).
6. Stephen Knight, "Asylum from Trafficking: A Failure of Protection," *Immigration Briefings* 07-07 (2007): 3. The one exception in the CGRS database is Case #3579, of a Ukrainian male victim of labor trafficking, heard by an asylum officer in 2005. Other organizations that represent or work with asylum seekers also only published comments about sex-trafficking cases, or cases that combined sex trafficking with some element of forced labor.
7. Ibid.
8. Tina Javaherian, "Seeking Asylum for Former Child Soldiers and Victims of Human Trafficking," *Pepperdine Law Review* 29, no. 2 (2012): 423–82.
9. Ibid., 447–52.
10. See Jessika Johnson, "Recent Development: Rreshpja v. Gonzales: The Sixth Circuit's Failure to Consider Gender's Place in Asylum Claims," *Tulane Journal of International and Comparative Law* 14 (2006): 623–41.
11. *Gjura v. Holder*, 695 F. 3d 223 (2d Cir. 2012).
12. Center for Gender and Refugee Studies, "Sexual Slavery and Human Trafficking," accessed July 3, 2014, http://cgrs.uchastings.edu/our-work/sexual-slavery-human-trafficking.
13. Molly Redden, "A Sex Trafficking Victory That Shows Just How Broken the System Is," *New Republic*, August 29, 2013, accessed September 3, 2014, http://cgrs.uchastings.edu/sites/default/files/New%20Republic%20August%202013.pdf.

14. *Cece v. Holder*, 733 F. 3d 662 (7th Cir. 2013).
15. Lynsay Gott, "Unrealistic Burdens: How the T Visa and Asylum Law Fail to Protect Many Victims of Trafficking," *Immigration and Nationality Law Review* 26 (2005): 718.
16. Knight, "Asylum from Trafficking," 7–8.
17. Ibid., 6.
18. Ibid., 4.
19. Ibid., 12.
20. Gott, "Unrealistic Burdens," 718.
21. World Organization for Human Rights USA, "Guide for Establishing the Asylum Eligibility of Victims of Human Trafficking and Forced Marriage" (2011), accessed June 5, 2012, http://www.uscrirefugees.org/2010Website/5_Resources/5_4_For_Lawyers/5_4_3_Human_Trafficking_Resources/5_4_3_3_Human_Trafficking_Links/Guide_to_Establishing_Asylum_Trafficking_Lynsey_Gott.pdf, 28–41.
22. Mohamed Y. Mattar, "Interpreting Judicial Interpretations of the Criminal Statutes of the Trafficking Victims Protection Act: Ten Years Later," *Journal of Gender, Social Policy and the Law* 19, no. 4 (2011): 1247–304. While this book is about asylum, I consider the T visa a form of immigration relief that is intended to protect.
23. For a description of the events leading up to the TVPA, see MaryAnne McReynolds, "The Trafficking Victims Protection Act: Has the Legislation Fallen Short of Its Goals?" *Policy Perspectives* 15 (2008): 33–56.
24. US Department of Justice Civil Division, "Report on the Tenth Anniversary of the Trafficking Victims Protection Act," October 29, 2010, accessed February 25, 2014, http://www.justice.gov/crt/about/crm/trafficking_newsletter/tvpaanniversaryreport.pdf, 4.
25. These estimates are based on reports by the US Department of State and other governmental agencies. Polaris Project, "Human Trafficking Statistics," accessed June 15, 2014, http://www.cicatelli.org/titleX/downloadable/Human%20Trafficking%20Statistics.pdf.
26. "Green Card for a Victim of Trafficking," US Citizenship and Immigration Services, n.d., accessed January 4, 2015, http://www.uscis.gov/green-card/other-ways-get-green-card/green-card-victim-trafficking-t-nonimmigrant.
27. Gott, "Unrealistic Burdens," 710.
28. 8 CFR § 214.11(g)(2) (2002).
29. H.R. 3244, 106th Congress 7(f)(4) (2000), cited in Gott, "Unrealistic Burdens," 170.
30. April Rieger, "Missing the Mark: Why the Trafficking Victims Protection Act Fails to Protect Sex Trafficking Victims in the United States," *Harvard Journal of Law and Gender* 30 (2007): 252–53.
31. World Organization for Human Rights USA, 7.
32. The first publicized story was a police raid in 1995 of a garment factory in El Monte, California. The second was in 1997 when the New York City Police Department busted a labor-trafficking ring of deaf-mute Mexican nationals. See Mary Catherine Hendrix, "Enforcing the U.S. Trafficking Victims Protection Act in Emerging Markets: The Challenge of Affecting Change in India and China," *Cornell International Law Journal* 43 (2010): 183.
33. Cited in Department of Homeland Security, "Immigration Remedies for Trafficking Victims," accessed December 5, 2014, http://www.dhs.gov/files/programs/gc_1270569897006.shtm.

34. Jayashri Srikantiah, "Perfect Victims and Real Survivors: The Iconic Victim in Domestic Human Trafficking Law," *Boston University Law Review* 87 (2007): 157–211.
35. US Immigration and Customs Enforcement, "Continued Presence: Temporary Immigration Status for Victims of Human Trafficking," accessed July 12, 2014, http://www.ice.gov/doclib/human-trafficking/pdf/continued-presence.pdf.
36. Training material, "Human Trafficking and the T visa," accessed December 5, 2014, http://www.vaw.umn.edu/documents/humantrafficking/humantrafficking.pdf.
37. New York Anti-Trafficking Network Legal Subcommittee. In 2007 the Trafficking in Persons Reports started to collect data on prosecutions and convictions. See US Department of State, "Trafficking in Persons Report," June 2014, accessed July 23, 2014, http://www.state.gov/documents/organization/226844.pdf, 45.
38. New York Anti-Trafficking Network Legal Subcommittee, 9.
39. I only included sex slavery claims in the data analysis when paired with trafficking, as other sex slavery claims were paired with domestic violence, rape, or female genital cutting claims.
40. U.S. Citizenship and Immigration Services, "Service-Wide Receipts, Approvals, and Denials," accessed July 23, 2014, http://www.immigration.com/sites/default/files/t_u_visas_stat.pdf.
41. Gott, "Unrealistic Burdens."
42. United Nations Office on Drugs and Crime, "Global Report on Trafficking in Persons," February 2009, accessed June 20, 2014, http://www.unodc.org/documents/Global_Report_on_TIP.pdf, 6.
43. International Labour Organization, "ILO Action against Trafficking in Human Beings," 2008, accessed February 15, 2014, http://www.ilo.org/wcmsp5/groups/public/@ed_norm/@declaration/documents/publication/wcms_090356.pdf, 3.
44. Srikantiah, "Perfect Victims," 184–85.
45. Alison Siskin and Liana Sun Wyler, "Trafficking in Persons: U.S. Policy and Issues for Congress," *Congressional Research Service*, February 19, 2013, 29 n. 137, 30, 149, 31 n. 151. These numbers include *all* investigations of trafficking cases, so trafficking investigations include not only victims who are foreign nationals but also US citizens.
46. Srikantiah, "Perfect Victims," 177.
47. Ronald Weitzer, "The Social Construction of Sex Trafficking: Ideology and Institutionalization of a Moral Crusade," *Politics and Society* 35, no. 3 (2007): 447–75.
48. Nicole Footen Bromfield and Moshoula Capous-Desyllas, "Underlying Motives, Moral Agendas and Unlikely Partnerships: The Formulation of the U.S. Trafficking in Victims Protection Act through the Data and Voices of Key Policy Players," *Advances in Social Work* 13, no. 2 (2012): 243–61.
49. George W. Bush, "President Bush Addresses United Nations General Assembly," September 23, 2003, quoted in Meghana Nayak, "Orientalism and 'Saving' US State Identity after 9/11," *International Feminist Journal of Politics* 8, no. 1 (2006): 55.
50. Cited in U.S. Department of Justice Civil Division, "Report on the Tenth Anniversary of the Trafficking Victims Protection Act," October 29, 2010, accessed July 23, 2014, http://www.justice.gov/crt/about/crm/trafficking_newsletter/tvpaanniversaryreport.pdf, 2.

51. Elizabeth Bernstein, "Carceral Politics as Gender Justice: The 'Traffic in Women' and Neoliberal Circuits of Crime, Sex, and Rights," *Theory and Society* 41, no. 3 (2012): 233–59; Carole S. Vance, "Innocence or Experience: Melodramatic Narratives of Sex Trafficking and Their Consequences for Law and Policy," *History of the Present* 2, no. 2 (2012): 200–218.
52. Srikantiah, "Perfect Victims," 187.
53. US Department of State, "Trafficking in Persons Report" (2007), accessed June 15, 2014, http://www.state.gov/documents/organization/82902.pdf.
54. Wendy Chapkis, "Trafficking, Migration, and the Law: Protecting Innocents, Punishing Immigrants," *Gender and Society* 17, no. 6 (2003): 926.
55. Trafficking Victims Protection Act, sec. 103 (9) cited in ibid., 927.
56. Chapkis, "Trafficking, Migration," 927.
57. Ibid., 925.
58. Ibid., 924.
59. New York Anti-Trafficking Network Legal Subcommittee, "Identification and Legal Advocacy for Trafficking Survivors, third edition," January 2009, accessed February 20, 2011, http://aaldef.org/docs/T visa-manual-3rd-ed%281208%29.pdf, 7–8.
60. Leticia Saucedo, "A New 'U': Organizing Victims and Protecting Immigrant Workers," *University of Richmond Law Review* 42 (2008): 101–65.
61. See also Salvador A. Cicero-Dominguez, "Assessing the U.S.-Mexico Fight against Human Trafficking and Smuggling: Unintended Results of U.S. Immigration Policy," *Northwestern Journal of International Human Rights* 4, no. 2 (2005): 303–30.
62. United Nations Office on Drugs and Crime, "Human Trafficking FAQs: How Is Human Trafficking Different from Migrant Smuggling?" accessed June 20, 2014, http://www.unodc.org/unodc/en/human-trafficking/faqs.html#How_is_human_trafficking_different_to_migrant_smuggling.
63. Cicero-Dominguez, "Assessing the U.S.-Mexico Fight," 305.
64. Jacqueline Bhabha and Monette Zard, "Smuggled or Trafficked?" *Forced Migration Review* 25 (2006): 6–8.
65. Srikantiah, "Perfect Victims," 188.
66. Ibid., 192.
67. Janie Chuang, "The United States as Global Sheriff: Using Unilateral Sanctions to Combat Human Trafficking," *Michigan Journal of International Law* 27 (2006): 437–94.
68. Jacqueline Bhabha, "Internationalist Gatekeepers? The Tension between Asylum Advocacy and Human Rights," *Harvard Human Rights Journal* 15 (2002): 172.
69. Dina F. Haynes, "Used, Abused, Arrested and Deported: The Case for Extending Immigration Benefits to Protect Victims of Trafficking and Secure the Prosecution of Traffickers," *Human Rights Quarterly* 26, no. 2 (2004): 244.
70. Ibid., 232, emphasis added.
71. Ibid., 257.
72. On the issue of agency and how trafficking female victims are constructed, see Lobasz, "Beyond Border Security."
73. "Boy Used in Smuggling Scheme Can Stay in U.S.," CNN Online, July 24, 2001, accessed August 3, 2014, http://www.cnn.com/2001/LAW/07/23/human.trafficking, cited in Chapkis, "Trafficking, Migration," 934.
74. Chapkis, "Trafficking, Migration," 935.

75. The White House National Security Council, "Transnational Organized Crime: A Growing Threat to National and International Security," accessed July 3, 2014, http://www.whitehouse.gov/administration/eop/nsc/transnational-crime/threat.
76. Arthur Rizer and Sheri R. Glaser, "Breach: The National Security Implications of Human Trafficking," *Widener Law Review* 17 (2011): 84.
77. Chapkis, "Trafficking, Migration," 934.
78. Jacqui True, *The Political Economy of Violence against Women* (New York: Oxford University Press, 2012), 71.
79. Rieger, "Missing the Mark."
80. Lobasz, "Beyond Border Security."
81. Haynes, "Used, Abused," 241.
82. Mary Catherine Hendrix, "Enforcing the U.S. Trafficking Victims Protection Act in Emerging Markets: The Challenge of Affecting Change in India and China," *Cornell International Law Journal* 43 (2010): 205.
83. TVPA § 110(d)(4), 114 Stat. 1464, 1483.
84. TVPA § 110(d)(5).
85. Hendrix, "Enforcing," 196.
86. Josh Rogin, "Will the State Department Sanction China and Russia for Human Trafficking," *Foreign Policy*, April 18, 2013, accessed May 15, 2013, http://thecable.foreignpolicy.com/posts/2013/04/18/will_the_state_department_sanction_china_and_russia_for_human_trafficking.
87. Chuang, "United States as Global Sheriff," 438–39.
88. Rebecca L. Wharton, "A New Paradigm for Human Trafficking: Shifting the Focus from Prostitution to Exploitation in the Trafficking Victims Protection Act," *William and Mary Journal of Women and the Law* 16, no. 3 (2010): 771–72.
89. Jo Doezema, "Ouch! Western Feminists' 'Wounded Attachment' to the 'Third World Prostitute,'" *Feminist Review* 67, no. 1 (2001): 16–38; Chapkis, "Trafficking, Migration." For more on the debates of the use of the tier system, see Memorandum from the Office of the Press Secretary to the Secretary of State, "Presidential Determination with Respect to Foreign Governments' Efforts Regarding Trafficking in Persons," October 17, 2008, accessed November 15, 2013, http://2001-2009.state.gov/g/tip/rls/prsrl/08/111083.htm; Susan W. Tiefenbrun, "Updating the Domestic and International Impact of the U.S. Victims of Trafficking Protection Act of 2000: Does Law Deter Crime?," *Case Western Reserve Journal of International Law* 38, no. 2 (2006–7): 268; Meril Eugene Anthes Jr., "Regarding Women & Children: Using International Trade Relations to Stem the Growing Tide of the Sexual Exploitation of Women and Children," *Currents: International Trade Journal* 14, no. 1 (2005): 69–81; Alexandra Webber and David Shirk, "Hidden Victims: Evaluating Protections for Undocumented Victims of Human Trafficking," *Immigration Policy in Focus* 4, no. 8 (2005), accessed July 13, 2014, http://www.ilw.com/articles/2006,0503-webber.shtm.
90. Kathleen Kim and Grace Chang, "Reconceptualizing Approaches to Human Trafficking: New Directions and Perspectives from the Field(s)," *Stanford Journal of Civil Rights and Civil Liberties* 3 (2007): 331.
91. Sean T. Masson, "Cracking Open the Golden Door: Revisiting U.S. Asylum Law's Response to China's One-Child Policy," *Hofstra Law Review* 37 (2009): 1135–68.
92. Illegal Immigration Reform and Immigrant Responsibility Act of 1996 ("IIRIRA"), Pub. L. No. 104-208, § 601(a)(1), 110 Stat. 3009-689 (codified as amended at 8 U.S.C. § 1101(a)(42)(2006))

93. See also Nicholas Cutaia, "A Circuit Split on Judicial Deference: Interpreting Asylum Claims by Fiancés and Boyfriends of Victims of China's Coercive Family Planning Policies," *St. John's Law Review* 80, no. 4 (2006): 1307–34.
94. 8 U.S.C. § 1101(a)42.
95. Kimberly Sicard, "Section 601 of IIRIRA: A Long Road to a Resolution of Untied States Asylum Policy Regarding Coercive Methods of Population Control," *Georgetown Immigration Law Journal* 14, no. 4 (2000): 927–40.
96. Katherine L. Vaughns, "Retooling the 'Refugee' Definition: The New Immigration Reform Law's Impact on United States Domestic Asylum Policy," *Rutgers Race and the Law Review* 1 (1998): 78.
97. *Matter of Chang*, 20 I&N. Dec. 38 (BIA 1989), 43.
98. Thomas L. Hunker, "Generational Genocide: Coercive Population Control as a Basis for Asylum in the United States," *Journal of Transnational Law and Policy* 15 (2005): 143.
99. Jessica Marsden, "Domestic Violence Asylum after *Matter of L-R-*," *Yale Law Journal* 123, no. 7 (2014): 2134–573.
100. For a discussion of the emergence and role of the US pro-life movement, see Ziad W. Munson, *The Making of Pro-Life Activists: How Social Movement Mobilization Works* (Chicago: University of Chicago Press, 2008).
101. See Sylvia A. Law and Lisa F. Rackner, "Gender Equality and the Mexico City Policy," *New York University International Law and Politics* 20 (1987): 193–228; Sharon Camp, "The Impact of the Mexico City Policy on Women and Health Care in Developing Countries," *New York University International Law and Politics* 20 (1987): 35–52.
102. Robert Pear, "Chinese Foes of One-Child Plan Get U.S. Asylum," *New York Times*, August 6, 1988, accessed July 2, 2014, http://www.nytimes.com/1988/08/06/world/chinese-foes-of-one-child-plan-get-us-asylum.html.
103. George H. W. Bush, "Memorandum of Disapproval for the Emergency Chinese Immigration Relief Act," November 30, 1989, assigned June 10, 2014, http://www.presidency.ucsb.edu/ws/?pid = 17883.
104. Charles E. Schulman, "The Grant of Asylum to Chinese Citizens Who Oppose China's One Child Policy: A Policy of Persecution or Population Control?" *Boston College Third World Law Journal* 16, no. 2 (1996): 313–37.
105. Kirk Semple, Joseph Goldstein, and Jeffrey E. Singer, "Asylum Fraud in Chinatown: An Industry of Lies," *New York Times*, February 22, 2014, accessed March 15, 2014, http://www.nytimes.com/2014/02/23/nyregion/asylum-fraud-in-chinatown-industry-of-lies.html?_r = 0 .
106. 21 I&N Dec. 915 (BIA 1997).
107. Kyle R. Rabkin, "The Zero-Child Policy: How the Board of Immigration Appeals Discriminates against Unmarried Asylum Seekers Fleeing Coercive Family Planning Measures," *Northwestern University Law Review* 101, no. 2 (2007): 965–96.
108. Raina Nortick, "Singled Out: A Proposal to Extend Asylum to the Unmarried Partners of Chinese Nationals Fleeing the One-Child Policy," *Fordham Law Review* 75, no. 4 (2007): 2168.
109. 24 I. & N. Dec. 1, 4 (B.I.A. 2006).
110. Nortick, "Singled Out," 2181.
111. Ibid.
112. Masson, "Cracking Open," 1136.
113. Nortick, "Singled Out," 2154, 2189, 2189 n. 258.

114. Megan Dempsey, "Misplaced Bright-Line Rule: Coercive Population Control in China and Asylum for Unmarried Partners: A Note," *Iowa Law Review* 92 (2006): 213–44.
115. See Dorothy Roberts, *Killing the Black Body: Race, Reproduction, and the Meaning of Liberty* (New York: Pantheon, 1997); feminists and reproductive rights/justice advocates confront the harmful stereotype of the unmarried promiscuous women when they mobilize for wider access to birth control and for freedom of choice in deciding how many children to have.
116. *Matter of Zhang*, 434 F. 3d (7th Cir. 2006) at 1004, cited in Jamie Jordan, "Ten Years of Resistance to Coercive Population Control: Section 601 of the IIRIRA of 1996 to Section 101 of the REAL ID Act of 2005," *Hastings Women's Law Journal* 18, no. 2 (2007): 242.
117. Center for Gender and Refugee Studies, "Li v. Ashcroft," 356 F. 3d 1153 (9th Cir. 2004), accessed August 3, 2014, http://cgrs.uchastings.edu/our-work/li-v-ashcroft.
118. Ibid.
119. Ibid.
120. Ibid.
121. *Matter of M-F-W and L-G-* 24 I&N Dec. 633 (BIA 2008).
122. *Matter of M-F-W and L-G-* 24 I&N Dec. 633 (BIA 2008).
123. Hunker, "Generational Genocide," 135.
124. Connie G. Oxford, "Protectors and Victims in the Gender Regime of Asylum," *NWSA Journal* 17, no. 3 (2005): 34.
125. Sunna K. Símonardóttir, "The Good, the Bad and the Innocent," *Þjódarspegillinn* (2013), accessed June 1, 2014, http://skemman.is/stream/get/1946/16782/39039/3/SunnaSimonardottir_Felman.pdf. See also Rosalind Petchesky, *Abortion and Women's Choice: The State, Sexuality, and Reproductive Freedom* (Boston: Northeastern University Press, 1990).
126. Lori K. Walls, "The Persecutor Bar in U.S. Immigration Law: Toward a More Nuanced Understanding of Modern 'Persecution' in the Case of Forced Abortion and Female Genital Cutting," *Pacific Rim Law and Policy Journal* 16, no. 1 (2007): 243.
127. Sara McKinnon, "The Discursive Formation of Gender in Women's Gendered Claims to U.S. Asylum," PhD diss., Arizona State University, 2009, 180.
128. Juliette Y. Hua, "The Object of 'Rights': Third World Women and the Production of Global Human Rights Discourse," PhD diss., University of California, San Diego, 2006.
129. Julian Baird Gewirtz and Rachel Kauder Nalebluff, "Chinese Villager Caught in U.S. Abortion Debate," *Huffington Post*, July 17, 2012, accessed August 3, 2012, http://www.huffingtonpost.com/julian-baird-gewirtz/china-abortion_b_1672917.html.
130. "House Foreign Affairs Committee Votes to Defund UNFPA," *Ms. Magazine*, October 6, 2011, accessed June 5, 2013, http://www.msmagazine.com/news/uswirestory.asp?ID = 13256.
131. Katherine Marshall, "Navigating the Turbulent Waters of Religion and Women's Rights: An Interview with Thoraya Obaid," *Huffington Post*, January 15, 2011, accessed June 3, 2014, http://www.huffingtonpost.com/katherine-marshall/courageous-in-navigating-_b_806313.html.
132. Even though the European Union and Friends of UNFPA (previously Americans for the UNFPA) aimed to fill in the gap left by the US denial/withdrawal of funding by the George W. Bush administration, those relying on the earmarked

US funds found their services interrupted. Also, the denial of funds directly contradicted the US proclaimed commitment to women's reproductive health and choice.

133. Paula Abrams, "Population Politics: Reproductive Rights and U.S. Asylum Policy," *Georgetown Immigration Law Journal* 14 (2000): 897–898.
134. McKinnon, "Discursive Formation," 181.
135. United Nations Convention on the Elimination of Discrimination Against Women, 1979; Abrams, "Population Politics."
136. Staff member at Global Justice Center, in discussion with author, October 14, 2013.
137. Michelle Goldberg, "Twice Victimized: U.S. Policy Obstructs Care for War-Rape Victims," *AlterNet*, May 16, 2011, accessed January 3, 2014, http://www.alternet.org/story/150958/twice_victimized%3A_u.s._policy_obstructs_care_for_war-rape_victims.
138. Editorial, "Humanitarian Aid for Rape Victims," *New York Times*, September 7, 2011, accessed October 3, 2012, http://www.nytimes.com/2011/09/08/opinion/humanitarian-aid-for-rape-victims.html?_r = 1.
139. Global Justice Center, "Submission to the UN Universal Periodic Review," April 2010, accessed February 3, 2014, http://www.globaljusticecenter.net/index.php?option = com_mtree&task = att_download&link_id = 34&cf_id = 34, 3; Global Justice Center, "Q&A: How President Obama Can—and Must—Save the Lives of Girls and Women Raped in War by Lifting the Abortion Ban Attached to US Humanitarian Aid," September 25, 2013, accessed February 3, 2014, http://globaljusticecenter.net/index.php?option = com_mtree&task = att_download&link_id = 20&cf_id = 34, 3.
140. Global Justice Center, "Submission to the UN Universal Periodic Review," 3–5, 7; Akila Radhakrishnan, in discussion with author, August 30, 2012.
141. Kristina Kallas and Akila Radhakrishnan, "Why Is the U.S. Waging War on Women Raped in War?" *RH Reality Check*, August 15, 2011, accessed February 15, 2013, http://www.rhrealitycheck.org/blog/2011/08/15/taking-war-on-women-to-women-in-war; Akila Radhakrishnan and Kristina Kallas, "Foreign Policy, Akin-Style: How the U.S. Denies Abortions to Women Raped in War," *Atlantic*, August 21, 2012, accessed February 15, 2013, http://www.theatlantic.com/international/archive/2012/08/foreign-policy-akin-style-how-the-us-denies-abortions-to-women-raped-in-war/261382/.
142. Global Justice Center, "Submission to the UN Universal Periodic Review," 11.
143. Ibid., 4.
144. Global Justice Center, "Submission to the UN Universal Periodic Review"; Akila Radhakrishnan, discussion with author, August 30, 2012.
145. Global Justice Center, "A Call for European Union Member States to Ensure Access to Safe Abortion Services for Female Rape Survivors in Armed Conflict," June 2014, accessed August 28, 2014, http://globaljusticecenter.net/index.php?option = com_mtree&task = att_download&link_id = 414&cf_id = 34; Akila Radhakrishnan, discussion with author, August 30, 2012.
146. Global Justice Center, "Submission to the UN Universal Periodic Review," 6; Akila Radhakrishnan, discussion with author, August 30, 2012.

CHAPTER 5

1. David Valentine, *Imagining Transgender: An Ethnography of a Category* (Durham, NC: Duke University Press, 2007), 30.

2. As Michael Warner argues, "Queer rejects a minoritizing logic of toleration or simple political-interest representation in favor of a more thorough resistance to regimes of the normal." Michael Warner, "Introduction," in *Fear of a Queer Planet: Queer Politics and Social Theory*, ed. Michael Warner (Minneapolis: University of Minnesota Press, 1993), xxvi, quoted in Eithne Luibhéid, "Introduction: Queering Migration and Citizenship," in *Queer Migrations: Sexuality, U.S. Citizenship, and Border Crossings*, ed. Eithne Luibhéid and Lionel Cantú, Jr. (Minneapolis: University of Minnesota Press, 2005), x.
3. Judith Butler, *Gender Trouble: Feminism and the Subversion of Identity* (New York: Routledge, 1990); Butler, *Bodies That Matter: On the Discursive Limits of "Sex"* (New York: Routledge, 1993); Warner, "Introduction"; Judith Halberstam, *In a Queer Time and Place: Transgender Bodies, Subcultural Lives* (New York: New York University Press, 2005); Jane Ward and Susan Mann, "Postmodernism, Poststructuralism, Queer, and Transgender Theories," in *Doing Feminist Theory: From Modernity to Postmodernity*, Susan Archer Mann (Oxford: Oxford University Press, 2012), 211–55.
4. V. S. Peterson and Anne Sisson Runyan, *Global Gender Issues*, 2nd ed. (Boulder, CO: Westview Press), 46–47.
5. Laura J. Shepherd and Laura Sjoberg, "Trans-bodies in/of War(s): Cisprivilege and Contemporary Security Strategy," *Feminist Review* 101 (2012): 6.
6. Kate Bornstein, *Gender Outlaw: On Men, Women, and the Rest of Us* (New York: Routledge, 1994).
7. Shepherd and Sjoberg, "Trans-bodies in/of War(s)," 6.
8. Lisa Duggan, *The Twilight of Equality? Neoliberalism, Cultural Politics, and the Attack on Democracy* (Boston: Beacon Press, 2003), 50.
9. Roderick A. Ferguson, "Race-ing Homonormativity: Citizenship, Sociology and Gay Identity," in *Black Queer Studies: A Critical Anthology*, ed. E. Patrick Johnson and Mae G. Henderson (Durham, NC: Duke University Press, 2005), 52–67; see Nan Seuffert, "Same-Sex Immigration: Domestication and Homonormativity," University of Wollongong Research Online (2009), accessed June 15, 2014, http://ro.uow.edu.au/cgi/viewcontent.cgi?article = 1597&context = lawpapers .
10. Jasbir Puar, *Terrorist Assemblages: Homonationalism in Queer Times* (Durham, NC: Duke University Press, 2007).
11. For a brief history of the legislation, see Lena Ayoub and Shin-Ming Wong, "Separated and Unequal," *William Mitchell Law Review* 32, no. 2 (2006): 559–97.
12. Ibid., 564 n. 14, 565.
13. Timothy J. Randazzo, "Social and Legal Barriers: Sexual Orientation and Asylum in the United States," in Luibhéid and Cantú, *Queer Migrations*, 32.
14. Ibid., 32–33.
15. *Matter of Toboso-Alfonso*, 20 I&N Dec. 819 (BIA 1990), 822, quoted in Randazzo, "Social and Legal Barriers," 33, emphasis added.
16. *Matter of Toboso-Alfonso.*
17. Keith Southam, "Who Am I and Who Do You Want Me to Be: Effectively Defining a Lesbian, Gay, Bisexual, and Transgender Social Group in Asylum Applications," *Chicago Kent Law Review* 86 (2011): 1370–71.
18. Robert C. Leitner, "A Flawed System Exposed: The Immigration Adjudicatory System and Asylum for Sexual Minorities," *University of Miami Law Review* 58, no. 2 (2004): 679–99.

19. L. G. Shoop, "Health-Based Exclusion Grounds in United States Immigration Policy: Homosexuals, HIV Infection and the Medical Examination of Aliens," *Journal of Contemporary Health Law Policy* 9 (1993): 527.
20. *Matter of Tenorio,* A72-093-558, IJ, July 26, 1993.
21. Randazzo, "Social and Legal Barriers," 35.
22. Ibid.
23. Howard Merkel and Alexandra Minna Stern, "The Foreignness of Germs: The Persistent Association of Immigrants and Disease in American Society," *Millbank Quarterly: A Multidisciplinary Journal of Population Health and Health Policy* 80, no. 4 (2002): 757–88.
24. John Medeiros, "Immigration after DOMA: How Equal Is Marriage Equality?" *Hamline University's School of Law's Journal of Public Law and Policy* 35, no. 1 (2014): 200–201.
25. Fiona McKinnon and Ellen Kemp, "Immigration and HIV," *The Body*, Fall 2006, accessed August 2, 2014, http://www.thebody.com/content/art38433.html.
26. See, for example, *Karouni v. Gonzales*, 399 F. 3d 1163 (9th Cir. 2005); *Boer-Sedano v. Gonzales*, 418 F. 3d 1082 (9th Cir. 2005).
27. *Karouni v. Gonzales.*
28. Victoria Neilson and Aaron Morris, "The Gay Bar: The Effect of the One-Year Filing Deadline on Lesbian, Gay, Bisexual, Transsexual, and HIV-Positive Foreign Nationals Seeking Asylum or Withholding of Removal," *New York City Law Review* 8 (2005): 263.
29. Sharita Gruberg, "Dignity Denied: LGBT Immigrants in U.S. Immigration Detention," Center for American Progress, November 2013, accessed February 10, 2014, http://cdn.americanprogress.org/wp-content/uploads/2013/11/ImmigrationEnforcement.pdf.
30. See Immigration Equality's Asylum Manual, available at www.immigrationequality.org.
31. Grace Poore, "Three Movements in a Minor: Lesbians and Immigration," *Off Our Backs*, August–September 1996, 12, quoted in Luibhéid, "Introduction," xxxvi n. 10.
32. Medeiros, "Immigration after DOMA," 205 n. 42, 206.
33. Ibid.; see also Shannon Minter, "Sodomy and Public Morality Offenses under U.S. Immigration Law," *Cornell International Law Journal* 26 (1993): 771–818.
34. Karel Raba, "Thirty Years of Adams v. Howerton: Changed Circumstances, DOMA, and a Vision of a DOMA-Free World," *Chapman Law Review* 17 (2013): 265–94.
35. Rebecca Isaacs, "Op-ed: DOMA, the First Battle in the Immigration War," Advocate.com, July 2, 2013, accessed August 2, 2013, http://www.advocate.com/commentary/2013/07/02/op-ed-doma-first-battle-immigration-war.
36. Bijal Shah, "LGBT Identity in Immigration," *Columbia Human Rights Law Review* 45 (2013): 100–213.
37. Raba, "Thirty Years."
38. Randazzo, "Social and Legal Barriers," 48–49.
39. Ibid., 49–50.
40. Neilson and Morris, "The Gay Bar," 264.
41. Ibid.
42. Ibid., 265.

43. For example, almost every law review or immigration organization publication I read about LGBT asylum seekers mentioned examples of people who did not want to apply for asylum for the reasons named.
44. Randazzo, "Social and Legal Barriers," 51.
45. Ibid., 52.
46. C. T. Turney, "Give Me Your Tired, Your Poor, and Your Queer: The Need and Potential for Advocacy for LGBTQ Immigrant Detainees," *UCLA Law Review* 58 (2011): 1350.
47. Ibid., 1352.
48. Ibid., 1353; see also note 52, 1353.
49. Pooja Gehi, "Struggles from the Margins. Anti-immigrant Legislation and the Impact on Low-Income Transgender People of Color," *Women's Rights Law Reporter* 30 (2009): 326.
50. Ibid., 321.
51. See also Félix E. Gardón, "The REAL ID Act's Implications for Transgender Rights," *Women's Rights Law Reporter* 30 (2009): 352–56.
52. Turney, "Give Me Your Tired," 1359.
53. See James McGrath, "Are You a Boy or a Girl? Show Me Your REAL ID," *Nevada Law Journal* 9 (2009): 368–406; Melanie A. Conroy, "Real Bias: How REAL ID's Credibility and Corroboration Requirements Impair Sexual Minority Asylum Applicants," *Berkeley Journal of Gender Law and Justice* 24 (2009): 2–3.
54. Gehi, "Give Me Your Tired," 332.
55. 8 C.F.R. 208.4(a) (5) (2004).
56. Jeffrey Martins, "Running Out of Time: Staying One Step Ahead of the One-Year Asylum Deadline," *Immigration Law Today*, September/October (2007): 36.
57. Gehi, "Give Me Your Tired," 329.
58. US Citizenship and Immigration Services, "Affirmative Asylum Procedures Manual," November 2007, revised July 2010, accessed November 13, 2013, http://www.uscis.gov/sites/default/files/USCIS/Refugee%2C%20Asylum%2C%20and%20Int%27l%20Ops/Asylum/AffrmAsyManFNL.pdf, 64–65.
59. Quoted in ibid., 64.
60. Ibid., 65.
61. Fatima Mohyuddin, "United States Asylum Law in the Context of Sexual Orientation and Gender Identity: Justice for the Transgendered?" *Hastings Women's Law Journal* 12 (2001): 387–410.
62. *Hernandez-Montiel v. I.N.S.*, 225 F. 3d 1084 (9th Cir. 2000).
63. *Hernandez-Montiel v. I.N.S.* See Suzanne B. Goldberg, "Give Me Liberty or Give Me Death: Political Asylum and the Global Persecution of Lesbians and Gay Men," *Cornell International Law Journal* 26 (1993): 605–23; Naomi Mezey, "Dismantling the Wall: Bisexuality and the Possibilities of Sexual Identity Classification Based on Acts," *Berkeley Women's Law Journal* 10 (1995) 98–133 .
64. *Reyes-Reyes v. Ashcroft*, 3 84 F. 3d 782 (9th Cir. 2004).
65. *Reyes-Reyes v. Ashcroft.*
66. *Hernandez-Montiel v. I.N.S.*
67. Joseph Landau, "Soft Immutability and Imputed Gay Identity: Recent Developments in Transgender and Sexual-Orientation-Based-Law," *Fordham Urban Law Journal* 32 (2004): 237–63, quoted in Laurie Berg and Jenni Millbank, "Developing a Jurisprudence of Transgender Particular Social Group," University of Technology Sydney Faculty of Law Legal Studies Research Paper Series No. 2013/1 (2013), 15.

68. Berg and Millbank, "Developing a Jurisprudence," 14–15.
69. See David Valentine, *Imagining Transgender: An Ethnography of a Category* (Durham, NC: Duke University Press, 2007), 29.
70. Victoria Neilson, "Uncharted Territory: Choosing an Effective Approach in Transgender-Based Asylum Claims," *Fordham Urban Law Journal* 32, no. 2 (2004): 116.
71. Ibid., 120.
72. Berg and Millbank, "Developing a Jurisprudence," 16–17.
73. Southam, "Who Am I," 1373; see also Landau, "Soft Immutability."
74. Southam, "Who Am I," 1374. See also Fatma Marouf, "The Emerging Importance of 'Social Visibility' in Defining a 'Particular Social Group' and Its Potential Impact on Asylum Claims Related to Sexual Orientation and Gender," *Yale and Law Policy Review* 27 (2008): 63.
75. To develop this section, I also consulted Barry O' Leary, "'We Cannot Claim Any Particular Knowledge of the Ways of Homosexuals, Still Less of Iranian Homosexuals . . .': The Particular Problems Facing Those Who Seek Asylum on the Basis of Their Sexual Identity," *Feminist Legal Studies* 16, no. 1 (2008): 87–95; E. Luibhéid, *Entry Denied: Controlling Sexuality at the Border* (Minneapolis: University of Minnesota Press, 2002); Deborah A. Morgan, "Not Gay Enough for the Government: Racial and Sexual Stereotypes in Sexual Orientation Asylum Cases," *Law and Sexuality Review* 15 (2006): 135–61; Goldberg, "Give Me Liberty"; E. Luibhéid, "Queer/Migration: An Unruly Body of Scholarship," *GLQ* 14, nos. 2–3 (2008): 169–90; Marisa Silenzi Cianciarulo, "Terrorism and Asylum Seekers: Why the REAL ID Act Is a False Promise," *Harvard Journal on Legislation* 43 (2006): 101–43; "The Real ID Act: Bad Law for Our Community," National Center for Transgender Equal and Transgender Law Center, accessed February 23, 2014, http://www.realnightmare.org/images/File/NCTE%20realid.pdf; Sonia Katyal, "Exporting Identity," *Yale Journal of Law and Feminism* 14 (2002): 97–176; Morgan, "Not Gay Enough."
76. Deborah Anker and Sabrineh Ardalan, "Escalating Persecution of Gays and Refugee Protection: Comment on Queer Cases Make Bad Law," *N.Y.U. Journal of International Law and Politics* 44 (2012): 543.
77. Ibid., 546.
78. Quoted in ibid., 547.
79. Ibid., 547–48.
80. Ibid., 550.
81. James Hathaway and Jason Pobjoy, "Queer Cases Make Bad Law," *International Law and Politics* 44 (2012): 325. While Hathaway and Pobjoy focus on Australia and the United Kingdom, their analyses are relevant in terms of the need to prove well-founded fear of persecution.
82. Ibid., 326.
83. Dan Bilefsky, "Gays Seeking Asylum in U.S. Encounter a New Hurdle," *New York Times*, January 28, 2011, accessed September 15, 2013, http://www.nytimes.com/2011/01/29/nyregion/29asylum.html?_r = 0&adxnnl = 1&pagewanted = all&adxnnlx = 1404762256-FFgu3M9losO5241z11Ui8w.
84. Stephanie Mencimer, "Immigration Judge to Asylum Seeker: You Don't Look Gay," *Mother Jones*, October 7, 2010, accessed September 15, 2013, http://www.motherjones.com/mojo/2010/10/bush-immigration-judge-gay-asylum seeker.

85. V. Neilson, "Homosexual or Female: Applying for Gender-Based Asylum Jurisprudence to Lesbian Asylum Claims," *Stanford Law and Policy Review* 16, no. 2 (2005): 418.
86. Susan Berger, "Production and Reproduction of Gender and Sexuality in Legal Discourses of Asylum in the United States," *Signs* 34, no. 3 (2009): 659–85.
87. Ibid., 675.
88. See *Tavera Lara v. Attorney General*, No. 05-16094 (11th Cir. 2006), quoted in ibid., 674.
89. Neilson, "Homosexual or Female," 425.
90. Ibid., 432.
91. Ibid., 433.
92. Ibid., 437.
93. Ibid., 426, emphasis mine.
94. See also the discussion of body scanning in Shepherd and Sjoberg, "Trans-bodies in/of War(s)."
95. Victoria Neilson, "Asylum Pitfalls May Await the Transgender Applicant," *On The Issues*, Summer 2009, accessed July 13, 2014, http://www.ontheissuesmagazine.com/2009summer/2009summer_Neilson.php.
96. Ibid.
97. See Melissa Bourdeaux, "Living a Lie: Why 'Don't Ask Don't Tell' Presents an Unworkable View of Personhood," *Boston College Third World Law Journal* 31, no. 3 (2011): 9.
98. Hollis V. Pfitsch, "Homosexuality in Asylum and Constitutional Law: Rhetoric of Acts and Identity," *Law and Sexuality* 15 (2006): 59–89; Diane S. Meier, "Gender Trouble in the Law: Arguments against the Use of Status/Conduct Binaries in Sexual Orientation Law," *Washington and Lee Journal of Civil Rights and Social Justice* 15 (2008): 147–89.
99. Berg and Millbank, "Developing a Jurisprudence," 30.
100. Ibid., 2.
101. Ibid.
102. The White House Office of the Press Secretary, "Presidential Memorandum—International Initiatives to Advance the Human Rights of Lesbian, Gay, Bisexual, and Transgender Persons," December 6, 2011, accessed February 12, 2014, http://www.whitehouse.gov/the-press-office/2011/12/06/presidential-memorandum-international-initiatives-advance-human-rights-l.
103. Samantha Power, "U.S. Leadership to Advance Equality for LGBT People Abroad," White House Blog, December 13, 2012, accessed January 18, 2013, http://www.whitehouse.gov/blog/2012/12/13/us-leadership-advance-equality-lgbt-people-abroad.
104. Mark Bromley, "Building a Strategy for an LGBT-Inclusive U.S. Foreign Policy," Council for Global Equality, November 2007, accessed January 18, 2013, http://www.globalequality.org/storage/documents/pdf/lgbt_foreign_policy_project-discussion_paper.pdf.
105. Power, "U.S. Leadership."
106. Hathaway and Pobjoy, "Queer Cases," 315–18.
107. Paul Canning, "New York Times Gay Asylum Article Misled, Say Advocates," *LGBT Asylum News*, February 7, 2011, accessed January 18, 2013, http://madikazemi.blogspot.com/2011/02/new-york-times-gay-asylum-article.html.
108. Luibhéid, "Introduction," xxix.

109. Leonard Birdsong, "A Legislative Rejoinder to 'Give Me Your Gays, Your Lesbians, and Your Victims of Gender Violence, Yearning to Breathe Free of Sexual Persecution . . . ,'" *William Mitchell Law Review* 35, no. 1 (2008): 204.
110. Lionel Cantú, with Eithne Luibhéid and Alexandra Minna Stern, "Well Founded Fear: Political Asylum and the Boundaries of Sexual Identity in the U.S.-Mexico Borderlands," in Luibhéid and Cantú, *Queer Migrations*, 58.
111. Ibid., 63.
112. *Doe v. Holder*, No. 09-72161 (9th Cir. 2013), accessed August 13, 2014, http://cdn.ca9.uscourts.gov/datastore/opinions/2013/11/27/09-72161.pdf.
113. "U.S. Court Reviews Gay Russian's Asylum Case, *Moscow Times*, December 2, 2013, accessed August 15, 2014, http://www.themoscowtimes.com/news/article/us-court-reviews-gay-russians-asylum-case/490595.html.
114. Bob Egelko, "Court Backs Asylum for Gay Russian Man," *SF Gate*, November 28, 2013, accessed February 20, 2014; Arthur S. Leonard, "US Ninth Circuit Revives Russian Gay Asylum Seeker's Bid," *Daily Queer News*, December 5, 2013, accessed February 20, 2014, https://dailyqueernews.wordpress.com/2013/12/05/us-ninth-circuit-revives-russian-gay-asylum-seekers-bid/.
115. Priyanka Gupta, "LGBT Exodus from Russia: Stories of Exile," *Huffington Post*, March 29, 2014, accessed April 15, 2014, http://www.huffingtonpost.com/priyanka-gupta/lgbt-exodus-from-russia-s_b_4671241.html.
116. Michael K. Lavers, "Gay Asylum Seeker Flees Violence in Putin's Russia," *Washington Blade*, September 24, 2014, accessed September 28, 2014, http://www.washingtonblade.com/2014/09/24/gay-russian-asylum-seeker-hopes-find-sanctuary-u-s/.
117. Aaron Sussman, "Expanding Asylum Law's Pattern-or-Practice-of-Persecution Framework to Better Protect LGBT Refugees," *University of Pennsylvania Journal of Law and Social Change* 16, no. 2 (2013): 111–31.
118. Shankar Vedantam, "Jamaica's Gays Finding Refuge by Applying for U.S. Asylum," *Washington Post*, February 11, 2011, http://www.washingtonpost.com/wp-dyn/content/article/2011/02/11/AR2011021106013.html?sid = ST2011021106030, accessed February 15, 2014.
119. Lucy H. Halatyn, "Political Asylum and Equal Protection: Hypocrisy of United States Protection of Gay Men and Lesbians," *Suffolk Transnational Law Review* 22 (1998): 133–62.
120. John M. Becker, "U.S. Policies Fail LGBT Asylum seekers," *Bilerico Project*, January 9, 2014, accessed February 14, 2014, http://www.bilerico.com/2014/01/us_policies_fail_lgbt_asylum seekers.php.
121. Scott James, "With Ban on H.I.V. Immigrants Now History, Relief and Revision," *New York Times*, March 19, 2010, accessed April 15, 2013, http://www.nytimes.com/2010/03/19/us/19sfmetro.html?_r = 0.
122. Luibhéid, "Introduction," xxv.
123. Ibid., xxvi.
124. Alisa Solomon, "Trans/Migrant: Christina Madrazo's All-American Story," in Luibhéid and Cantú, *Queer Migrations*, 3–29.
125. Ibid., 4, 22.
126. Ibid.
127. Quoting interview with author and transcript from panel, "Shifting Grounds for Asylum: Female Genital Surgery and Sexual Orientation," October 16, 1997, New York University School of Law, published in *Columbia Human Rights Law Review*, Spring 1998, 29, 467–532, in ibid., 20.

CHAPTER 6

1. Richa Nagar and Amanda Swarr, "Introduction: Theorizing Transnational Feminist Praxis," in *Critical Transnational Feminist Praxis*, ed. Amanda Swarr and Richa Nagar (Albany: State University of New York Press, 2010), 1–22.
2. Ibid., 5, emphasis original.
3. Emanual Adler and Steven Bernstein, "Knowledge in Power: The Epistemic Construction of Global Governance," in *Power in Global Governance*, ed. Michael Barnett and Raymond Duvall (Cambridge: Cambridge University Press, 2005), 294–318.
4. Jaya Ramji-Nogales, Andrew I. Schoenholtz, and Philip G. Schrag, "The Immigration Courts," in *Refugee Roulette: Disparities in Asylum Adjudication and Proposals for Reform*, ed. Jaya Ramji-Nogales, Andrew I. Schoenholtz, and Philip G. Schrag (New York: New York University Press, 2009), 45.
5. Ibid.
6. Ibid., 45–46.
7. Ibid., 46.
8. Emily Heller, "Asylum Cases Keep Reed Smith Pro Bono Counsel on Cutting Edge," *National Law Journal*, January 14, 2010, accessed February 20, 2014, http://www.law.com/jsp/article.jsp?id = 1202437934421.
9. Elisabeth Prügl, "Diversity Management and Gender Mainstreaming as Technologies of Government," *Politics and Gender* 7 (2011): 71–89.
10. Jennifer Coffman, "Producing FGM in U.S. Courts: Political Asylum in the Post-Kasinga Era," *Africa Today* 53, no. 4 (2007): 79.
11. Anthony Good, "'Undoubtedly an Expert?' Anthropologists in British Asylum Courts," *Journal of the Royal Anthropological Institute* 10 (2004): 113–33.
12. Country of Origin Research and Information, "Events: International Conference—10th and 11th June 2010," accessed August 1, 2014, http://www.cori.org.uk/3.html.
13. Lionel Cantú Jr. with Eithne Luibhéid and Alexandra Minna Stern, "Well-Founded Fear: Political Asylum and the Boundaries of Sexual Identity in the U.S.-Mexico Borderlands," in *Queer Migrations: Sexuality, U.S. Citizenship, and Border Crossings*, ed. Eithne Luibhéid and Lionel Cantú Jr. (Minneapolis: University of Minnesota Press, 2005), 61–74.
14. Center for Gender and Refugee Studies, "Get Involved," accessed June 20, 2014, http://cgrsdrupal.uchastings.edu/about/get-involved.
15. Chitra Aiyar, conversation with author, August 13, 2012.
16. Maria Eriksson Baaz and Maria Stern, "Why Do Soldiers Rape? Masculinity, Violence, and Sexuality in the Armed Forces in the Congo (DRC)," *International Studies Quarterly* 53, no. 2 (2009): 495–518.
17. US Immigration and Citizenship Services Refugee, Asylum, and International Office Directorate Officer Training, "Guidance for Adjudicating Lesbian, Gay, Bisexual, Transgender, and Intersex (LGBTI) Refugee and Asylum Claims," December 28, 2011, accessed January 20, 2013, http://www.uscis.gov/sites/default/files/USCIS/About%20Us/Directorates%20and%20Program%20Offices/RAIO/lgbtir-guidance-for-adjudicating-lesbian-gay-bisexual-and-intersex-claims.pdf.
18. Marysia Zalewski and Jane L. Parpart, "Introduction: Rethinking the Man Question," in *Rethinking the Man Question: Sex, Gender and Violence in International Relations*, ed. Jane L. Parpart and Marysia Zalewski (London: Routledge, 2008), 7–8.

19. Christina Gerken, "Neo-liberalism and Family Values in 1990s Immigration Reform Discourse," *Roots and Routes* 17 (2008): 44–71.
20. "Gayatri Chakravorty Spivak," in *The Present as History: Critical Perspectives on Global Power*, ed. Nermeen Shaikh (New York: Columbia University Press, 2007), 193.
21. Lila Abu-Lughod, "Seductions of the 'Honor Crime,'" *differences* 22, no. 1 (2011): 16–63.
22. Ibid., 44.
23. Inderpal Grewal, "Outsourcing Patriarchy: Feminist Encounters, Transnational Mediations and the Crime of 'Honor Killings,'" *International Feminist Journal of Politics* 15, no. 1 (2013): 1–19; Elora Halim Chowdhury, "Rethinking Patriarchy, Culture and Masculinity: Transnational Narratives of Gender Violence and Human Rights Advocacy," *Journal of International Women's Studies* 16, no. 2 (2015): 98–114. Both authors point out that representations of backwardness play a role *within* non-Western countries as well.
24. Aisha Gill, "'Honour'-Based Violence Runs Deep and Wide," *Guardian*, February 1, 2012, accessed June 14, 2013, http://www.guardian.co.uk/commentisfree/2012/feb/01/honour-based-violence-deep-wide.
25. Abu-Lughod, "Seductions," 34.
26. Ibid., 32.
27. US Citizenship and Immigration Services Refugee, Asylum, and International Operations Asylum Division, "Asylum Officer Basic Training Course: Female Asylum Applicants and Gender-Related Claims," March 12, 2009, accessed January 10, 2014, http://www.uscis.gov/sites/default/files/USCIS/Humanitarian/Refugees%20%26%20Asylum/Asylum/AOBTC%20Lesson%20Plans/Female-Asylum-Applicants-Gender-Related-Claims-31aug10.pdf, 26.
28. Carol Bohmer and Amy Shuman, *Rejecting Refugees: Political Asylum in the 21st Century* (New York: Routledge, 2008), 126–27.
29. Megan Gaucher, "Keeping It in the Family: The (Re)production of Conjugal Citizens Through Canadian Immigration Policy and Practice," PhD diss., Queen's University, 2013, 53, accessed April 20, 2014, http://qspace.library.queensu.ca/bitstream/1974/7845/1/Gaucher_Megan_N_201303_PhD.pdf.
30. Law Commission of Canada, "Beyond Conjugality: Recognizing and Supporting Close Personal Adult Relationships," December 21, 2001, accessed March 10, 2014, https://ecf.cand.uscourts.gov/cand/09cv2292/evidence/DIX0093.pdf.
31. Ibid., 18.
32. Ibid., 43.
33. Shani M. King, "U.S. Immigration Law and the Traditional Nuclear Conception of Family: Toward a Functional Definition of Family That Protects Children's Fundamental Human Rights," *Columbia Human Rights Law Review* 41 (2010): 509–66.
34. Victoria Degtyareva, "Defining Family in Immigration Law: Accounting for Nontraditional Families in Citizenship by Descent," *Yale Law Journal* 120 (2011): 862–908.
35. Rachel Lewis, "Lesbians under Surveillance: Same-Sex Immigration Reform, Gay Rights, and the Problem of Queer Liberalism" *Social Justice* 37, no. 1 (2010–11): 98.
36. Eithne Luibhéid, "Heteronormativity and Immigration Scholarship: A Call for Change," *GLQ* 10, no. 2 (2004): 227–35; Debanuj DasGupta, "Queering

Immigration: Perspectives on Cross-Movement Organization," *Scholar and Feminist Online* 10.1–10.2 (Fall 2011–Spring 2012), http://sfonline.barnard.edu/a-new-queer-agenda/queering-immigration-perspectives-on-cross-movement-organizing/; see also Queer Migration Research Network, accessed April 15, 2014, www.queermigration.com.

37. Karma Chavez, "Border (IN)Securities: Normative and Differential Belonging in LGBTQ and Immigrant Rights Discourse," *Communication and Critical/Cultural Studies* 7, no. 2 (2010): 136–55.
38. Monisha Das Gupta, "'Don't Deport Our Daddies': Gendering State Deportation Practices and Immigrant Organizing," *Gender and Society* 28, no. 1 (2014): 83–109.
39. Ibid., 99–101.
40. Pooja Gehi and Soniya Munshi, "Connecting State Violence and Anti-violence: An Examination of the Impact of VAWA and Hate Crimes Legislation on Asian American Communities," *Asian American Law Journal* 21 (2014): 5–35.
41. Dan Levine and Kristina Cooke, "Special Report: U.S. Visa Program For Crime Victims Is Hit-or-Miss Prospect," Reuters, October 21, 2014, accessed November 18, 2014, http://www.reuters.com/article/2014/10/21/us-usa-immigration-uvisa-specialreport-idUSKCN0IA1H420141021.
42. Gehi and Munshi, "Connecting State Violence."
43. Maxine Baca Zinn, "Feminism and Family Studies for a New Century," *Annals of the American Academy of Political and Social Science* 57, no. 1 (2000): 42–56.
44. For these examples, I draw upon the following: Dorothy Roberts, *Killing the Black Body: Race, Reproduction, and the Meaning of Liberty* (New York: Pantheon, 1997); Ananya Bhattacharjee and Jael Silliman, eds., *Policing the National Body: Race, Gender and Criminalization in the United States* (Cambridge, MA: South End Press, 2002); Joan C. Chrisler, ed. *Reproductive Justice: A Global Concern* (Santa Barbara, CA: Praeger, 2012).
45. Per the Genocide Conventions and the Rome Statute, genocide means "any of the following acts committed with intent to destroy, in whole or in part, a national, ethnical, racial or religious group, as such: (a) Killing members of the group; (b) Causing serious bodily or mental harm to members of the group; (c) Deliberately inflicting on the group conditions of life calculated to bring about its physical destruction in whole or in part; (d) Imposing measures intended to prevent births within the group; (e) Forcibly transferring children of the group to another group."
46. Alyson M. Drake, "Aimed at Protecting Ethnic Groups or Women? A Look at Forced Pregnancy under the Rome Statute," *William and Mary Journal of Women and the Law* 18 (2012): 618.
47. Forced pregnancy can be charged as a crime against humanity if there is (1) "intent" to change or affect the "ethnic composition" of any population can be proven; (2) the forced pregnancy occurred as a widespread or systematic attack; or (3) the perpetrator knew that forced pregnancy was "part of or intended" to be a part of a widespread of systematic attack. Forced pregnancy as a war crime has similar elements that need to be proven: (1) establish "intent" of affecting the ethnic composition "or carrying out other grave violations of international law"; (2) establish the crime occurred in the context of an armed conflict; and, (3) establish that the perpetrator was aware of the existence of the armed conflict.

48. Drake, "Aimed at Protecting."
49. René Degni-Segui, Special Rapporteur of the Commission on Human Rights, "Report on the Situation of Human Rights in Rwanda," Economic and Social Council, United Nations, E/CN.41996/68, January 29, 1996, accessed January 10, 2013, http://www1.umn.edu/humanrts/commission/country52/68-rwa.htm.
50. Mary Valentich, "Rape Revisited: Sexual Violence against Women in the Former Yugoslavia," *Canadian Journal of Human Sexuality* 3, no. 1 (1994): 53–64.
51. *Prosecutor v. Akayesu*, Case. No. ICTR-96-4-T, Judgment 507.
52. *Prosecutor v Karadzic*, Case No. IT-95-5/18-I, 2006.
53. *Kadic v. Karadzic*, 70 F. 3d (2d Cir. 1996).
54. *Doe v. Karadzic: Brief Amici Curiae from Alliances*, 94-9035, United States Court of Appeals for the Second Circuit, accessed January 20, 2013, http://avalon.law.yale.edu/diana/5june.asp.
55. Drake, "Aimed at Protecting," 606 n. 80.
56. Siobhan K. Fisher, "Occupation of the Womb: Forced Impregnation as Genocide," *Duke Law Journal* 46 (1996): 91–133; R. Charli Carpenter, "Forced Maternity, Children's Rights and the Genocide Convention: A Theoretical Analysis," *Journal of Genocide Research* 2, no. 2, (2000): 223; Claudia Card, "The Paradox of Genocidal Rape Aimed at Enforced Pregnancy," *Southern Journal of Philosophy* 46 (2008): 178; Robin May Schott, "War Rape, Natality and Genocide," *Journal of Genocide Research* 13, no. 1–2 (2011): 5–21.
57. Maria Eriksson Baaz and Maria Stern, "Why Do Soldiers Rape? Masculinity, Violence, and Sexuality in the Armed Forces in the Congo (DRC)," *International Studies Quarterly* 53, no. 2 (2009): 495–518.
58. Akila Radhakrishnan and Kristina Kallas, "Foreign Policy, Akin-Style: How the U.S. Denies Abortions to Women Raped in War," *Atlantic*, August 21, 2012, accessed June 15, 2014, http://www.theatlantic.com/international/archive/2012/08/foreign-policy-akin-style-how-the-us-denies-abortions-to-women-raped-in-war/261382/.
59. Alexandra Minna Stern, "Sterilized in the Name of Public Health: Race, Immigration, and Reproductive Control in Modern California," *American Journal of Public Health* 95, no. 7 (2005): 1128–38, http://www.ncbi.nlm.nih.gov/pmc/articles/PMC1449330/.
60. Nilmini Gunuratne Rubin, "A Crime against Motherhood," *Los Angeles Times*, May 13, 2012, http://articles.latimes.com/2012/may/13/opinion/la-oe-rubin-eugenics-mothers-day-20120513.
61. Lawyer, name withheld, in discussion with author, February 16, 2012.
62. Center for Gender and Refugee Studies, "CGRS/FGC Asylum Advisory," accessed August 15, 2013, http://www.cap-press.com/files/refugee3e/AT_and_AK%20Memo.pdf, 4.
63. Sara Meger, "Rape of the Congo: Understanding Sexual Violence in the Conflict in the Democratic Republic of Congo," *Journal of Contemporary African Studies* 28, no. 2 (2010): 119–35; Felicia Wairagu, "Congo-Kinshasa: The Forgotten Rape Capital of the World," *All Africa*, March 7, 2012, http://allafrica.com/stories/201203070912.html.
64. Caritas, "Rape Destroying Congo's Communities, Says Cariatas Psychologist," accessed February 20, 2013, http://www.caritas.org/activities/emergencies/RapeDestroyingCongo.html.
65. Ricci Shryock, "Rape Counseling Centers in DRC Address Unwanted Pregnancies," Voice of America, November 24, 2010, accessed February 20, 2013,

http://www.voanews.com/content/rape-counseling-centers-in-drc-address-unwanted-pregnancies-110660219/156915.html; Danielle Shapiro, "Mothers in Congo Get Help in Raising Children of Rape," *Christian Science Monitor*, May 9, 2010, accessed February 20, 2013, http://www.csmonitor.com/World/Africa/2010/0509/Mothers-in-Congo-get-help-in-raising-children-of-rape.

66. Bureaucracy of Democracy, Human Rights, and Labor, U.S. Department of State, "2011 Human Rights Report: Democratic Republic of the Congo," May 24, 2012, accessed June 15, 2014, http://www.state.gov/j/drl/rls/hrrpt/2011/af/186183.htm.
67. Radhakrishnan and Kallas, "Foreign Policy, Akin Style."
68. Akila Radhakrishnan, Staff Attorney, Global Justice Center, in discussion with author, August 30, 2012.
69. Immigration Equality, "Chapter Three: Asylum Basics: Elements of Asylum Law," accessed February 24, 2013, http://www.immigrationequality.org/issues/law-library/lgbth-asylum-manual/asylum-basics-elements-asylum-law/.
70. Alison Watson, R. Charli Carpenter, McEvoy-Levy, and Michael Goodhart, "Sins of the Fathers: War Rape, Wrongful Procreation, and Children's Human Rights," *Journal of Human Rights* 6, no. 3 (2007): 307–24.
71. Rebecca Bresnick, "Bearing Children: The Right to Decide," *Human Rights* 22, no. 1 (1995): 22–25; R. Charli Carpenter, "Surfacing Children: Limitations of Genocidal Rape Discourse," *Human Rights Quarterly* 22, no. 2 (2000): 428–77; Watson et al., "Sins of the Fathers."
72. World Health Organization, "Unsafe Abortion: Global and Regional Estimates of the Incidence of Unsafe Abortion and Associated Mortality in 2008, Sixth Edition," accessed February 15, 2013, http://whqlibdoc.who.int/publications/2011/9789241501118_eng.pdf?ua = 1, 27.
73. Stephanie Johanssen, in discussion with author, October 24, 2012. The Beijing Platform for Action and the International Conference on Population and Development mentions that legal, safe abortions should be available.
74. Kevin Sieff, "Access Denied," *Texas Observer*, February 20, 2009, accessed August 14, 2014, http://www.texasobserver.org/2963-access-denied/; Mia Giardina, "Reproductive Injustice: Immigration, Birthing, and the Prison System," Public Education Project, February 2010, accessed August 14, 2014, http://protectchoice.org/article.php?id = 680.
75. Sieff, "Access Denied."
76. Alexandria Walden, "Abortion Rights for ICE Detainees: Evaluating Constitutional Challenges to Restrictions on the Right to Abortion for Women in ICE Detention," *University of San Francisco Law Review* 43 (2009): 979–1012.
77. Planned Parenthood, "Immigration Reform," accessed August 14, 2014, http://www.plannedparenthoodaction.org/issues/immigration-reform/; National Latina Institute for Reproductive Health, "Latina Immigrants and Abortion Fact Sheet," July 2005, accessed August 14, 2014, http://latinainstitute.org/sites/default/files/Latina_Immigrants_and_Abortion_Final.pdf.
78. Center for Reproductive Rights, "Fulfilling Unmet Promises: Securing and Protecting Reproductive Rights and Equality in the United States" (2013), accessed February 20, 2014, http://reproductiverights.org/sites/crr.civicactions.net/files/documents/CRR_ICCPR%20Shadow%20Report%202013_Final.pdf.

79. April Rieger, "Missing the Mark: Why the Trafficking Victims Protection Act Fails to Protect Sex Trafficking Victims in the United States," *Harvard Journal of Law and Gender* 30 (2007): 231–56; Jayashri Srikantiah, "Perfect Victims and Real Survivors: The Iconic Victim in Domestic Human Trafficking Law," *Boston University Law Review* 87 (2007): 157–211.
80. The United Nations Office on Drugs and Crimes and U.S. governmental agencies do generally discuss the rights of smuggled migrants. However, I point to the need for more sustained attention to the violence the smuggled migrants specifically experience, such as at the hands of smugglers as well as US Border Patrol, and how female smugglers often *protect* women fleeing violent situations. See David Spener, "Global Apartheid, *Coyotaje*, and the Discourse of Clandestine Migration," in *Global Human Smuggling: Comparative Perspectives*, ed. David Kyle and Rey Koslowski (Baltimore, MD: Johns Hopkins University Press, 2011), 157–85.
81. Julia Ann Simon-Kerr, "Moral Turpitude," *Utah Law Review* 2 (2012): 1007, 1009.
82. See also Angela DeVolld, "Refugee Roulette: Wagering on Morality, Sexuality, and Normalcy in U.S. Asylum Law," *Nebraska Law Review* 92, no. 3 (2014): 627–54.
83. Brian C. Harms, "Redefining 'Crimes of Moral Turpitude': A Proposal to Congress," *Georgetown Immigration Law Journal* 15 (2001): 259–88; Ann Marie Nicolosi, "Female Sexuality, Citizenship, and Law: The Strange Case of Louise Camacho," *Journal of Contemporary Criminal Justice* 18, no. 3 (2002): 329–38; Pooja R. Dadhania, "The Categorical Approach for Crimes Involving Moral Turpitude after *Silva-Trevino*," *Columbia Law Review* 111 (2011): 313–55; Julia Ann Simon-Kerr, "Moral Turpitude," *Utah Law Review* 2 (2012): 1001–69.
84. Nate Carter, "Shocking the Conscience of Mankind: Using International Law to Define 'Crimes Involving Moral Turpitude' in Immigration Law," *Lewis and Clark Review* 10, no. 4 (2006): 955–88.
85. Dadhania, "Categorical Approach," 319.
86. Immigration Act of 1917, chapter 29, 3, 39 Stat. 874, 875–76.
87. Human Rights Watch, "Forced Apart: Families Separated and Immigrants Harmed by United States Deportation," 19, no. 3, July 17, 2007, accessed August 14, 2013, http://www.hrw.org/sites/default/files/reports/us0707_web.pdf, 24.
88. Harms, "Redefining Crimes."
89. Sara M. Walsh, Krista Eckhardt, and Steve Russell, "Sex, Lies, and Law: Moral Turpitude as an Enforcer of Gender and Sexuality Norms," *Sexuality Research and Social Policy* 3, no. 2 (2006): 38.
90. Ibid., 46.
91. Ibid., 48.
92. Ibid., 41.
93. Ibid.
94. Ibid., 48.
95. Adrien Katherine Wing, ed., *Global Critical Race Feminism: An International Reader* (New York: New York University Press, 2000); Shahnaz Khan, *Zina, Transnational Feminism, and the Moral Regulation of Pakistani Women* (Vancouver: University of British Columbia Press, 2006); Joetta L. Carr, "The SlutWalk Movement: A Study in Transnational Feminist Activism," *Journal of Feminist Scholarship* 4 (2013): 24–38.
96. Ann Stoler, "Making Empire Respectable: The Politics of Race and Sexual Morality in 20th Century Colonial Cultures," *American Ethnologist* 16, no. 4 (1989): 634–60.

97. Isabelle R. Gunning, "Female Genital Surgeries and Multicultural Feminism: The Ties That Bind; The Differences That Distance," *Third World Legal Studies* 13, no. 2 (1995): 17–47.
98. Catherine Lee, "'Where the Danger Lies': Race, Gender, and Chinese and Japanese Exclusion in the United States, 1870–1924," *Sociological Forum* 25, no. 2 (2010): 248–71. For a different context about the racialization of prostitution, see Philippa Levine, *Prostitution, Race and Politics: Policing Venereal Disease in the British Empire* (New York: Routledge, 2003).
99. The case and legal strategy challenging the case are discussed at Immigrant Defense Project, "Crimes Involving Moral Turpitude," accessed June 20, 2014, http://immigrantdefenseproject.org/litigation/crimes-involving-moral-turpitude.
100. "Confronting 'Crime,' Confronting Harm," accessed June 20, 2014, http://criticalresistance.org/wp-content/uploads/2012/06/Ab-Toolkit-Part-3.pdf.
101. Karma R. Chávez, *Queer Migration Politics: Activist Rhetoric and Coalitional Possibilities* (Champaign: University of Illinois Press, 2013).
102. Queer Migration Research Network, accessed April 15, 2014, www.queermigration.com.
103. Iván Espinosa-Madrigal, "The LGBT Community Should Condemn Arizona's Anti-immigrant Law, SB 1070," *Huffington Post*, April 23, 2012, accessed August 12, 2014, http://www.huffingtonpost.com/ivan-espinozamadrigal/arizona-sb-1070_b_1446809.html.
104. Kari Lerum, Kiesha McCurtis, Penelope Saunders, and Stéphanie Wahab, "Using Human Rights to Hold the US Accountable for Its Anti-Sex Trafficking Agenda: The Universal Periodic Review and New Directions for U.S. Policy," *Anti-trafficking Review* 1 (2012): 80–103. See also Best Practices Policy Project, Desiree Alliance, and Sexual Rights Initiative, "Report on the United States of America 9th Session of the Universal Periodic Review," November 2010, accessed January 14, 2014, http://lib.ohchr.org/HRBodies/UPR/Documents/session9/US/JS5_%20HSRI_Joint%20submission5_JS.pdf.
105. United Nations General Assembly Human Rights Council, "Report of the Working Group on the Universal Periodic Review: United States of America," A/HRC/16/11, January 4, 2011, accessed January 14, 2014, http://daccess-dds-ny.un.org/doc/UNDOC/GEN/G11/100/69/PDF/G1110069.pdf?OpenElement.
106. Human Rights Watch, "Sex Workers at Risk: Condoms as Evidence of Prostitution in Four US Cities" (2012), accessed January 3, 2014, http://www.hrw.org/sites/default/files/reports/us0712ForUpload_0.pdf, 78–79. See also US Department of State, "US Response to UN Human Rights Council Working Group Report," March 10, 2011.
107. Human Rights Watch, "Sex Workers at Risk."
108. Ibid., 87–88.

CHAPTER 7

1. Amy Shuman and Carol Bohmer, "Representing Trauma: Political Asylum Narrative," *Journal of American Folklore* 111, no. 466 (2004): 394–414; Carol Bohmer and Amy Shuman, *Rejecting Refugees: Political Asylum in the 21st Century* (London: Routledge, 2008).
2. Caitlin Steinke, "Male Asylum Applicants Who Fear Becoming the Victims of Honor Killings: The Case for Gender Equality," *CUNY Law Review* 17 (2013): 233–62.

3. Rebecca Stringer, *Knowing Victims: Feminism and Victim Politics in Neoliberal Times* (New York: Routledge, 2014).
4. Center for Gender and Refugee Studies, "Thousands of Girls and Women Are Fleeing Rape, Sexual Violence and Torture in Honduras, El Salvador and Guatemala," accessed September 25, 2014, http://cgrs.uchastings.edu/talking_points_and_stories.
5. Lawyer, name withheld, in discussion with the author, July 14, 2014.
6. Public Law 110-457-Dec. 23, 2008, 112 Stat. 5044.
7. *Matter of W-G-R*, 26 I&N Dec. 208 (BIA 2014); *Matter of M-E-V-G*, 26 I&N Dec. 227 (BIA 2014); National Immigrant Justice Center, "Particular Social Group Advisory: Applying for Asylum after *Matter of M-E-V-G* and *Matter of W-G-R*," accessed September 3, 2014, https://www.immigrantjustice.org/sites/immigrantjustice.org/files/NIJC%20PSG%20Practice%20Advisory_Final_3.4.14.pdf.
8. Gary J. Gates, "LGBT Adult Immigrants in the United States," Williams Institute, March 2013, accessed August 13, 2014, http://williamsinstitute.law.ucla.edu/wp-content/uploads/LGBTImmigrants-Gates-Mar-2013.pdf.
9. Queers for Economic Justice estimates that the number is closer to 1 million sexual minorities. Quoted in Debanuj DasGupta, "Queering Immigration: Perspectives on Cross-Movement Organizing," *Scholar and Feminist Online* 10.1–10.2 (Fall 2011–Spring 2012), accessed August 13, 2014, http://sfonline.barnard.edu/a-new-queer-agenda/queering-immigration-perspectives-on-cross-movement-organizing/.
10. Crosby Burns, Ann Garcia, and Philip E. Wolgin, "Living in Dual Shadows: LGBT Undocumented Immigrants," Center for American Progress, March 2013, accessed August 13, 2014, http://www.americanprogress.org/wp-content/uploads/2013/03/LGBTUndocumentedReport-6.pdf, 24.
11. Ibid.
12. Isabelle Gunning and Hope Lewis, "Cleaning Our Own House: 'Exotic' and Familiar Human Rights Violations," *Buffalo Human Rights Law Review* 4 (1998): 130–31.
13. Sharon Pickering, *Women, Borders, and Violence: Current Issues in Asylum, Forced Migration, and Trafficking* (New York: Springer, 2011); Efrat Arbel and Alletta Brenner, "Bordering on Failure: Canada-U.S. Border Policy and the Politics of Refugee Exclusion," Harvard Immigration and Refugee Law Clinical Program, 2013.
14. Amy Lind and Jill Williams. "Engendering Violence in De/Hyper-nationalized Spaces: Border Militarization, State Territorialization, and Embodied Politics at the U.S.-Mexico Border," in *Feminist (Im)mobilities in Fortress(ing) North America: Rights, Citizenships, and Identities in Transnational Perspective*, ed. Anne Sisson Runyan, Amy Lind, Patricia McDermott, and Marianne Marchand (Surrey, UK: Ashgate, 2013), 95–114.
15. Rutvica Andrijasevic, "Sex on the Move: Gender, Subjectivity and Differential Inclusion," *Subjectivity* 29 (2009): 396.
16. Alison Mountz, "Where Asylum Seekers Wait: Feminist Counter-topographies of Sites between States," *Gender, Place and Culture* 18, no. 3 (2011): 381–99.
17. Immigrations and Customs Enforcement, "Enforcement and Removal Facility Locator," accessed August 12, 2014, http://www.ice.gov/detention-facilities/.
18. Alison Mountz, Kate Coddington, R. Tina Catania, and Jenna M. Loyd, "Conceptualizing Detention: Mobility, Containment, Bordering, and Exclusion," *Progress in Human Geography* 37, no. 4 (2012): 522–41.

19. Michael Flynn, "There and Back Again: On the Diffusion of Immigration Detention," *Journal on Migration and Human Security* 2, no. 3 (2014): 166.
20. Ibid., 174–75.
21. Melanie Montpetit-Richter, "Empire, Desire and Violence: A Queer Transnational Feminist Reading of the Prisoner 'Abuse' in Abu Ghraib and the Question of 'Gender Equality,'" *International Feminist Journal of Politics* 9, no. 1 (2007): 38–59; Liz Philipose, "The Politics of Pain and the End of Empire," *International Feminist Journal of Politics* 9, no. 1 (2007): 60–81; Laura Sjoberg, "Agency, Militarized Femininity, and Enemy Others," *International Feminist Journal of Politics* 9, no. 1 (2007): 82–101; Lauren Wilcox, "Dying Is Not Permitted: Sovereignty, Biopower, and Force-Feeding at Guantanamo Bay," in *Torture: Power, Democracy and the Human Body*, ed. Shampa Biswas and Zahi Zalloua (Seattle: University of Washington Press, 2011), 101–28; Christine Sylvester, *War as Experience: Contributions from International Relations and Feminist Analysis* (New York: Routledge, 2013), 69–70.
22. Johanna Kantola, "The Gendered Reproduction of the State in International Relations," *British Journal of Politics and International Relations* 9 (2007): 270–83.
23. Gil Loescher, "Blaming the Victims: Refugees and Global Security," *Bulletin of the Atomic Scientists* 58, no. 6 (2002): 52.
24. Mountz et al., "Conceptualizing Detention," 526–27.
25. Ibid., 528.
26. Christine Fialho, "A Model Immigration Detention Facility for LGBTI?," *Forced Migration Review* 42 (2013), accessed August 1, 2014, http://www.fmreview.org/sogi/fialho.
27. Molly Redden, "No Water, No Toilet Paper, No Tampons: How the US Treats Border Detainees," *Mother Jones*, June 5, 2014, accessed August 1, 2014, http://www.motherjones.com/politics/2014/06/immigrant-detention-customs-border-protection-lawsuit.
28. Natalie J. Sokoloff and Susan C. Pearce, "Locking Up Hope: Immigration, Gender, and the Prison System," *Scholar and Feminist Online* 6, no. 3 (2008): 1–6, accessed August 1, 2014, http://sfonline.barnard.edu/immigration/sokoloff_pearce_01.htm; Mark Brunswick and Alejandra Matos, "Detained Immigrant Teen Assaulted by Registered Sex Offender in Sherburne County Jail," *Star Tribune*, April 14, 2014, accessed August 1, 2014, http://www.startribune.com/local/255046481.html.
29. Joanne Lin, "End Near for Shackling of Pregnant Women," American Civil Liberties Union, January 21, 2014, accessed January 28, 2014, https://www.aclu.org/blog/immigrants-rights-reproductive-freedom/end-near-shackling-pregnant-women.
30. César Cuauhtémoc García Hernández, "The Perverse Logic of Immigration Detention: Unraveling the Rationality of Imprisoning Immigrants Based on Markers of Race and Class Otherness," *Columbia Journal of Race and Law* 1, no. 2 (2012): 357–58.
31. Dylan Rodríguez, "'I Would Wish Death on You . . .': Race, Gender, and Immigration in the Globality of the U.S. Prison Regime," *Scholar and Feminist Online* 6, no. 3 (2008), accessed August 1, 2014, http://sfonline.barnard.edu/immigration/; Martha D. Escobar, "Neoliberal Captivity: Criminalization of Latina Migrants and the Construction of Irrecuperability," PhD diss., University of California–San Diego, 2010, accessed November 14, 2013. http://escholarship.org/uc/item/6cm3n9q7.

32. Marie Gottschalk, "Hiding in Plain Sight: American Politics and the Carceral State," *Annual Review of Political Science* 11 (2008): 235–60.
33. Jan Jindy Pettman, "Body Politics: International Sex Tourism," *Third World Quarterly* 18, no. 1 (1997): 105.
34. Laura J. Shepherd and Laura Sjoberg, "Trans-bodies in/of War(s): Cisprivilege and Contemporary Security Strategy," *Feminist Review* 101 (2012): 10.
35. Catherine Eschle and Bice Maiguashca, "Rethinking Globalised Resistance: Feminist Activism and Critical Theorising in International Relations," *British Journal of Politics and International Relations* 9, no. 2 (2007): 284–301; Meghana Nayak and Eric Selbin, *Decentering International Relations* (London: Zed Books, 2010); L. H. M. Ling, *The* Dao *of World Politics: Towards a Post-Westphalian, Worldist International Relations* (London: Routledge, 2014).
36. Cynthia Enloe, "Foreword," in *Gender Matters in Global Politics*, ed. Laura J. Shepherd (New York: Routledge, 2010), xviii.

INDEX